Did you ever wonder why Jesus, the King of kings and Lord of lords, said, "It is better I go and He come"? Must be something special to come. Ken Hemphill answers many questions that have been misunderstood as you read this biblical analysis of the Holy Spirit. You may allow the power to come back into your life and ministry.

—Evangelist William Fay
Share Jesus Without Fear

Few people have demonstrated a greater love for the church and the body of Christ. Dr. Ken Hemphill has written much in the area of giftedness and how we use those gifts to enhance God's kingdom and to see it enlarged as we live up to our calling and giftedness. You will be blessed, challenged, and encouraged by this book.

—Dr. Johnny M. Hunt
Senior Pastor, First Baptist Church, Woodstock, Georgia
President, Southern Baptist Convention

I have read this book from cover to cover. It is worth it! As the pastor of a local congregation, I need help! There is too much to do, too many people to love, and too few to help. Drawing on his many years of ministry, Ken Hemphill has written a book that will open the eyes of your understanding about the issue of gifts, drive home God's provision for His church, and provide for biblical solutions. This book is deeply theological in content and highly practical in application. Ken does not avoid the subjects we most often avoid and leaves his reader solidly equipped to seek and find those God-given gifts designed to produce maximum potential in the body of Christ. It is well written, well presented, and is an essential tool for all who sincerely desire to serve the Savior to the best of their ability.

—Don Wilton
Senior Pastor, First Baptist Church, Spartanburg, South Carolina

Wrong understandings associated with spiritual gifts have not changed much since the first century. Some seek the most obvious gifts just to show how gifted they are. Others believe they are not gifted and thus have little to offer. Still others fear that any study of spiritual gifts will lead them to be "charismatic." Ken Hemphill addresses these concerns in this helpful and needed work. Recognizing that the Bible—not experience or tradition—must guide our understanding of gifts, he calls believers to use their gifts for God's glory in the context of the church. Read this book and be challenged by it. Learn from it, even if you don't agree with every conclusion about this controversial topic. Apply it by using your gifts. Then teach others to do the same.

—Chuck Lawless
Dean, Billy Graham School of Missions, Evangelism and Church Growth
The Southern Baptist Theological Seminary

You Are Gifted is a well-crafted work to help pastors and laity discover ways to put their spiritual gifts to work. Ken Hemphill has done a masterful job in dealing with an often misunderstood topic.

—Dr. Geoff Hammond
President, North American Mission Board, SBC

Much has been written about spiritual gifts, and Christians often strive to understand a personal application from complex interpretations of the subject. Ken Hemphill has written a balanced and refreshing perspective that is practical and inspiring. His thorough and balanced exegesis of Scripture passages on spiritual gifts give assurance to every believer of God's grace and gifting. *You Are Gifted* is a book that will contribute to one's growth and equipping to serve God effectively.

> —Dr. Jerry Rankin
> President, International Mission Board, SBC

You Are Gifted is a biblical and practical resource for pastors as we fulfill our task of "equipping the saints to do the work of the ministry." Dr. Hemphill shares the secrets of locating and motivating volunteers in our churches from being spectators to becoming participators in God's grand scheme of redeeming the world to Himself! Read it, apply it, and people will be reached and blessed.

> —Dr. John Cross
> Senior Pastor, South Biscayne Church, North Port, Florida

How do you mobilize people from spectating in the pews to participation in ministry? Is there a place for me? Can God use me? Do I fit in the church? If so, how and where? These are the questions that are often asked by pastors and parishioners. Ken Hemphill carefully and clearly answers both sets in his book *You Are Gifted*. Through sound biblical exegesis, Ken provides a solid blueprint given by God for the mobilization of persons from spectators to participants and the meaning that each receives as a result. God's blueprint has been and continues to be spiritual gifts. In this book the believer receives clarity around whom God fits within the body, how God fits us within the body, where God fits us within the body, and why God fits us within the body. He also sounds the call for gifted leaders to equip gifted members.

If there was ever a time when pastors and people needed to take hold of the empowering and gifting ministry of the Holy Spirit within the church, it is now. Ken Hemphill provides a clear understanding of how it can be done.

> —Claude Alexander
> Bishop, The Park Ministries, Charlotte, North Carolina

Few people are more qualified to write a book on spiritual gifts. His own experiences as a pastor, his extensive study of the New Testament, much of it in 1 Corinthians, under some of the world's greatest New Testament scholars, help the church to catch something of its apostolic fervor and provide some of the keenest insight of any of the numerous books on spiritual gifts.

> —Roy J. Fish, ThD
> Distinguished Professor of Evangelism Emeritus
> Southwestern Baptist Theological Seminary
> Fort Worth, Texas

YOU ARE
GIFTED

YOU ARE
GIFTED

YOUR SPIRITUAL GIFTS AND
THE KINGDOM OF GOD

KEN HEMPHILL

Foreword by Johnny Hunt

PUBLISHING GROUP

NASHVILLE, TENNESSEE

978-0-8054-4862-7

Published by B&H Publishing Group
Nashville, Tennessee

Dewey Decimal Classification: 234.13
Subject Heading: SPIRITUAL GIFTS / KINGDOM OF GOD /
CHRISTIAN LIFE

2 3 4 5 6 7 8 9 10 • 22 21 20 19 18

Contents

Acknowledgments

I have a lifelong love affair with the church. My parents taught me to love the church from the day I was born. My dad was a pastor; and Mom, like many pastors' wives, was involved in Sunday school, choir, missions, and any other task that needed to be done. My love affair has only grown in intensity and depth as I have served the church in the role of a pastor, and then later as seminary president, and now as national strategist for Empowering Kingdom Growth. I have written this book as a love letter to the church. It is my constant prayer and the burden of my life that the church would catch the vision for what God intends it to be. If we could replace apathy with passion for the kingdom and recapture our heritage, the church could express the fullness of God in our world today. This book is dedicated to that end.

I have been privileged to serve as national strategist for the initiative called Empowering Kingdom Growth for nearly six years. From the beginning we have acknowledged and declared that the Holy Spirit is the One who empowers all kingdom activity. For that reason we have focused on providing biblical materials that would help believers and their church families grow in their kingdom commitment.

This book is about the work of the Holy Spirit as He empowers and gifts believers to accomplish their kingdom work in their sphere of influence. We have often shied away from talking about the ministry of the Holy Spirit, particularly related to spiritual gifts, for fear that it might lead to confusion and dissension. Our failure to teach the wonderful truths about spiritual gifts has itself led to confusion and has also greatly hindered the ministry of the local church. Every believer is created in God's image, redeemed by His grace, empowered and gifted by His Spirit to serve alongside Him for kingdom advance. I pray that every reader will have the joy of discovering, developing, and deploying their gift for the edification of the body and the glory of the King.

Most books are a team effort, and this one is no exception. Dr. John Polhill, my professor at Southern Seminary, was the first to encourage me to research and write on this topic, which he believed to be critical to the church. Professor C. F. D. Moule guided my research for three years in Cambridge as I prepared my PhD dissertation on the topic of spiritual gifts. B&H Publishing

Group has worked with me as I have published several books on this vitally important subject. Also thanks to Kim Stanford, managing editor, who has greatly improved the original manuscript.

I am thankful that Dr. Morris Chapman, president of the Executive Committee of the Southern Baptist Convention, had the vision and courage to call Southern Baptists to kingdom living. I am grateful that he allowed me to serve with him in this critical task. My colleagues at the Executive Committee continue to give me encouragement as I speak and write on the kingdom. Mary Creson, my administrative assistant, has helped to assemble the manuscript and get it to my colleagues at LifeWay Christian Resources and its publishing division, B&H Publishing Group.

I have been greatly encouraged by George Williams, whose vision and passion led me to look again at spiritual gifts from a kingdom perspective. This is my first opportunity to work with Tom Walters, and it has been a delightful experience.

Our children and their husbands are living examples of uniquely gifted laborers. Kristina, Brett, and Lois continue their ministry to the ends of the earth. Rachael, Trey, Emerson, and Ward are now in Scotland furthering their education for the sake of the kingdom. Katie, Daniel, Aubrey, and Sloane continue to exercise the gift of hospitality as they open their home to friends from church.

This book is dedicated to my wife and kingdom partner. She not only supported me throughout the process of research and writing while I was completing my PhD on this topic, but she has continued to encourage me to write and speak on this subject. She is a gifted woman who has employed her many gifts through the church, the seminary, and now the International Mission Board.

My beloved professor and mentor, C. F. D. Moule died during the writing of this book. No words could ever express the debt I owe to him.

Much of the material for this book was originally developed as part of my project for my PhD from Cambridge. For that project I consulted numerous sources and commentaries on these various passages and have attempted to stay abreast of new resources printed since that time. Because of the desire to make this material usable to the broader church audience, I have attempted to keep footnotes to a minimum. That does not suggest that I have not learned from or depended on the scholarship of others. I am greatly indebted to many who have written materials on the various passages discussed in this book and have probably borrowed from many of them. If you recognize your work, I thank you and apologize that I have not given everyone the credit they deserve.

Preface

When I think of the subject of spiritual giftedness, Ken Hemphill's name always comes to mind. For more than a dozen years I have read and been enlightened, blessed, and encouraged by the books that seem to always speak along the lines of this great subject.

We now have, in our hands, *You Are Gifted*. It is almost as though Dr. Hemphill has taken everything that he has learned through the years and combined it into one great study. He deals with the church at Thessalonica, which happens to be one of my favorite churches to study in all of the sixty-six books of the Bible. Whether it is history that you are looking for in order to know the particular context of spiritual gifts, or defining spiritual gifts, or helping your people to know the guidelines for the use of giftedness in the context of the local church, knowing what motivates a person through their spiritual giftedness, how to identify spiritual leaders for the church, you will find that all of these subjects are wonderfully illustrated and offer great help to each of us in order to better get our arms around these subjects.

Dr. Hemphill has proven himself to be a student of God's Word as well as a student of the church of the Lord Jesus. He has deep insight into spiritual truth and great clarity as to how the church needs to function. I feel confident that those of us who take the time to read and study these principles will have a better handle on how to equip the generation that we are ministering to and prepare them to pass the spiritual baton to the generation who comes behind. Oftentimes a local church finds itself confused and, yes, maybe even experiencing fear somewhat concerning spiritual gifts. I believe that as you grasp with a clearer and greater understanding of spiritual gifts and how God allows them to operate within the context of an individual's life and the local church, it will remove the fear and confusion forever.

There is a great need, in the context of those who are called out by Christ as part of His body, not only to discover where their giftedness lies but to develop and employ that giftedness for the glory of God. Adrian Rogers used to say,

"Spiritual gifts are not toys to play with but gifts to build with." This book will show you how to take those gifts and build the kingdom of God in a way that God would be glorified, the church would be edified, and deep in our own hearts we would be able to one day close our eyes as we transition from this life to the next, knowing that we were satisfied in our spirit and that we had done the best we could to equip our people.

Last, but not least, we are in a war in the Christian church! It has been said that the church is not a playground but a battlefield. Spiritual gifts can be used in your life to equip you for the spiritual warfare that takes place within this world and in the context of the church. May God bless you as you read this book, and then pass it along to others.

—Johnny Hunt
President, Southern Baptist Convention
Pastor, First Baptist Church, Woodstock, Georgia

Confronting Reality

Our church was experiencing phenomenal growth. That's both the good news and the bad news. The pains that come with such growth are as real as the physical growth pains I felt when I was a preteen. When my joints ached and my stretching muscles screamed for relief, the only solace I could find was my dad's assurance that I would be taller in the morning. I made regular and solemn treks to the door frame in my bedroom to record the progress being made, attempting to prove to myself that the gain was worth the pain.

While we were always in need of money, our greatest growth need at the time was for members of the body of Christ to step forward and do their fair share of the ministry. We simply would not reach our community and our world if we couldn't find people willing to serve. The preschool area of our ministry was voracious in its demands for help. It takes a lot of hands to handle a growing preschool. But that was not our only area of need. There was the growing worship ministry and its need for choir and orchestra members. Each area of the Sunday school was experiencing growth, and with that came the need for people to assume ministry roles.

What were we to do? If all else failed, I'd preach a particularly "convicting message" about the demand for service. To ensure that everyone got the message, I determined to lace it with all the guilt-laden phrases I could muster. Surely such a message would motivate the masses! I was both shocked and distraught when my sermon on service produced little visible results.

A Life-Changing Conversation

Still reeling from the lack of response, I left my office to make my hospital rounds. As I walked through the lobby of the Leigh Memorial Hospital, I smiled at a local candy striper, a volunteer who wore a pink, candy-striped uniform and gave countless hours of free service to the local hospital. This lady smiled brightly as she waved at her pastor. That's right: she was a member of my flock.

Her smile and the immediate recognition on my part that she was giving freely of her time to serve persons in the hospital caused me to think of my vain appeal for help. I sensed the Holy Spirit prompting me to ask her about her service to the hospital and lack of service through the church. I made my way to the reception desk and asked the questions that led to a radical transformation in my ministry.

"How many hours of service do you give each week through the hospital?" I asked.

Smiling brightly, she answered that she gave more than twenty hours a week.

I first complimented her on her servant spirit and then asked permission to ask a personal question. Just to break the ice, I asked, "Were you at church yesterday?"

She responded with a weak "yes" and then dropped her eyes, anticipating the next question.

"Did you hear my message?" A slight nod of the head indicated a "yes" response. "What did you think of it?" I queried. She responded that she couldn't understand why no one would respond to such an appeal.

With complete innocence she asked, "Why do we have such trouble getting people to serve?"

I was stunned to find that she was actually asking the same question I had been asking myself. I cautiously proceeded, "Have you ever thought of volunteering even a few hours a week for service through the church?"

Her vulnerability was unnerving. "Pastor, you don't know how I dream of being of service to the Lord through the church."

I must confess that I was thoroughly confused. I was thinking to myself that I could certainly answer her dream. Why were my pleas for help and her desire for service simply not connecting?

"You have not because you ask not!" So I asked! "Why have you never stepped forward and volunteered your service in our church?"

Her face spoke of her agony and her shame. "Oh, pastor, I am not worthy, and I am not capable."

We Are Worthy and Capable

The Holy Spirit spoke to me through this laywoman. I had no idea concerning this woman's past or of her present struggles, but I now knew that she was like a large number of people who listened to me every Sunday. Every time I would talk about getting involved in the ministry of the church, their hearts stirred within them, but just as quickly their hopes were extinguished by the adversary who convinced them that they were simply not worthy. I began to examine my preaching ministry and to work harder to communicate the truth that we are new creatures in Christ. I underlined the truth that God's redemption impacts all of our life and thus He has declared us worthy of serving Him. This theme seemed to deal with the issue of worth, but it left one plea unanswered.

What about her concern about being capable? After all, we are talking about spiritual ministry. Serving the King and advancing the kingdom should never be taken lightly. At this juncture I began to teach more fully about the ministry of the Holy Spirit as He empowers and gifts believers for ministry. The King has gifted us for service in the body, and that alone makes us capable.

> *When you understand that God created you in His image, redeemed you by His grace, gifted and empowered you by His Spirit, and specifically chose you to serve alongside Him to advance His kingdom, your life will be forever changed.*

I began to repeat a simple truth that transformed my thinking and my ministry. When you understand that God created you in His image, redeemed you by His grace, gifted and empowered you by His Spirit, and specifically chose you to serve alongside Him to advance His kingdom, your life will be forever changed.

Do you understand that you have been uniquely and specifically gifted by the Holy Spirit? Do you know what your gifts are? Are you using them through your local church to advance the kingdom here on earth? I think you will find this book both stimulating and challenging as we investigate the truth of God's Word concerning spiritual gifts.

Spiritual gifts are individualized endowments of grace from the Father, equipping you to play a vital role in His plan for the advance of His kingdom and the reaching of the nations. Thus the discovery of your unique giftedness is not an option. It is a necessity. God created you with intentionality, and He placed you in His body just as He chose (see 1 Cor. 12:18).

The Progression of the Study

This book is about finding your gifts and putting them to work. We will first begin by examining the relevant passages about spiritual gifts. Many believers have ignored some of these passages because they have been misinterpreted or misused in an arrogant and sometimes hurtful way by persons who claim that the possession of certain gifts proves them to be more spiritual than others who lack such gifts. You will find that this is an age-old problem. Yet we shouldn't allow this fog of misunderstanding to keep us from unwrapping the wonderful gifts the Father has for us. You can be assured that our Father only gives "good gifts" (Matt. 7:11).

Many books on this subject move directly to the well-known gift passages such as 1 Corinthians 12–14; Romans 12; and Ephesians 4. We will look at these passages in due time, but we must first lay a good foundation by looking at one of the earliest passages in the story of the development of the New Testament church. By studying 1 Thessalonians 5, we will discover some wonderful foundational truths that help us understand the other gift passages later in the Pauline letters. We will examine the pertinent passages in the order they were written by Paul to assist the developing early church.

Further, we will look at the gift passages in their immediate and larger contexts. This process should help us avoid the pitfall of debating secondary issues that seem to consume so much energy and provide so little assistance in helping believers find their rightful place in the body of Christ. *The central thrust of Scripture is that spiritual gifts are graciously given by God to enable believers to participate fully in the edification of the church and the advance of the kingdom.*

This approach will provide the maximum benefit to the church. At the same time we must deal honestly with the entire teaching of Scripture. While we will not focus on the controversial issues surrounding the gift passages such as the nature and role of tongues, we will attempt to deal with them honestly and carefully as we come to them in the natural progression of our study of the Pauline letters.

A study guide, DVDs, and administrative materials are available for individual or small group study. Free materials are available from www.auxano press.com, www.empowerkingdomgrowth.com, www.lifeway.com, and www.youaregifted.org. Study guides and DVDs are available from LifeWay Stores, online at www.lifeway.com, by calling 1-800-251-3225, and at www.auxano press.com. All materials are keyed to this book. Read the material with your Bible open for the greatest possible impact. Be prepared for a great kingdom adventure as the Spirit applies God's truth to your life.

1 | An Insider's View of the Emerging Church

A Study of 1 Thessalonians 5

The topic of this book is spiritual gifts, but gifts should never be studied in a vacuum as if they are a curious phenomenon to be discussed, debated, and then dissected and discarded. The topic of gifts should never frighten the believer since our Father can only give good gifts. But gifts should never be sought with selfish desire for self-aggrandizement as if they are evidence of spiritual ascendancy. While there is a great deal of interest—both fascination and fear—concerning spiritual gifts, they are not an end in themselves. We are to seek the Giver and not the gift.

Gifts are not given to people for their amusement or for the amazement of their friends and neighbors.

Gifts prove nothing about the *spirituality* of the believer but everything about the *graciousness* of the Giver.

Gifts have a singular purpose. They enable us to participate in the advancement of God's kingdom to the ends of the earth in preparation for the return of the King.

Spiritual gifts are always given and exercised in the larger context of the church. They enable us to edify other members of the body of Christ and to evangelize those still waiting to enter the kingdom.

> *Gifts have a singular purpose. They enable us to participate in the advancement of God's kingdom to the ends of the earth in preparation for the return of the King.*

Gifts are the manifestation of the grace of God and thus distributed by His royal design. Gifted persons are the gift of the resurrected King to His church, enabling it boldly and effectively to advance His kingdom. They are the ministry of the Holy Spirit, the Helper sent by the Father, who enables us to advance the kingdom through His supernatural empowering.

Gifts are an expression of God's love and thus are to be studied, sought, and used with His eternal purpose in mind.

The church is the chosen instrument of the King—gifted with the keys of the kingdom, empowered by the Spirit, and tasked with the discipling of the nations. Thus it is critical for us to study spiritual gifts in the context of the emerging New Testament church. We will begin with one of the earliest churches founded by Paul and move sequentially as we study the churches at Corinth, Rome, and Ephesus. I pray that you will find the study enlightening, inspirational, and transformational. This study is not intended simply to inform you concerning spiritual gifts. It is designed to help you discover and employ your gifts for the pleasure of the King.

The Founding of the Church in Thessalonica

Our pilgrimage to understand better the role of spiritual gifts in advance of the kingdom through the church takes us to Thessalonica, the largest and most important city in Macedonia. This seaport town was a wealthy and flourishing center of trade. Paul regarded the planting of a kingdom-centered church in this city as pivotal to the resurrected Lord's command that the disciples should expand the kingdom to Jerusalem, Judea, Samaria, and the ends of the earth (Acts 1:8).

According to Luke's account of Paul's ministry in Thessalonica, Paul began his work there by teaching the local residents in the synagogue. For three Sabbaths he reasoned with them about the coming of the Messiah (King) (Acts 17:1–10). He demonstrated that Jesus' suffering, death, and resurrection were all a part of God's sovereign plan. Some people persuaded by this message joined with Paul and Silas, thus becoming the nucleus of the church in Thessalonica. Luke specifically mentions the response of a large number of God-fearing Greeks and leading women.

The Jews, jealous of the success of Paul's teaching, fomented a riot by co-opting scoundrels from the marketplace. The resulting uproar turned the city into a cauldron of unrest. The mob attacked Jason's house looking for the missionaries. When they discovered that Paul and Silas were nowhere to be found, they drug Jason and some of the brothers before the city officials.

The jealous Jews argued that the missionaries were turning the world upside down. In truth they were turning it right-side up. What was the message that led to both joyous acceptance and hostile rejection? "These men who have upset the world have come here also; and Jason has welcomed them, and they all act contrary to the decrees of Caesar, saying that there is another king, Jesus" (Acts 17:6–7). Their message of the rightful King and His kingdom was, at once, unsettling and exciting.

We have the same message, and we are empowered and gifted by the same Spirit. Why is no one accusing us of turning the world upside down? Is it possible that we have not had the boldness to declare the truth to a world in need of a King?

Why is no one accusing us of turning the world upside down?

The city authorities heard the accusations but could do little to appease the angry mob since Paul and Silas had not been located. Jason and the brethren were released after the authorities received a pledge that the trouble would cease. Paul and Silas were sent off to Berea after nightfall. The city authorities may have considered the matter closed, but some of the angry Jews followed Paul to Berea and continued to harass the believers who constituted the church at Thessalonica.

In order to discredit and destroy the new believers, Paul's detractors mounted a slander campaign against Paul and his work in Thessalonica. Read Paul's impassioned self-defense in 1 Thessalonians 1–3, and you will see that their attack may have met with some measure of success. Paul expresses sincere concern for the welfare of the young believers and their relationship to him.

You might wonder how such trumped-up charges against the apostle could meet with any measure of success. It is possible that "Jason and some brethren" (Acts 17:6) refers to a small inner circle of believers. To save Paul from being delivered to the authorities, they had secreted him away at night. A rescue of this nature could hardly be publicized among all the church members. Thus, many of the believers were unaware of the details of his departure. They only knew that Paul was conspicuously absent and they were suffering from hostility aimed at him. Thus the accusations brought against him may have seemed to some to have an element of truth.

Paul's sudden disappearance and his failure to return to Thessalonica provided detractors with a golden opportunity to raise doubts about the preacher and his message.

If Paul was a charlatan and his message was false, then there was no basis for the existence of the church. This could explain why Paul devoted much of the first three chapters of 1 Thessalonians to a defense of his tactics, behavior, message, and results while in Thessalonica. He assured his readers that his message did not spring from "error or impurity or by way of deceit" (1 Thess. 2:3). He could not be accused of greed since he worked night and day to support himself (2:5–9).

Paul first sent Timothy to strengthen the church in Thessalonica, and then he sent them a personal letter to remind them of his teaching and to clarify any points of confusion. First Thessalonians is among the earliest letters of Paul. By reading this letter, we can gain understanding about the structure and function of the developing early church. One of the most important features of this letter is the provision Paul makes for the ongoing life of the community. Paul was well aware that the future of Christianity in Thessalonica depended on the ability of believers to encourage and minister to one another. All the problems that would be faced by this community could best be met by the mutual encouragement one of another and by the loving recognition of leaders who have charge over the brethren in the Lord.

Let's underline a few basic principles that we will find in this community ministry passage. First, the community of believers is designed for mutual encouragement. Every believer is competent and responsible for ministry to others. Second, some members of the community are gifted to provide spiritual and administrative oversight. Third, when gifted leaders and gifted members work together in harmony, the church functions with maximum potential.

One of the dangers inherent in spiritual gifts is that they can create introverted and selfish desires. *The discovery and employment of spiritual gifts must always be anchored in the context of Christian community.* God gives the spiritual gifts with the good of the community in view, and therefore we must remain biblically and practically anchored to the local church in our desire for and use of gifts.

The Overarching Value of Relationships

When I lead conferences on church kingdom growth, I often hear horror stories about internal struggles over power and authority. Sometimes these battles involve the pastor and deacons or elders, and in other instances they involve various members of the church. In many cases the results of these internal struggles are inactivity on the part of many church members and a resulting lack of kingdom advance. The attitude seems to be, "I'll let these folks hash it out; I've got better things to do with my time." Many gifted members have moved to the sidelines from where they watch others engage in kingdom activity. Relationships are at the heart of the church, and they are the foundation for kingdom activity. We must, therefore, focus on attitudes and relationships for ministry that will provide a stable platform for the proper exercise of spiritual gifts and enable positive kingdom advance.

Paul concludes the first letter to the Thessalonians with a passage that focuses on the proper functioning of the Christian community (1 Thess. 5:12–22). Paul's first remarks have to do with the proper relationship between the "brethren" and "those who . . . have charge over you in the Lord" (v. 12). The concept that all members of the body are gifted for service does not conflict with God's design for pastoral leadership in the church. They are not conflicting ideas but complimentary ones. The relationship between leaders and gifted members is foundational for proper kingdom ministry in the body.

The church is like a family, and if the church becomes dysfunctional, then its work is hampered, and its members are wounded. The proper context for discovering and using one's giftedness is a healthy community of believers. We must make a firm commitment to develop and maintain proper relationships throughout the church family so that our mission is unhindered and individual members are affirmed in their unique giftedness.

Paul first exhorts the Thessalonians to "appreciate" (v. 12) and "esteem . . . highly in love" (v. 13) those who labored among them in leadership positions. Little effective leadership can occur when those who have been gifted for and called to this task are not appreciated. But respect is not enough to bind the brethren to their leaders. Esteem that flows from love is also needed. Examine the text carefully, and you will discover that the love is based not on the personality of the individual but on the significance of the work being accomplished (v. 13). The church deals with issues that impact eternity, and we cannot allow personal preferences and personality conflicts to impact negatively our ministry.

Paul's hasty departure may have created some tension in the church. Who was in charge after his departure may not have been entirely clear. Some members may have grown weary of what appeared to be power struggles between "Jason and the brethren" and other self-appointed leaders that Paul dubs as the "unruly" (5:14). *Unruly* translates a military term that means "to stand out of rank." These would-be leaders were out of formation and thus causing dissension which had led to a disdain for all leaders.

Further information provided by 2 Thessalonians 3:7–11 suggests that the refusal to work was a central element of their unruly behavior. These men had disobeyed Paul's teaching and had spread dissent in the community by behaving like busybodies. The cartoon character Lucy in the *Peanuts* comic strip illustrates this nagging, destructive sort of behavior. Unruly persons polarize people and destroy unity. They seek to lead by intimidation, and they keep many members from discovering their unique ministry within the community.

Paul's first concern in the discussion of community ministry is to identify and undergird the true leaders of the church so that peace and unity would mark the fellowship. Notice that the result of healthy relationships between leaders and brethren is the ability to "live in peace with one another." This phrase from 1 Thessalonians 5:13 is the unifying theme of this entire letter. Paul's desire is to establish harmonious relationships within the community so that individual members could encourage one another in the face of persecution, and the community could command the respect of those outside the church (4:12). Our unity is critical to our witness. The atmosphere of respect, love, and peace provides the platform for all the gifted members of the church to accomplish their work unhindered.

Over the years I have seen the work of many fine churches hampered because they lacked healthy interpersonal relationships. Every community has at least one church where there has been a constant parade of preachers. None of them stay long. They all leave for different stated reasons. One preaches too long; another, not long enough. One is too authoritative; the next is unwilling to lead. This parade of pastors not only affects the witness of that church in the community; it also impacts the spiritual self-image of the members. This church will stagger from one church split to the next as factions choose up sides over leadership issues.

Individual members, who have been hurt by the bickering and disputes, often move to another church hoping to get away from such pettiness. Many of these wounded transfer members remain reluctant to use their God-given abilities in their new church family. Their spiritual self-esteem has been wounded, and thus their gifts lie unused. They don't want to get burned again. This is a double tragedy. Gifted believers who are unengaged impact the kingdom ability of the local church.

The first step in gift discovery is the identification with a local church where healthy family relationships can be developed. In a healthy church you will receive teaching by example as well as instruction. Leaders will model the attitudes and behaviors they call for in others' lives. The context of love and mutual esteem will provide the natural climate for gift discovery and employment.

The Ministry of Gifted Leaders

What is the role of leaders in the life of the church? How does their gifted ministry enable other members of the body to discover and develop their own gifts? We will find answers to these critical questions in all of the Pauline gift passages. In 1 Thessalonians 5:12–13 we will find several foundational truths that Paul would build upon in later passages.

The church in Thessalonica needed to embrace their leaders for numerous reasons. The hostility to the ministry of Paul resulted in his premature departure, leaving the church in need of further instruction. Paul's absence, coupled with the harassment from Jewish leaders, created a need for stability and clear direction—a need for leadership. Paul considered the mission of the church to be so central to the evangelization of the world that the healthy relationship between the leaders and members of the church could not be taken lightly.

Paul uses three different phrases—"labor among you," "have charge over you," and "give you instruction" (5:12)—to describe both the identity and the scope of the work of authentic leaders in the church.

Labor Among

The term translated *labor among* underlines the magnitude of the intense physical exertion required of those in leadership. Paul uses this same phrase in several contexts to speak of the manual labor by which he maintained himself while doing missionary service (1 Thess. 2:9; 1 Cor. 4:12; and 2 Thess. 3:8). He employs the same word for his evangelistic

> *The work of the ministry is hard work.*

activity (1 Cor. 15:10; Gal. 4:11; and Phil. 2:16). Paul's point is clear: the work of the ministry is hard work. Those flippant "preacher jokes" about wanting a job where one only has to work on Sunday and Wednesday demeans the hard work involved in ministry. This, in turn, depreciates the eternal significance of ministry through the church.

As discussed above, some men in Thessalonica wanted to be in leadership positions, but they were unwilling to work. These men had become a divisive factor in the community and were creating challenges for the authentic leaders. Paul's emphasis on the hard work of ministry would make clear which leaders should be given respect. Today we find church members who like positions of leadership for the honor and prestige they bestow, but they are unwilling to fulfill the heavy commitment of work that authentic leadership requires.

The term "labor among" also suggests what we refer to as the pastoral function of the leader who works among and alongside his flock. He nurtures the flock placed under his care. Like a shepherd he gently leads and protects those in his care. He leads by example and encouragement. A unique aspect of the nurturing ministry of the pastor is the enabling of members in the discovery and employment of their giftedness through the church for eternal impact.

Have Charge Over

One of the primary functions of the pastoral leader is that of leading or managing. The Greek term Paul employs has two meanings—"preside or lead" and "protect or care for." In 1 Timothy 3:4–5 Paul mentions the administrative work of the pastor by comparing it to the function of the father as head of the home. In the home a father rules over his family and protects them. We should conclude that both administrative leadership and pastoral protection are in view in each of these texts. Pastoral leaders that are biblical and effective will lead in such a manner that they provide protection and care for all the members of the church.

A church without a clearly identified leader is likely to attempt to move in all directions at one time, which causes confusion and ultimately harms the body. The church must have strong pastoral leadership to aid all the individual members to be empowered to fulfill their unique gifted role. The pastor's leadership must reflect the mature, patient, and loving concern of a father whose desire is to see the total development of his children.

Earlier in this letter Paul compares his labor among them to the nursing mother who "tenderly cares for her own children" (1 Thess. 2:7). He speaks then of his fond affection that caused him to impart his own life along with the gospel. He reminds them of the hardships he endured and the integrity of his work as he exhorted and encouraged them, "imploring each one of you as a father would his own children" (2:11). He is calling the leaders of the church to practice the style of leadership he modeled while he was among them.

Any leader, pastor or otherwise, will do well to remember that authority to lead is inextricably tied to one's love and care for those being led. The phrase "in the Lord" places a clear boundary on the leader's authority and indicates that leadership is a service that the individual owes to the Lord. Leadership is a stewardship given by the Lord and takes place only in the realm of the spiritual affairs of those being led. It is "given by the Lord," but it is "earned" by the sweat of the brow. It is exercised in the care of the flock, but it is presented to the Lord as our "reasonable service."

Recently we have seen a healthy and biblical emphasis on the shared ministry of all church members. The outdated concept that the paid pastor is the only one qualified or required to provide ministry is quickly becoming extinct. Not too soon, I might add! Paul saw the church as a unified group of Spirit-empowered members, some of whom were specifically gifted for leadership. Understanding spiritual gifts should give strong encouragement for all members of the body to fulfill their appropriate roles in ministry. Yet we must not allow the discovery of shared ministry to cause us to depreciate the work of those called by God to "have charge over" the church. Like parents in the healthy family, these persons will care for the congregants, oversee the work of the church, and give instruction.

We must renew our commitment to follow the biblical pattern for church leadership. Gifted members must allow those gifted and called to leadership to fulfill their God-given task of providing visionary direction. The church cannot treat the pastor as a hireling who is given little say in the direction of the ministry, or the church will continue to flounder in the morass of ineffectiveness. Nonetheless, pastors must not attempt to exert their authority in a strong-handed manner. Leadership authority is given by the Lord, but it is earned by laboring among and caring for the flock. Church is no game. Eternity is at stake. We are God's kingdom community, and we cannot allow dysfunctional relationships to hamper our work.

Give You Instruction

The final term used to describe the work of the pastoral leaders indicates a teaching function. The term used for instruction includes the idea of warning and correction. The pastor as teacher seeks to influence the mind and disposition of the church family by appropriate biblical instruction, wise counsel, warning, and correction. We don't like the suggestion that warning and correction may be required, but they are as essential to healthy church relationships as they are to healthy family relationships. Warning directs people away from destructive behavior, and correction moves them toward positive personal growth.

Some churches have ignored the corrective aspect of biblical teaching because it can be difficult and unpleasant. It reminds me of my dad's standard line before he punished me: "Son, this hurts me more than it does you." I had trouble believing that as a child, but now that I am a parent and a grandparent, I know it is true. Confrontation with the purpose of bringing constructive warning and correction may be painful, but it is necessary to enable the church family to fulfill its mission and the individual members to discover their giftedness. Paul's letters provide numerous illustrations of corrective teaching with the goal of strengthening the church. We discover that Paul always administered correction in pastoral love and for the good of the church.

The goal of all instruction is the health and welfare of the body. When there must be correction, its goal must always be healing and restoration. While the pastor may provide most corrective teaching, all the members of the church must be willing to invest the time and energy required to assist in the healing of those who have received correction. The goal of ministry is to equip the members of the body for effective kingdom service.

If the pastor is assigned by God the task of teaching, he must be given sufficient time to prepare for his teaching/preaching ministry. One of the first growth barriers that confronted the early church was the complaint that the apostles were neglecting the needs of the Hellenistic widows. The church responded by electing servants (deacons) to assist in meeting this need so that the apostles could "devote ourselves to prayer and the ministry of the word" (Acts 6:4). Tragically, we often choose to "pile on" when someone complains about the lack of attention the pastor pays to someone in need rather than look for a biblical solution that will enable the pastor to spend adequate time in his study and still allow the church to meet legitimate needs of its members.

The giftedness of every member of the church ensures that the church can meet the needs of the growing congregation and still provide the pastor with adequate time for prayer and preparation for teaching. I might add one final thought on the teaching ministry of the pastor. For the teaching ministry of the church to be effective, members must make worship attendance and small-group Bible study high priorities.

The three pastoral functions that Paul laid out in this early letter to the Thessalonians are as vital today as they were in the first century. They are essential to the healthy growth of the church, vital in the discovery of individual giftedness, and crucial to the involvement of every member in meaningful ministry.

The Shared Ministry of the Body

Paul begins this section (1 Thess. 5:12) by requesting that the "brethren" appreciate their leaders. In verse 14 he repeats the word *brethren*, this time with a slightly stronger appeal: "We urge you." He uses the repetition of the word *brethren* to draw attention to the responsibility for ministry that is applicable to every member of the Thessalonian church. He is no longer looking at the responsibility of a small group of leaders, but he now turns his attention to the privilege and responsibility of every member to participate in the life and ministry of the church.

Admonish the Unruly

The specific issues Paul mentions here are tailored to the unique needs in Thessalonica, but they establish a mandate for "every member ministry," and they are as relevant today as ever. The brethren are first urged to "admonish the unruly."

We have already touched on the "unruly" members in Thessalonica who were in special need of warning. They are "standing out of rank," refusing to work, and thus their idleness has created a burden for the community. Refusal to work may have been related to their mistaken conviction that the Lord would return with such haste that earthly labor had little meaning. In 2 Thessalonians 3:6–15 Paul gives specific directions concerning the ministry to these persons. He first exhorts those who are behaving properly not to become weary in their own work. He then instructs them not to associate with those behaving in an undisciplined manner. They are not to regard the person as an enemy "but admonish him as a brother" (v. 15).

We would do well to follow Paul's instructions in our churches today. We may be tempted to throw up our hands and "drop out" of ministry duties when we see others in the church consuming the ministries of the church without contributing to the church's mission with their financial resources or their time. We must not become weary in doing good. We should also not give encouragement to those who, through their idleness, have become busybodies. We must refuse to listen to their complaining and refuse to cater to their whims so that they find their "unruly" behavior has no impact. We must admonish them as we would our own family member. The relationships of family and the work of the church are too vital for us to ignore the demand to "admonish the unruly."

Encourage the Fainthearted

Next Paul urges them to "encourage the fainthearted" (1 Thess. 5:14). This term may refer to members who have been distressed by persecution, discouraged by the death of a community member, or confused by the delay of the Lord. I mention these three items together because they may have been interrelated in the thinking of the "fainthearted." Paul devotes a portion of chapters 4 and 5 to a discussion of persons "who have fallen asleep in Jesus" (4:14) and speculation concerning "the times and the epochs" (5:1). Paul ends his discussion of the day of the Lord with a similar call to mutual encouragement. "Therefore encourage one another and build up one another, just as you also are doing" (5:11).

Persons who are disconsolate and discouraged for any reason must be consoled and encouraged. These persons do not need to be admonished, but they need to be encouraged. When we attempt to correct those who are discouraged, it compounds their problem and further alienates them from the life of the church.

For example, some may attempt to teach Sunday school, believing that teaching is their gift. In the process they discover that they are not serving in their gifted area, and they become discouraged and quit. They now feel like a failure and are tempted to leave the church. Such people don't need correction as quitters; they need encouragement and support.

Help the Weak

Community members are to "help the weak" (1 Thess. 5:14). The "weak" may refer to members whose faith has become shaky and unsettled. The word *help* is too weak a translation. These persons must be "clung to." People who are "weak" easily slip through the cracks of our church fellowship. They are often too frail and hurting to ask for help. They may drop out of church activities and become isolated, leading to an even greater need. Those who are stronger may inadvertently give the impression that these weak members need to suck it up and get on with life. The apparent strength of others can actually serve to further discourage those who are struggling in their faith.

Galatians, another early letter of Paul's, gives similar advice for restoring those who have stumbled because of a personal weakness. "Brethren, even if anyone is caught in any trespass, you who are spiritual, restore such a one in a spirit of gentleness; each one looking to yourself, so that you too will not be tempted. Bear one another's burdens, and thereby fulfill the law of Christ" (Gal. 6:1–2). By the nature of its giftedness, the community is designed for mutual care.

Be Patient with Everyone

The call to patience is not so much a ministry activity as it is an attitude for community. Patience is an essential element in all ministry. "Unruly," "fainthearted," and "weak" believers are not always easy to work with, and therefore patience is the indispensable element for the ministering community. As our study of spiritual gifts progresses through the various community ministry passages, you will see a demand for patience in every passage where the life and ministry of the community are in view.

The church is the family of faith; and close interpersonal relationships, like those we experience in our own family, require patience. The church member who feels the "call" to criticize every program of the church, the single adult who feels his or her needs are not being met, the child who demands constant attention—all call for patience from the ministering community. We sometimes forget that the church will always be made up of individuals who are at different levels of spiritual maturity. We must provide a safe, loving environment for every member to receive the necessary care from the body as members' minister to one another.

While we must show patience to all the brethren, we cannot allow those who feel called to criticize every program to disrupt the mission and ministry of the church. Thus we must remember that this section began with the instruction that we admonish the unruly. Church members must show patience and express love, but we must keep before us the preeminent mission of the church to advance the kingdom.

Never Repay Evil with Evil but Seek the Good

Paul would need to remind his readers that the community of faith is no place for someone to return evil for evil. First, we would hope that evil would never rear its ugly head in the church, and yet tragically it does. Christians have not yet reached a state of perfection. They are simply forgiven and moving toward conformity to Christ. When evil does manifest itself, we pray that it would not be returned in kind.

When you think about the church in terms of family, we can see why working with "unruly, fainthearted, weak" believers can create situations where someone responds in an evil manner to those who are members of the family. But this evil cannot be nurtured by allowing someone to repay evil with evil. That is how the world responds, not the church. We put an end to the cycle of evil by always seeking "after that which is good for one another and for all people" (1 Thess. 5:15). Notice that Paul not only prohibits getting even, he requires that we go the additional mile and "seek after that which is good." Redemptive behavior requires that we take the initiative to minister good to those who do evil to us.

A child once wrote a letter to God, saying, "Did you really mean do unto others as they do unto you, because if You did, then I'm going to fix my brother."[1] Misinterpretations of Scripture, such as this childish one, coupled with basic human nature, often bring out the "I am going to fix my brother" attitude in us. It takes a humble and patient spirit provided by the Holy Spirit to desire the best for those who do evil to us. That is the nature of the radical Christian community.

The pastoral leader(s) may be called to provide for caring, teaching, and administrating the church; but all members of the church are called by God, and gifted by the Spirit, to build up the fellowship of the church by ministering to one another. Many of the duties we have assigned to the professional staff are here commanded of all the brethren. Have you ever found yourself wondering about what the pastor is going to do for people who have their feelings hurt and have quit coming to church? Maybe they are members of the "unruly" or the "weak" that God is calling you to minister to.

The Inner Resources for Ministry

In 1 Thessalonians 5:16–18 Paul links together three brief exhortations: "Rejoice always; pray without ceasing; in everything give thanks" by indicating that these are "God's will for you in Christ Jesus." The quality of inner life provided by these three related activities will enable one to live and minister effectively in the context of community, which is often spoiled by our human failings. Our ability to encourage the fainthearted, to show patience, and to refuse to return evil for evil but to seek the good for the one offering evil depends on the work of the Spirit who produces His fruit in our lives. This joyful approach to life and ministry is produced by the intimacy of our relationship to God, nurtured through prayer and thanksgiving.

The source of divine power necessary for effective ministry is tapped as we worship both privately and corporately. During corporate worship the community is knit together and built up through the event of worship.

Rejoice Always

Before you pass over this section by arguing that it is not natural for anyone to respond to adverse circumstances with joy, you must note that this is an imperative, "be joyful." Joy does not refer to our natural attitude. Joy is not the natural response of happiness that we easily manifest when things go our way. Joy is the undergirding strength of our life produced by the Holy Spirit and is unrelated to our circumstances, personality type, or natural ability. Believers can manifest joy during times of sorrow (2 Cor. 6:10), adversity (cp. Matt. 5:10–12), or persecution (Luke 6:22–23). Earlier, in 1 Thessalonians 1:7, Paul referenced their experience of joy provided by the indwelling Holy Spirit when they received the word in much tribulation.

Joy comes from the same Greek stem as the word *grace*. Our experience of grace enables us to manifest joy in the midst of every circumstance of life. Joy is based on our understanding of the majesty of God who is at work in every circumstance of our lives, working for our good and conforming us to the image of His Son (Rom. 8:28–29). It is the firm assurance that nothing and no one can separate us from the love of God in Christ Jesus our Lord (8:31–39).

Pray without Ceasing

The three commands are all interrelated. The abiding prayer life of the believer provides the undergirding resource of joy. The word Paul uses here is a general word that would include all forms of prayer. Notice that prayer is not an activity of set times and places. It is not confined to buildings of worship or liturgical calendars. It is our attitude toward life itself. It is the breath of Christian existence. Nothing can be accomplished for God that is not bathed by prayer, and thus it is the life of the Christian.

Not long ago I had the joy of visiting with a friend who works in a predominately Muslim city. One evening we had dinner with a young Muslim woman. After giving me a gift of handmade Muslim prayer beads, she asked me why Christians did not pray with the regularity that Muslims prayed. I must confess that I felt the pain of conviction concerning those moments and days when I attempt ministry in my own strength with little attention to prayer.

Once I recovered from my internal struggle, I told her about the intimacy of our prayer life, which is like an all-day dialogue with our Father. "Christians," I told her, "are not limited to certain times and periods when we pray. We are privileged to live consciously in the presence of our Father, conversing with Him without ceasing." It was apparent that this was a novel idea that she had not considered from her Muslim background, where prayer occurs with specified regularity as the call to prayer echoes from the mosque five times a day. As they finger their prayer beads, they repeat the ninety-nine names of Allah, none contain the idea that he is "father" to the Muslim.

Here is the question I want to pose. Do we pray with the intimacy of a child who must stay in constant contact with the Father? Do we live consciously in His presence, or do we only address Him when we have tried everything else?

In Everything Give Thanks

We are looking at an attitude of life that comes from the understanding of grace and issues from our constant state of prayerfulness. In Romans 1:21 Paul indicates that a lack of gratitude is characteristic of unbelief. Christians, on the other hand, are marked by their attitude of gratitude.

> *When we understand that we deserved death because of our sinful rebellion but that we have been granted life as a free gift of God's grace, we are compelled to give thanks in every circumstance.*

When we understand that we deserved death because of our sinful rebellion but that we have been granted life as a free gift of God's grace, we are compelled to give thanks in every circumstance. We not only give thanks for our redemption, but we give thanks for our assurance that God is at work in all our circumstances to conform us to the image of His Son.

This does not suggest that we glibly give thanks for difficult circumstances such as sickness or persecution as if they cause us no pain. The call for "universal thanks" does not suggest that we believe God is the author of evil that we encounter. God is incapable of tempting us to evil (James 1:13). We give thanks that God is bigger than all our circumstances and thus is able to work through them for our good and His glory. We can thank God that He can work in everything for our good. Our good is conforming to His image. We give thanks because we know that our sovereign God is at work in every event to make us like His Son.

We have the resources for daily living and for ministry in the community of faith provided for us in Christ Jesus. We access those resources both privately and corporately through worship. The three imperatives we have considered are linked together as God's will for us in Christ. Prayer is at the heart of our ability to manifest joy in every circumstance, and the fruit of the Spirit's work in our lives enables us to give thanks in everything. The Spirit enables us to live and work together for the cause of the kingdom. He provides the unity necessary for the diversely gifted body to work in unity.

Five Imperatives for Spirit-Empowered Ministry

Paul concludes this section with five interrelated imperatives addressed to the entire community. Since these verbs are in the imperative, they are not suggestions but commands for community ministry.

Do Not Quench the Spirit; Do Not Despise Prophetic Utterances

The first two negatives—"Do not quench the Spirit; do not despise prophetic utterances" (1 Thess. 5:19–20)—may indicate that Paul has in mind specific practices that are already in existence in the community. In other words, someone in Thessalonica is guilty of quenching the Spirit by ignoring the teaching of authentic prophecy.

A word of warning! We must be careful not to read the issues that Paul will face in Corinth into this passage, such as an exaggerated emphasis on tongues and the resulting spiritual pride. Many commentators read this brief passage while wearing their "Corinthian spectacles." These five brief imperatives do not provide us with sufficient information to conclude that the Thessalonian community was struggling with specific issues related to the abuse of spiritual gifts as was the church in Corinth. If there had been a serious issue related to the exercise of gifts, we should assume that Paul would have addressed it in greater specificity as he does when he writes to the Corinthians.

These two negative imperatives make clear that Paul desires the church to allow for freedom in the exercise of spiritual gifts, particularly prophecy. Paul has taught them that each Christian has received the Holy Spirit (1:5, 7 and 4:8). This early community ministry passage in 1 Thessalonians does not contain the detailed teaching that we find later in the Corinthian and Roman letters, but the idea that all are gifted for ministry is clearly implied in 5:14–15. To prohibit gifted members of the body from exercising their God-given abilities in ministry would quench the Spirit. The image of quenching the Spirit suggests the putting out of a flame or light.

Have we allowed our fear over charismatic excess to create such fear concerning spiritual gifts that we are in danger of putting out the flame of the Spirit? The Spirit is the gift of the Father through the Son, and He is only capable of giving good gifts.

The only gift mentioned specifically by Paul in this context is prophecy. If Paul has in mind the same definition for prophecy in this passage that he articulates in 1 Corinthians 14:3, then we are not looking at a "predictive gift" that provides new revelation. Rather we are looking at an intelligible message, whose content is from the Lord, spoken with the purpose of "edification and exhortation and consolation."

The word translated *despise* is a particularly strong word and suggests that Paul has in mind the "prophetic utterances" of the authentic leaders in Thessalonica that were being ignored (1 Thess. 5:20). There were apparently various "prophetic voices" in Thessalonica, and not all of them had proved to be true, as 2 Thessalonians 2:2 clearly shows. If the Thessalonians responded to the prophetic confusion by despairing of all prophecy, they would forfeit the benefit of authentic prophecy.

It is equally possible that Paul had in view the "unruly" persons who were ignoring his commands (2 Thess. 3) and possibly challenging the teaching of those men Paul left in charge. Paul links "do not despise prophetic utterance" with "do not quench the Spirit" (1 Thess. 5:19) to underline the divine necessity of listening to those who speak an authentic word from the Lord.

Examine Everything Carefully; Hold Fast to That Which Is Good

The next two imperatives—"But examine everything carefully; hold fast to that which is good" (1 Thess. 5:21)—are positive. Rather than despising prophecy, they must "examine everything carefully." Paul feared the disastrous results of a wholesale rejection of prophetic speech, but he was equally aware that the possibility of spiritual fraud existed. Thus the unquestioned acceptance of all prophetic speech would be unsatisfactory. After careful examination of the attitude of the prophet and the content of the prophetic speech, they must "hold fast to that which is good; abstain from every form of evil" (vv. 21–22).

What are the criteria for evaluating prophetic utterance? The word *good* can be translated as "genuine." If we use that meaning, Paul would be suggesting a criterion that determines the source and the nature of the inspired utterance. Today we would ask whether the teaching aligns itself with the content of Scripture and whether the individuals prove themselves to be faithful servants through their hard work on behalf of the church. It is also possible that "good" means "ethically right" or "beneficial." This would cause us to look to the edifying nature of the prophetic message. Does this person glorify God and seek to edify the church?

Abstain from Every Form of Evil

While believers are to hold fast to the good, they must "abstain from every form of evil" (1 Thess. 5:22). "Evil" here might mean "spurious" and thus refer to false prophetic utterances. This principal could be applied to the use of any spiritual gift. We must not accept uncritically anything and everything that is presented as the work of the Spirit. On the other hand, we cannot reject spiritual manifestations because some may prove to be inauthentic. We must cling to those which are good with the same tenacity that we reject charlatans.

The brevity of the passage will not allow us to reach too many conclusions on the evaluation of the prophetic utterance. We can safely conclude that Paul wanted to strengthen the position of those who were the recognized leaders of the community. He wanted the church to embrace the manifestation of the Spirit's presence in their ongoing ministry, and not overreact to a few zealots and thus quench the Spirit. He seemed to have confidence that the God who gives the gifts would also provide the discernment to enable the church to know the difference between good and evil.

A Brief Overview

Paul's treatment of the gifted ministry of the church is basic in this passage. Yet many of the themes presented here are more fully developed in later gift passages. As is the case with all Pauline letters, the instructions given in this section are written in response to the particular needs being faced by the young church. They are facing affliction from without and dissension from within. Paul encourages them in numerous areas of spiritual growth, but he focuses on the unique role of the ministering community, made up of gifted leaders and members who must work together for the health of the community.

Several distinctive themes are found here.

- Every member is responsible for ministry in the community, and every member must be concerned for the other members' spiritual welfare.
- Even though all members are empowered for ministry, God has gifted and called some to perform leadership functions. They must be esteemed and loved for the sake of the ministry that must be accomplished. Three primary functions of the leaders emerge— pastoral ministry among the members, oversight of the ministry, and instruction of the brethren.
- The relationships forged between members of the community are critical to the health and ministry of the church.

Questions for Reflection

1. We have seen that God calls and gifts certain persons for leadership in the church. Who are these persons in your church family?

2. The recognition and acceptance of these persons by the community assures the success of their ministry and builds the unity of the church. What can you do to recognize and encourage those who serve in leadership functions?

3. The fundamental teaching of Scripture is that every member is gifted for service to the Lord through His church. How do you serve the Lord in your church? If you do not presently serve, what would you like to do?

4. How important do you believe the church is to your spiritual growth?

2 | A Visit to Corinth

The Historical Setting

Over the years I have had the pleasure of taking several trips to the Holy Land. I was thrilled to stand at the sight where Jesus may have delivered His great kingdom manifesto, the Sermon on the Mount. I had the privilege of reading selected passages to our tour group as the wind from the Sea of Galilee carried my words like an unseen public-address system. I was moved to tears when we visited where some believe the crucifixion and burial took place. I was amazed to watch tourists whisper, as if they were in a church, when they walked through the garden.

Yet I must admit that I was most excited about my visit to ancient Corinth. I spent the better part of three years of graduate study in this city. I wasn't there in person, but as I poured over the text of the Corinthian letters, I had attempted to imagine this city during Paul's ministry there. The site was nothing but excavated rubble. Standing atop the Acrocorinth, a towering plateau nearly two thousand feet above the surrounding land, I could see why Paul had been intent on establishing an outpost for the church in this pivotal site. As I walked the market street, I could almost see Paul in his market stall, selling hides and sharing the gospel.

Corinth had flourished as a Greek city-state before and after the golden years of Athens (fifth century BC). However, in the second century the city came into conflict with Rome and was subsequently destroyed by the Roman consul Lucius Mumius in 146 BC. The site lay dormant for nearly one hundred years until it was refounded by Julius Caesar as a Roman colony in 44 BC.

The strategic location of Corinth as the sentry city of a four and one-half mile isthmus that bridged the Peloponnese and the mainland and separated the

Saronic and Corinthian gulfs made Corinth a strategic and desirable site for a city. Most ship traffic found it safer and easier to take the inland route through Corinth than to go around the Peloponnese. Corinth not only had a growing population; it had a regular flow of visitors.

Corinth had everything necessary to make it a prosperous and licentious city. It had a supply of good water from the springs, a natural defense provided by the towering Acrocorinth, two harbors, which controlled East-West commerce, and it hosted the Isthmian games, which ranked just below the Olympics in importance. As you can imagine, a city like Corinth in the first century attracted inhabitants and guests like Las Vegas in the twenty-first century.

Corinth was first repopulated by freedmen from Rome. The rebirth of Corinth provided both a golden opportunity for a freedman to seize the moment for economic prosperity and a convenient way for Rome to rid itself of potential troublemakers. Corinth, with all of its natural advantages, attracted people from the East and the West. The Romans were dominant, and they brought with them their Roman gods and their culture. But the process of Hellenization (Greek influence) had already impacted Roman culture; and since Corinth was historically Greek, it maintained its ties with Greek religion, philosophy, and art.

Thus the religious environment of Corinth was a melting pot of religious practices from East and West. From the East came the mystery cults of Egypt and Asia; from Rome came the Roman gods. With the expulsion of the Jews from Rome by Claudius (Acts 18:2), Judaism with its synagogues and peculiar belief that there was only one God was added to the religious stew. To add a little spice, God tossed into the stew the greatest missionary of the first century, the apostle Paul. He quickly established a friendship with Aquila and Priscilla, Jews from Rome, who shared his profession as a tent maker. This church planter extraordinaire dedicated eighteen months to developing a Christian stronghold in this critical city (Acts 18:11).

The newly reestablished city of Corinth quickly developed an aristocracy based on wealth, which created a fiercely entrepreneurial spirit in the city. Not all the new inhabitants struck it rich in Corinth, so there were thousands of artisans and slaves—the working class—that made up the bulk of the population. Debauchery and religion flourished side by side. Old Corinth had gained such a reputation for sexual vice that Aristophanes (450–385 BC) coined the verb *korinthiazo,* which meant "to act like a Corinthian"—a shorthand expression for sexual fornication. Sexual sin was abundant in this seaport town where money flowed freely.[1]

Corinth may not look like the most receptive environment for church planting, but the gospel is good seed, and soon after Paul's arrival a thriving church was planted. As you might expect, the church reflected the community. The church seems to have been made up predominately of Gentiles from the lower socioeconomic strata. Nonetheless, several wealthy families were among the members. There were also a few leading Jews, including the leader of the local synagogue. The diverse community reflected the makeup of the community at large.

The Church and the Letters

Corinth may not look like the most receptive environment for church planting, but the gospel is good seed, and soon after Paul's arrival a thriving church was planted.

In the next four chapters we will look at the church at Corinth because most of the biblical material on spiritual gifts is found in 1 Corinthians. The church at Corinth may be typified by numerous terms, but *boring* would not be one of them. The lack of unity can be seen in the claims— "'I am of Paul,' and 'I of Apollos,' and 'I of Cephas,' and 'I of Christ'" (1:12). But their disunity, while a critical issue, is only the tip of the iceberg.

Some of the members of the church were engaged in a noisy court battle, which Paul declared a "total defeat" for the church (6:7). Everyone in the community seemed to insist on their own rights, whether it is the freedom to eat meat sacrificed to idols (chap. 8) or the freedom for the women to speak in the assembly with their heads uncovered (chap. 11). The church was scandalized by the word that a man was sleeping with his stepmother (5:1). The greater tragedy was that not everyone was upset with this abominable behavior, which Paul declared, "does not exist even among the Gentiles." Apparently some proudly saw such behavior as a sign of their advanced spirituality (5:2). The last time the church celebrated the Lord's Supper, some left hungry while the wealthier members were tipsy from too much wine (11:21).

The whole community seemed to be confused about the matter of spiritual gifts. Do certain gifts prove that some are spiritually elite? This must have been the question of many in Corinth. Some individuals may have claimed to speak with the tongues of angels (13:1). These people saw their abundance of gifts as sure proof of their spiritual ascendancy. The plethora of gifts possessed by those who claimed to be spirituals had caused others to doubt that they were gifted at all.

The detailed discussion of spiritual gifts in 1 Corinthians demands that we pay close attention to this letter in order to develop an understanding of spiritual gifts. We must give due consideration to the Corinthian situation in order to distinguish between basic principles concerning gifts and corrections of abuses unique to Corinth. Many commentators do not give sufficient attention to the central role that misunderstandings about gifts play in the difficulties plaguing the Corinthian church.

Paul's introductory paragraph in his letters often alerts the reader to the central issue being addressed by the letter. The first matter Paul addresses in the Corinthian letter is the abundance of spiritual gifts in evidence in Corinth. The mention of gifts actually precedes his mention of the various factions within the church, suggesting that gifts are more of an issue than the factions.

Immediately following his standard greeting, Paul speaks to the *abundance* of gifts possessed. First Corinthians 1:4–5 likely echoes the claims of some in Corinth. "I thank my God always concerning you for the grace of God which was given you in Christ Jesus, that in *everything* you were enriched in Him, in *all* speech and *all* knowledge" (my italics). While Paul cites this boast of *abundance* without any corrective in this first paragraph, he would later remind them that they didn't possess all knowledge, nor did any of them possess all the gifts.

Many people turn to Corinthians, without fully understanding its historical and situational context, to develop their theology of gifts. Passages are lifted out of their immediate and historical context and used to defend existing practice in a particular church or denomination. Or conversely, another passage is lifted from the same context to argue against a particular practice. One group quotes the first half of 1 Corinthians 14:5, "Now I wish that you all spoke in tongues," and argues that all Christians must speak in tongues. Another group quotes a portion of 1 Corinthians 13:8, "If there are tongues, they will cease," and concludes that no one today can speak in tongues. How can we reach contradictory conclusions from one man's writing?

A Wealth of Material

Fortunately the two Corinthian letters combined with Luke's account in Acts 18:1–17 provide us with the material to build a reasonably accurate picture of the church at Corinth. Paul arrived in Corinth on the heels of several difficult ministry ventures. At Philippi, Thessalonica, and Berea he had promising beginnings cut short by fanatical Jews who saw him as a dangerous heretic. He experienced little success in Athens. From Athens he journeyed to Corinth, and in his own words he came to Corinth "in weakness and in fear and in much trembling" (1 Cor. 2:3).

Paul began his ministry in Corinth by teaching in the synagogue. When many of the Jews resisted his message and uttered blasphemies, he relocated his ministry to the home of Titus Justus, a worshipper of God. Paul also refocused his ministry with a goal of reaching the Gentiles. Paul's early converts in Corinth were Jews, including Crispus, the leader of the synagogue, and devout Gentiles who had attached themselves to the synagogues. These people are often referred to as "God-fearers" in the Bible because they were seeking the one true God. They were often receptive to the gospel.

Paul's ministry in Corinth lasted eighteen months. Because of the success of his preaching, the Jews made a united attack on Paul and brought him before the judge's bench. The judge ruled that the accusations against Paul were nothing more than questions about words and names. This legal ruling actually served to legitimize Christianity in Corinth. Not long after this event Paul departed for Ephesus.

After Paul departed Corinth, the church was led by Stephanas, Fortunatus, and Achaicus (1 Cor. 16:17). During Paul's absence other leaders visited Corinth. Some, like Apollos, augmented Paul's message by watering where Paul had sown (3:6), but others seem to have created considerable confusion, particularly in regard to spiritual gifts.

Sometime after his departure Paul wrote a letter to the Corinthians that no longer exists. The evidence for the existence of this letter is found in 1 Corinthians 5:9: "I wrote to you in my letter not to associate with immoral people." Its contents were misunderstood; and that misunderstanding, along with other concerns, prompted the writing of the letter we call 1 Corinthians.

Paul had several sources of information that must have influenced the topics he chose to address in this lengthy letter. Members of the Corinthian church had kept Paul abreast of the happenings in the church at Corinth. We know, for example, that members of Chloe's household had brought Paul the disheartening news that quarrels existed and disunity reigned in the church (1:11–12).

Paul had received a letter from Corinth, perhaps brought to him by Stephanas, Fortunatus, and Achaicus (16:15–17). We can't be certain if this letter was commissioned by the entire church or was initiated by a portion of the members. The letter sought clarification on issues related to his original teaching and on other matters that had become divisive in his absence. Paul's answers to the concerns posed in this letter are prefaced by the phrase "now concerning." Paul's response to the letter from Corinth begins in 1 Corinthians 7:1 where he addresses marriage and sexual purity. Based on the sometimes combative nature of Paul's response, some individuals in Corinth likely disagreed with portions of his teaching and prohibitions. The section on spiritual gifts begins with the phrase "now concerning." This suggests that his lengthy teaching on gifts was actually prompted by confusion that had developed since his departure.

The Holy Spirit prompted Paul to write a powerful letter of correction and instruction, which also helps us today answer our questions about spiritual gifts. Accurate interpretation of individual texts depends on a clear understanding of the historical situation in Corinth. We will devote the remainder of this chapter to a description of the Corinthian community by allowing the letter itself to describe the environment of the Corinthian church.

A Closer Look at the Corinthian Church

The presence of party names in 1 Corinthians 1:12—"'I am of Paul,' and 'I of Apollos,' and 'I of Cephas,' and 'I of Christ'"—have caused many interpreters to attempt to explain the Corinthian difficulties by describing the belief system held by the different groups. First, this approach to interpreting the Corinthian correspondence flounders because the letters do not provide sufficient information to describe actual parties and their beliefs. Second, the letter itself suggests a friendly relationship between Paul and Apollos (3:4–9 and 4:6).

While the presence of organized groups of people with distinctive theological positions doesn't seem likely in Corinth, a number of individuals in the community shared similar beliefs and practices. They were not formed into actual factions because they relied not so much on theological understanding as they did on shared experience. We see a similar phenomenon today when people are drawn together based on a particular worship style or spiritual experience and have little regard for any denominational or theological foundation.

We Are Spirituals

At the core of the Corinthian difficulties was the conviction on the part of some that they were "spiritual persons" in an elitist sense. Spirituals or "spiritual persons" translates the Greek word *pneumatikos,* which is from the root *pneuma* meaning "spirit." This word occurs only twenty-four times in all the Pauline letters, and fifteen of them are found in 1 Corinthians. On five distinct occasions *pneumatikos* refers to spiritual persons (2:13–15; 3:1; 12:1; and

14:37). Frequently we can detect a polemic overtone to Paul's use of the word. For example, in 3:1 Paul states that he cannot refer to them as "spiritual men" because they are bickering and fighting like children. They wanted to claim advanced spiritual status, but their childish behavior indicated otherwise.

Paul begins the discussion of spiritual gifts in 1 Corinthians 12 by responding to a question posed by the Corinthians in their letter to him. Their question must have implied that they thought spiritual gifts provided proof of superior spiritual attainment. I have reconstructed the question as follows: "Doesn't the possession of spiritual gifts prove that we are spiritual persons?" After three chapters of corrective teaching, Paul concludes with a stern warning: "If anyone thinks he is a prophet or a spiritual (*pneumatikos*), let him recognize that the things which I write to you are the Lord's commandment" (14:37). Certain showy gifts are at the heart of the claim of some to be spiritual persons. They believe these gifts provide verifiable proof. Paul argues that the proof of spirituality will be their recognition of and conformity to his apostolic teaching.

It is unlikely that the spirituals were an identified group of people who actually organized themselves to oppose Paul's leadership and teaching. It doesn't appear that the people involved had a clearly defined theological understanding of gifts. Their zeal for gifts may have emerged from their fascination over the supernatural elements of Christian conversion and their desire for religious ecstasy. As new believers they were like excited children in a candy store.

Their zeal for gifts may have emerged from their fascination over the supernatural elements of Christian conversion and their desire for religious ecstasy. As new believers they were like excited children in a candy store.

Paul uses the word *zealous* (14:12) to describe the youthful and often immature enthusiasm for gifts and seeks to redirect their zeal for gifts toward edification. "So also you, since you are zealous of spiritual gifts, seek to abound for the edification of the church." Their misguided zeal had led them to jealous bickering over religious leaders (chap. 3). When we read 2 Corinthians, we notice that the zealous boasting in various leaders was related to the presumed possession of powerful gifts and claimed visionary experiences of these leaders.

Their spiritual zeal was primarily focused on gifts (1 Cor. 12:31; 14:1, 12, 39). They believed gifts provided the visible sign that they were spiritual.

Paul faced a dilemma. He did not want to quench the spiritual enthusiasm of these new believers, but he did want to direct it toward more mature purposes. My dad, who was a country preacher, used to say that he wasn't sure whether it was easier to warm up a spiritual corpse or cool down a zealot. Paul faced both problems. While some were zealous for ecstatic experiences, the next powerful teacher, and their own rights to express their gifts, others had responded with a calculated coolness toward spiritual matters.

We face the same issues in the twenty-first-century church. Some members flit from one church to another looking for the next powerful preacher, a dramatic show of the power of the Spirit, and the overwhelming religious experience. Other believers avoid any conversation about the Spirit or any demonstration of His power for fear that they will be drawn into excess. Both positions are in error.

Possession of certain dramatic gifts had given the spirituals a distorted and inflated image of themselves. In their own thinking, they were spiritual giants. The word translated "to make arrogant" or "to puff up" occurs only seven times in the entire New Testament, and six are found in 1 Corinthians. The word "boast" occurs fifty-three times in the New Testament, and thirty-five of them are in this letter. What does that tell us about the spirituals? The picture is clear. They saw the gifts as signs of their spiritual ascendancy, and thus they arrogantly boasted about their gifts and sought every opportunity to display them without any concern for the edification of the body.

Although Paul did not face opposition from an organized group of opponents, he did face opposition from various "spiritual persons" who found him to be lacking in powerful gifts. The spirituals, on the basis of their gifts, had placed themselves and their leaders above Paul. In their estimation he was lacking in spiritual wisdom and dramatic gifts. Paul reminds them that no matter how many teachers they might have, he is still their father and can thus bring reproof (4:14–21). He gives them this strong warning because "some have become arrogant, as though I were not coming to you" (4:18). When he returns, he promises that he will find out not the strength of the words of the arrogant but their power (4:19). In other words, their spirituality is based on the strength of their boasting and not the truth of their lives.

Paul does not approach the arrogant spirituals as enemies but as wayward children. "I do not write these things to shame you, but to admonish you as my beloved children" (4:14). Some of his children had chosen to assert their own rights rather than live up to the standards inherent in the gospel. Paul desires that his letter have a corrective impact so that he can come with love and a gentle spirit, but he fears that they might need a disciplinarian. The Corinthians' disrespect for Paul's God-given leadership had led to a distorted and overinflated view of themselves as spiritual giants.

A Superstitious View of Grace

With their immature view of the Christian life, we should not be surprised to discover that the spirituals had a crude, almost magical view of the spiritual existence. Paul uses the word "spiritual" three times in 10:3–4 where he compares the spiritual journey of the Corinthians to the Israelites sojourn under Moses. The use of the word *baptized* (v. 2), the reference to spiritual food and drink, and the ensuing discussion leads to the conclusion that some in Corinth believed that baptism and the Lord's Supper possessed or imparted spiritual power.

Therefore Paul reminds the Corinthians that the Israelites were baptized into Moses. They had eaten spiritual food and had drunk spiritual drink, a reference to the provision of manna and water from the rock. Yet they had been laid low in the wilderness because of their behavior. This example is intended to serve as a stern warning against spiritual arrogance based on baptism or participation in the Lord's table that is not accompanied by a true transformation of the heart.

Paul's immediate application of the story of the Israelites' failure in the wilderness was to the arrogant participation of some Corinthians in events that took place in a pagan temple. Many social events, such as weddings, would have been held in facilities dedicated to pagan worship. Thus the new believers rationalized their attendance at these events based on both their knowledge that an idol was nothing and their arrogant belief that they were too mature to fall into idolatry. Paul agrees that neither the idol nor the meat sacrificed to it are anything (10:19–20) but argues that the mature believer should have no part in anything related to the demonic (v. 20). Paul's main concern is the arrogance that led some to behave as if they were so spiritual that participation in such events could not influence them.

Their magical and superstitious view of the Lord's table had not only led to careless participation in events at a pagan temple; it had caused them to neglect the true purpose and meaning of the fellowship meal that often preceded the actual Lord's Supper. Instead of creating fellowship and mutual concern, their practice had caused dissension. Some wealthy members came early and ate and drank their rich food without concern for the poorer members (11:17–34). Paul rebukes them, telling them that these gatherings that demonstrate no concern for the unity of the body were in no way a participation in the Lord's Supper. A proper understanding of the table would lead to humility and unity. It would cause them to discern the body of Christ in the unity and fellowship of believers and thus to pursue behavior that would edify fellow Christians.

This magical view of grace may seem foreign to us, but it still exists today. Some people seem to think that if they are baptized into the church, this act alone will put them right with God and protect them from evil influences. Thus they walk the aisle and are baptized and then return to their former way of life assuming that their baptism assures them of heaven. A similar superstitious attitude is seen when someone uses the symbols of prayer or participation in Mass or the Lord's Supper as a religious crutch that grants them luck or makes them immune to bad circumstances. Some people wear religious jewelry like a good luck charm that offers divine protection. Still others today seek a deeper level of religious ecstasy, believing it assures them of greater spiritual authority.

Some people wear religious jewelry like a good luck charm that offers divine protection. Still others today seek a deeper level of religious ecstasy, believing it assures them of greater spiritual authority.

The belief that any religious activity or experience, not accompanied by true repentance and conversion, can make a person right with God, signals a magical view of the operation of grace. Any suggestion that a religious or ecstatic experience makes one spiritually elite and therefore not bound by the dictates of Scripture is dangerous religious superstition. These distorted views of grace are dangerous precisely because they can inoculate us from true spirituality. A proper understanding of grace will cause us to seek God for God alone, not for any supposed favors or gifts that might be forthcoming. Grace will always lead to humility and holiness and never to spiritual arrogance and immoral behavior.

Gifts without Limitations

Some in Corinth mistakenly believed that certain gifts had a "sign" value that proved them to be spiritually elite. For example, tongues and other miraculous gifts were cited as proof of one's advanced spirituality. That was not the only area of confusion related to gifts. The word "all" is frequently connected to certain gifts indicating a lack of understanding concerning both the appropriate role of gifts and the inherent limitations of gifts. We can see this exaggerated claim to gifts without limits in the opening paragraph of this letter. Paul may well be reflecting their boasts when he writes: "That in everything you were enriched in Him, in all speech and all knowledge" (1 Cor. 1:5).

One of the areas where their conviction that their gifts were without limitations had created problems was in the area of wisdom and knowledge. They believed that their wisdom and knowledge gave them special insight into the realities of Christian existence in the here and now. For example, a claim of special knowledge was used to justify eating meat offered to idols. Paul likely echoes accurately the boast of the spirituals in 8:1: "We know that we all have knowledge." Based on this exaggerated boast, they conclude that idols are nothing (v. 4) and thus decide that eating meat offered to idols is of no consequence.

Paul counters their arrogant boasting by assuring them that their knowledge is not as total as they believed. "If anyone supposes that he knows anything, he has not yet known as he ought to know" (8:2). True knowledge, in contrast to their arrogant knowledge, would lead them to avoid idol meat in regard for the brethren (vv. 7–13). The bottom line—their knowledge had led to arrogant disregard for the brethren, indicating it is less than "full" knowledge.

The spirituals believed that Paul's teaching lacked depth and spiritual insight, perhaps because he refused to base his teachings on visionary experiences. Paul admits that he did not come with "superiority of speech or of wisdom" (2:1). He determined rather to preach the simple message of the cross in genuine humility. His words, however, differed greatly from those of their vaunted wise teachers. "And my message and my preaching were not in persuasive words of wisdom, but in the demonstration of the Spirit and of power" (2:4). The evidence of Paul's "Spirit power" was their conversion (v. 5). They sought visible signs such as miraculous gifts; Paul sought the fruit of evangelism.

Paul's primary corrective concerning their wisdom is found in 2:6–16. Paul declares that he did speak wisdom among those who were mature, implying that they "didn't get it" because of their immaturity. Paul again uses the vocabulary of the spirituals only to turn the table and demonstrate the content of true knowledge. True wisdom was not someone's private insight into the mysteries of God, but it was a clear understanding of the cross of Christ. The "truly spiritual person" would thus recognize the gracious character of all of life. "Now we have received, not the spirit of the world, but the Spirit who is from God, so that we may know the things freely given to us by God" (1 Cor. 2:12).

We have come to one of the primary correctives for the exaggerated boasting of the spirituals based on an overevaluation of their gifts. An appropriate understanding of the cross of Christ will enable one to understand the gracious nature of all life. If all of spiritual life is an act of grace, why would anyone boast concerning any gift—knowledge, wisdom, tongues, or prophecy? The act of boasting is the undoing of their boast to be spiritual persons. They haven't understood Paul's corrective teaching because he speaks of things that can only be discerned by one who has the presence of the Spirit, who Himself communicates spiritual truths to spiritual men.[2] The powerful and blunt corrective of 3:1 can hardly be ignored: "And I, brethren, could not speak to you as to spiritual men, but as to men of flesh, as to infants in Christ."

> An appropriate understanding of the cross of Christ will enable one to understand the gracious nature of all life.

My granddaughter Emerson is nearly four and has reached the "why" stage of life. "Why" precedes virtually every sentence or even stands alone as a sentence. "Why is the sky blue?" is a question that can be answered by a detailed discussion of how atmospheric conditions determine the sky's visual appearance, but such an answer would be both foolish and counterproductive for a three-year-old. You do not want to discourage children from asking questions, but giving them more than they can comprehend will frustrate both you and the children. The situation in Corinth is similar. It is not that Paul cannot communicate matters of deep wisdom. Rather, the immaturity of the Corinthians had rendered them unable to comprehend the deep wisdom of the cross and the accompanying message of grace.

A true understanding of the cross will eliminate all boasting. This in turn would stop the foolish strife created by their pitting one wise leader against another.

I would like to tell you that the spirituals accepted Paul's deeper wisdom of the cross communicated in this letter, but evidence from 2 Corinthians indicates that their desire for wise teachers with visionary messages did not subside. In that letter Paul finally concedes that he too had a visionary experience. His experience was not communicable (12:1–4). Thus Paul preferred to teach the intelligible and edifying message of the cross rather than impart some mystical message from the Lord obtained in a vision.

This distorted mystical individualism so desired by the spirituals is not the purpose of the giving of the gifts. In fact such distortion has caused many Christians to avoid the topic of gifts altogether. But we cannot allow false emphases to keep us from experiencing the genuine empowering of the Spirit who enables and gifts us to advance God's kingdom.

> *A true understanding of the cross will eliminate all boasting.*

We Already Reign

Some in Corinth were clearly confused about issues related to the end of time. The word "spiritual" occurs four times in 1 Corinthians 15:44–46 in a manner that suggests that Paul needed to correct an *overrealized* eschatology. The word *eschatology* means the study of the end of time. The major topic of 1 Corinthians 15 is the resurrection of Christ and the coming resurrection of all believers. This is a passage most pastors read at funerals to bring comfort and assurance that death's sting has been removed through the resurrection.

To say that some in Corinth had an overrealized eschatology means they believed they *already* possessed all of the supernatural powers and blessings heaven has to offer. In other words they believed they were already enjoying *full* resurrection power now. It is possible that some thought their "unknown tongues" was the language of the angels (13:1) thus providing concrete proof of their exalted status and full participation in the kingdom. The spirituals had no place for weakness or dishonor in the present existence. To correct their over-realized eschatology, Paul insists that the *present* body is "perishable," "sown in dishonor," "sown in weakness," "sown a natural body."

Paul assures them that there will be a resurrection body. When it is given, it will be "raised in glory," "raised in power," "raised a spiritual body." The spirituals had gotten the cart before the horse. They were claiming *all* the powers and realities that belong to the future. They were claiming that they already participated in the full glory and power of the Lord. Paul agrees that there is "a spiritual body" (15:44), but it follows the planting (death) of the "natural body" (15:46). Notice that Paul concludes the discussion of the resurrection with a call to responsible Christian service in the *present.* "Therefore, my beloved brethren, be steadfast, immovable, always abounding in the work of the Lord" (15:58). The spirituals were so heavenly minded they were no earthly good. Paul wants them to come back down to earth and get busy in the work of the Lord.

This overrealized eschatology is actually reflected earlier in the letter. Paul summarizes their own understanding of their spiritual status thus: "You are already filled, you have already become rich, you have become kings without us" (4:8). Paul wistfully comments, "I wish that you had become kings so that we also might reign with you" (4:8b). In other words, if one believer was already reigning, the same would be true of all genuine believers.

> *The spirituals were so heavenly minded they were no earthly good.*

Paul contrasts their supposed present exalted status and greatness with the weakness and dishonor accorded the apostles. Notice Paul's emphasis on the "present" in his declaration—"To this present hour we are both hungry and thirsty, are poorly clothed, and are roughly treated, and are homeless" (4:11). He provides a tongue-in-cheek contrast when he writes, "We are fools for Christ's sake, but you are prudent in Christ; we are weak, but you are strong; you are distinguished, but we are without honor" (4:10).

Paul lovingly declares that he has no desire to shame them. His goal is to admonish them as beloved children. Their arrogant assessment of themselves as spiritual giants had caused them to neglect their God-given leader. Thus Paul reminds them that while they may have many tutors, he alone is their spiritual father.

We find a similar distorted, overrealized eschatology today in a more subtle form. You may have heard some popular preacher proclaim that the kingdom of God has already come in its full expression. He then assures the faithful that no Christian should be sick, suffer discouragement, or be poor. If such a condition exists, he argues that it must be the lack of understanding or of faith. Overrealized eschatology is at the heart of the "health, wealth, and success" gospel. Once again it is often joined closely to a distorted view of spiritual gifts which are sought for their "sign value" and displayed without concern for the edification of the body.

Nonetheless, we cannot allow a distorted view of gifts to cause us to fear the Holy Spirit or the grace gifts He desires to give. The grace gifts of God are designed to edify and enable the body of Christ to advance the kingdom to the ends of the earth. Here is a promise you can count on. "If you then, being evil, know how to give good gifts to your children, how much more will your Father who is in heaven give what is good to those who ask Him!" (Matt. 7:11).

We Play by Our Own Rules

These various characteristics displayed by the spirituals emerge from a deficient theological understanding of life. Their spiritual arrogance was a result of a failure to understand the graciousness of all life. Their arrogance in turn had led to a warped view of freedom. They actually believed that their freedom had lifted them above the normal rules of Christian morality, tradition, and sexual-role distinctions. Paul may have actually quoted their slogan in 1 Corinthians 6:12 and 10:23 when he writes, "All things are lawful." As you read the context, it is apparent that Paul did not teach, nor did he believe that everything was lawful for the believer. Thus it is likely that he takes their slogan and then proceeds to show them the error of their thinking.

Their "supposed freedom" had made sexual immorality irrelevant or even praiseworthy. Paul pays special attention to one flagrant case of immorality. A man was living with his stepmother in an incestuous relationship (5:1–6). There had been no attempt to conceal the affair. On the contrary, some were proud of the event because it demonstrated how completely freed they were from the moral restrictions of normal religious life. Paul summarizes their attitude: "You have become arrogant and have not mourned" (5:2).

Perhaps it seems hard to believe that someone would see sexual sin as an issue of spiritual pride. Yet today we see people who believe that their advanced spirituality places them above reproof. Recent newscasts have covered the story of a self-proclaimed messianic leader who believed he was "called" to have sexual relationships with multiple women in his compound. Some popular pastors and televangelists of differing denominations have been found guilty of sexual sin. Most have been truly repentant, but some give the impression that such behavior does not truly affect them. Their superior gifts and advanced spirituality has placed them on another level from the average believer.

This "my own rules" mentality is pervasive. What about unfaithful spouses who claim that God led them to divorce one spouse and then led them to a new one because God wanted them to be fulfilled? Do we justify lying or cheating or other wrong behavior based on a feeling of our freedom and advanced spirituality? Why not cheat on your taxes since the government wastes so much money?

Beware of the distorted view of spirituality that divorces itself from ethical behavior!

Other curious problems in Corinth emerged from an arrogant insistence on freedom. The matter of eating meat offered to idols or attending an event held at a pagan temple was for some an issue of their freedom. They boasted that they had spiritual knowledge that assured them the idol was nothing (8:4). Paul may again be quoting their arrogant assertion when he writes, "We know that there is no such thing as an idol in the world." Armed with such knowledge, they see no reason not to eat the meat offered to idols. So what if some of the weak believers are offended! That is their problem and is, in fact, a sign of their weakness.

The right of a woman to pray or prophesy in public almost certainly had become an issue of freedom for some of the spiritual women intent on making a public statement (chap. 11). Thus they flaunted their freedom by releasing their hair in a public place bringing reproach on their head, their husband, and their Lord. They neglected the traditions of the church about proper decorum in the worship service.

Paul corrects this distorted "my rules" mentality with the assurance that the truly mature spiritual person would surrender freedom for the sake of the gospel and the edification of the brethren. In fact he uses himself as an example of one who gave up certain freedoms to minister in Corinth and ultimately to win the more to Christ. "For though I am free from all men, I have made myself a slave to all, so that I may win more" (9:19). "I have become all things to all men, so that I may by all means save some. I do all things for the sake of the gospel" (9:22–23).

Summary

Many of the problems in Corinth can be traced to a spiritual emotionalism, which probably did not possess a developed set of teachings or exhibit any real unity. The stream of this spiritual emotionalism may have been fed by many tributaries. The environment of Corinth—including the various mystery religions extant, the teaching of others who followed Paul in Corinth, and a spontaneous religious zeal that accompanied the conversion of former pagans—all may have contributed to the situation depicted in the first letter to the Corinthians.

It is possible to understand this letter as Paul's attempt to redefine what it means to be a spiritual person. The primary correction is found in the cross and the underlying graciousness of all of life. First, truly spiritual persons will recognize that all is of grace (2:12) and therefore they find no grounds for boasting in any gift. Second and closely related, the spiritual person is one whose behavior is determined by love. Love will lead to the desire to edify the body and reach the lost, and this in turn will affect which gifts are most eagerly sought.

Several considerations must be kept in mind as we begin our study of 1 Corinthians 12–14. The historical context we have just discussed and the significance of the gifts to the spirituals must always be kept in our focus as we look at individual verses. For that reason 1 Corinthians 12–14 cannot be viewed as an isolated, unemotional, theological treatment of spiritual gifts. It is an intensely personal, robustly original, and fundamentally positive evaluation of gifts when they are used for the edification of the church and thus the advance of the kingdom.

While Paul's overall evaluation of the role of spiritual gifts is fundamentally positive (12:11), we cannot overlook that Paul's teaching was placed against an aberrant understanding of gifts that had resulted in numerous practical difficulties for the church. For that reason we must pay close attention to Paul's style of argument which contains subtle nuances of correction. We will need to concentrate on the central thrust of Paul's argument rather than become sidetracked over issues that might be of interest but can distract us from following the flow of Paul's teaching.

This will be especially important when we study chapter 14 where it sometimes appears that Paul seems to vacillate in his evaluation of tongues. Therefore we will not spend a great deal of time attempting to describe a certain gift that could cause us to miss the flow of the overall understanding of the purpose and meaning of gifts.

To understand fully Paul's assessment of spiritual gifts, we must treat 1 Corinthians 12–14 as a unified whole. Too often we are tempted to run to a particular verse or section of verses to prove a point and thus fail to understand the totality of Paul's teaching. Here is a simple outline which might help you to see the flow of these three critical chapters.

Chapter 12 is Paul's positive redefinition of what spiritual gifts are, how many are available, and how they are given to serve the body. Simply stated, Paul broadens the understanding of what sort of ministry flows from gifts. Their understanding of gifts was far too small, including only the more visible or audible ones.

Chapter 13 is not only integral to the argument of these three chapters, but it is central to the entire letter. Paul does not suggest that love is far superior to gifts, nor does he dub love the highest gift, or even establish love as the means for evaluating gifts. Love is the redefinition of the spiritual man. Gifts are not the evidence of the fullness of the Spirit; Christ's character revealed in our behavior is the singular evidence.

Chapter 14 then is Paul's guideline for demonstrating how the spiritual person, defined by love, would seek and use gifts in the gathered assembly. "So also you, since you are zealous of spiritual gifts, seek to abound for the edification of the church" (14:12). Not only are the most edifying gifts to be sought, but all gifts must be used with the edification of believers and the reaching of the lost clearly in view.

QUESTIONS FOR REFLECTION

1. Many of the difficulties in Corinth can be traced to an immature and arrogant reaction to spiritual matters. The underlying theological foundation was the mistaken idea that the full expression of the kingdom had already been made available to the Christian. Do you think you have "arrived" spiritually, or are you anxious to discover what God can do with your life to advance His kingdom? What evidence exists that you are still growing?

2. Spiritual gifts are the manifestation of grace and therefore provide no basis for spiritual boasting. This being the case, the more edifying gifts should be most eagerly sought. Are you willing to accept and develop any gift God should desire to give you? When you think of your church, what area of service are you most drawn to?

3. Paul's primary correctives for spiritual arrogance are grace and love. What actions and attitudes do you manifest that may be destructive to the fellowship of your church? Are you willing to leave those behind and seek to edify the body?

4. If we are to discover our gifted self, we must avoid distorted images of spiritual gifts that can lead to arrogance and disrupt the church. Do you need to lay aside any of these mistaken notions?
   - Spiritual gifts prove I am more spiritually mature than another believer.
   - Religious activities have a "magical" power that makes me immune to sin.
   - I have wisdom and knowledge that places me above others in the church.
   - I have already arrived spiritually.
   - I don't have to obey the rules that govern the Christian community.

3

Redefining Spiritual Gifts

A Study of 1 Corinthians 12

Johnny Carson made famous a fictitious character named Carnac the Magnificent. Carnac would state an answer to a question and then hold a sealed envelope to his elaborate headdress and pretend to receive the question through his psychic powers. It was all a show, and the questions were humorous and often unrelated to the original response. It is difficult to determine the unstated question that prompts a particular response.

That precise dilemma faces us as we look at 1 Corinthians 12:1–3 where Paul begins his detailed treatment of spiritual gifts. It is commonly agreed that the phrase "now concerning spiritual gifts" signifies that Paul was referring to an inquiry from the Corinthian community. That's the easy part of the equation! What was the question or questions?

Note that the Corinthians had found it necessary to ask Paul's opinion about spiritual gifts. Had Paul left them ignorant concerning the matter of gifts? Listen to his opening words. "Now concerning spiritual gifts, brethren, I do not want you to be unaware" (12:1). Teachers who arrived after Paul's departure may have created such confusion that the Corinthians needed a fresh reminder and further elucidation concerning spiritual gifts.

This inquiry, arising out of the Corinthian zeal for gifts and misunderstanding of their sign value, presented the opportunity and provided the catalyst for the emergence of Paul's most *comprehensive* treatment of spiritual gifts. The principles that are developed in this section will form the basis for the teaching we will find in Romans 12 and Ephesians 4.

Before attempting to reconstruct the question from the Corinthians, we might want to pose a few of our own.

- What gifts are available today?
- What is their purpose and value?
- Do all Christians possess gifts?
- Do I seek certain gifts, or are they simply given?
- Can they be controlled?
- Can they be developed?
- Are some gifts more important than others?

Now back to the question that prompted this long and detailed discussion on spiritual gifts and spiritual persons. The word translated "spiritual gifts" in most English translations could also be rendered "spiritual persons." It is a genitive plural in the Greek and thus could be either neuter or masculine. "Spiritual gifts" and "spiritual persons" were so closely connected in the thinking of the Corinthians that Paul used a word that could imply both. Perhaps the question could be restated as follows: "Don't the spiritual gifts prove that we are spiritual persons?"

We can relate to this question. Due to the popularity of the charismatic movement, there probably aren't many pastors who have not been asked questions about spiritual gifts that resemble these: "Must I speak in tongues to be filled with the Spirit? Are we missing out on something powerful here in our church?"

Many people have been confronted and confused by well-meaning friends who have had what they consider to be a profound spiritual experience related to certain gifts. They may testify to their newfound experience by pointing to an objective sign that proves to them that they have had a "valid" spiritual experience. Some of these people are zealous for us to share in this experience. Evangelists for spiritual gifts can leave us with the impression that we're missing out if we turn our back on their offer. They may even suggest that we do not have the Spirit unless we "manifest a particular gift." Some believers come away from these encounters feeling like second-class Christians.

We should appreciate that what is commonly called the "charismatic movement" has caused the church to examine carefully the ministry of the Holy Spirit, especially in regard to spiritual gifts, and has caused us to reevaluate our spiritual walk and to seek a deeper experience with Christ. Whatever our spiritual background, we can all agree that the Holy Spirit is the source of spiritual life and the empowering for ministry. The impotence of the average Christian and average church is directly related to our failure to appropriate the empowering of the Spirit. While we can hardily agree with our charismatic friends on such matters, we should not accept uncritically everything anyone in the charismatic community teaches about the Holy Spirit or gifts. We must all look to Scripture, rightly interpreted, for our understanding of the Spirit and the gifts.

First Corinthians 12–14, as a whole, is intended to answer the question that links spiritual gifts and spiritual persons. Paul *first* redefines and broadens the understanding of gifts available. *Second*, he provides a positive redefinition of the evidence for the presence of the Spirit (chap. 13). He gave a radically different answer to the question of what proves one to be a spiritual person. *Finally*, he supplies clear guidelines for seeking and using spiritual gifts for the good of the community (chap. 14).

Paul's treatment of spiritual gifts is framed by terms that stress "understanding." The statement "I do not want you to be unaware" may have been intended to deflate the pride of the spirituals who boasted about their knowledge. They believed themselves to have an abundance of gifts and to possess all knowledge. Thus we can sense more than a tinge of irony in Paul's introductory statement concerning gifts. But the full impact of this statement is not made clear until we finish reading the entire section. Listen to Paul's conclusion: "If anyone thinks he is a prophet or spiritual, let him recognize that the things which I write to you are the Lord's commandment" (14:37). If after reading Paul's Spirit-inspired writing, the spirituals remain "ignorant" (same Greek word translated "unaware" in 12:1) about the true nature of spiritual gifts, they will prove themselves not to be spiritual persons. "But if anyone does not recognize this, he is not recognized" (14:38).

The Fundamental Corrective: Jesus Is Lord

We are hardly prepared for Paul's first words of correction. Why does Paul appeal to their idolatrous past in 1 Corinthians 12:2: "You know that when you were pagans, you were led astray to the mute idols," and then introduce the shocking disclaimer, "No one speaking by the Spirit of God, says, 'Jesus is accursed'" (v. 3). Here clarity is gained by focusing on the whole and remembering the historical situation. Since the work of the Spirit (*pneuma*) and the resulting spiritual gifts (*pneumatika*, 12:1) was at the heart of the Corinthian difficulties, Paul focuses first on the work of the Spirit in the life of every believer.

In the first thirteen verses of chapter 12, we find twelve references to the Spirit. This discovery is made even more impressive when we notice that the Spirit is not mentioned in Romans 12 or Ephesians 4, the other two gift passages. Some in Corinth were obsessed with proving their spirituality; and, therefore, Paul first has to correct their exclusivist and aberrant view of the Spirit's work by underlining the ministry of the Spirit in and through all Christians.

You may still be wondering why the blunt and unexpected reference to the cursing of Jesus?[1] Perhaps you are thinking it is incomprehensible to think that a Christian speaking under the inspiration of the Spirit could ever say, "Jesus is accursed." You would be absolutely correct since the ministry of the Spirit is to bear witness to Jesus, not curse Him. Then why mention a truth so obvious it need not be stated? Simply because it is equally impossible for the Christian to say, "'Jesus is Lord,' except by the Holy Spirit" (12:3).

We could paraphrase verse 3 in this manner. "It is *apparent* to you that no one could curse Jesus when speaking by the Spirit; it should be equally *apparent* that every person who truly confesses that Jesus is Lord does so by the Spirit." The confession "Jesus is Lord" was the earliest Christian confession. It was repeated at baptism as a verbal confession of one's faith. Thus these words of confession would have been etched in the memory of all the believers in Corinth.

Verses 2 and 3 are bound together by a strong Greek connective translated "therefore." Paul is not interested in comparing pagan and Christian inspiration, nor is he giving a guide for the discerning of spirits, whether they be Christian or demonic. The last phrase of verse 2, "however you were led," is a rather casual remark demonstrating a lack of interest in any pagan inspiration. Paul reminds them of their pre-Christian experience for one purpose alone. He wants to underline the work of the Spirit in their conversion experience. Before Paul can discuss gifts in a positive fashion, he must first establish that every believer is a *spiritual person* in the most fundamental sense because redemption and its accompanying confession, "Jesus is Lord," can only be uttered by the work of the Spirit.

> The confession "Jesus is Lord" was the earliest Christian confession.

We have a popular equivalent to this sort of argumentation in our modern-day vernacular. For example, someone walking out into the rain might say, "It's raining!" That observation is usually followed by a good natured barb like: "Really Sherlock, what was your first clue?" What we mean is that the rain running down our face is such an obvious testimony to the presence of rain, that it need not be mentioned. In the same manner Paul uses something obvious and agreed upon—"No one speaking by the Spirit of God, says, 'Jesus is accursed'"—to dramatize an equally obvious truth: "No one can say, 'Jesus is Lord,' except by the Holy Spirit."

Thus Paul's first concern is to refute the exclusivist claim by the spirituals that they alone possessed the Spirit. Paul appeals to the most basic truth of Christian experience—redemption through the work of the Spirit—to prove his point.

This first corrective ought to comfort those who have been told that they do not have the Spirit unless they manifest a sign gift like unknown tongues. You cannot be saved apart from the ministry of the Spirit. It should also serve as a warning to anyone who has become spiritually arrogant because they have been taught that their possession of a certain gift elevates them above other believers. Both of these ideas are wrong and can create dissension and harmful division in the body of Christ today as it did in Corinth.

Paul's singular purpose in the first three verses is to establish the truth that every believer is a spiritual person since the basic confession of faith—"Jesus is Lord"—cannot be uttered except by the Spirit. Further, the reference to "Jesus is Lord" brings the discussion of gifts under the umbrella of the kingship of Christ. This allows Paul to underline the sovereign activity of God placing the members in the body by His own design (12:18). This in turn leads to the focus on those gifts that more readily edify the body (chap. 14). Thus it is in the context of one's personal relationship with the King and the common possession of the Spirit that Paul can put forth his corrective teaching on gifts.

Following the three introductory verses, Paul continues his emphasis on the work of the Spirit, which is shared by all believers. As you read verses 4 through 11, notice the repetition of phrases such as "same Spirit," "the one Spirit," and "one and the same Spirit" in verses 4, 9, and 11. Verses 7 and 11 frame the first listing of gifts and underline the central purpose of Paul's teaching. "But to each one is given the manifestation of the Spirit for the common good. . . . But *one and the same* Spirit works all these things, distributing to *each one* individually just as He wills" (emphasis added).

The emphasis on the common work of the Spirit is made more explicit by the repetition of "Spirit" four times in the listing of gifts in verses 8–10 in phrases such as "according to the same Spirit" and "by the one Spirit." This section of chapter 12 is then linked to the image of the human body in verses 14–24 by the important reminder: "For by *one Spirit we all* were baptized into one body . . . and *we all* were made to drink of *one Spirit*" (v. 13, emphasis added). To dispel any possible confusion about who is "spiritual," Paul assures them that every Christian in Corinth had been baptized into the one body of

Christ, His church, by the one Spirit. Thus the baptism of the Spirit rightly understood occurs the moment of conversion when one confesses "Jesus is Lord" and incorporates every believer into the body of Christ.

Paul makes the same emphasis in his letter to the Romans. He writes, "But if anyone does not have the Spirit of Christ, he does not belong to Him" (Rom. 8:9). Further he declares, "For all who are being led by the Spirit of God, these are sons of God" (8:14). He then speaks of the spirit of adoption that enables us to cry out, "Abba! Father!" (v. 15). Affirmation of the work of the Spirit in the life of the believer is the assurance of our salvation. "The Spirit Himself testifies with our spirit that we are children of God" (8:16). The baptism of the Spirit is the common experience shared by every believer that occurs the moment we are saved, and it involves the incorporation of that believer into the body of Christ.

The Grace Corrective

Now that Paul has clearly established that the Spirit works in all Christians from the point of conversion, he takes another step as he assures the Corinthians that *all believers* are gifted for service to the King. Verse 7 can hardly be more pointed in this regard: "But to each one is given the manifestation of the Spirit for the common good" (1 Cor. 12:7). The possession of gifts does not prove that a person is spiritual in any sense that could lead to boasting. On the contrary all believers have spiritual gifts and should lead to service in the body for the good of all.

Paul introduces a new word to describe the "gifts" they possessed. The word translated "spiritual gifts" (*pneumatikon*) in 12:1 is from the root word for Spirit (*pneuma*). This term was preferred by those in Corinth who believed that these gifts had sign value for proving one's spirituality. Paul answers their question about gifts, but he substitutes the word *charismata,* which comes from the Greek word for "grace." Thus we could translate *charismata* as "manifestation of grace." The change of Greek words to discuss gifts is not obvious in most English translations, but it has tremendous significance. It provides the platform for introducing the "grace corrective."

The Greek term *charismata* is the word from which we get "charismatic." In many instances when I hear this word used today, the meaning given to it is actually what the Corinthians meant when they used *pneumatika.* For that reason many evangelical believers will quickly clarify that they are not charismatics. In truth, all believers are charismatics since we all alike have received "manifestations of grace" for ministry. Paul's substitution of the word *charismata* for *pneumatika* introduces another level of correction; it brings gifts under the umbrella of grace, a prominent theme of this letter. Gifts tell us nothing about the possessor, but they tell us everything about the Giver!

Think of it this way. Some friends give you a beautiful vase for your new home. You proudly display the vase in a prominent place, and visitors to your home frequently compliment you on the vase. Truth is, the vase tells the visitor little about its present possessor, but it speaks volumes about the grace of the donors. It speaks of their taste and their generosity. God is gracious not only to redeem us while we were yet sinners; His grace overflows in His willingness to grant us gifts for service that enable us to join Him in advancing His kingdom.

Paul actually brings gifts and grace together several times in the introduction to this letter. In his prayer of thanksgiving in 1 Corinthians 1:4–9, he thanks God "for the grace of God which was given you in Christ Jesus" (v. 4). He immediately relates this to the abundance of gifts they claim to manifest: "that in everything you were enriched in Him, in all speech and all knowledge . . . so that you are not lacking in any gift" (vv. 5 and 7). You might be interested to know that Paul actually introduces the term *charisma* in verse 7. The introduction of the term in the first paragraph and the linking of it with grace foreshadows the discussion of gifts in chapters 12–14.

The corrective of grace is again found in 1:27–31 where Paul indicates that human boasting is excluded before God because He alone is the source of life. In chapter 2 Paul contrasts the "wisdom" of the spirituals with the true wisdom of God. Christians have been given the Spirit of God "so that we may know the things freely given to us by God" (2:12). In other words, the Spirit makes us aware of the graciousness of all of life.

The grace corrective is central to Paul's teaching in chapter 3. Paul indicates that he could not refer to the Corinthians as spiritual persons but as babes. The issue was their strife and arrogant exaltation of one leader over another. The root cause of their strife was a lack of true wisdom. If they possessed true wisdom, they would have understood that Paul and Apollos were servants through whom God worked. They had different roles in ministry, but God caused the growth through their ministries (3:6). Paul indicates that he laid the foundation, "according to the grace of God which was given to me" (v. 10). But all ministries are grace empowered, and thus all praise must be God directed.

In chapter 4 Paul confronts the arrogant boasting of the spirituals in an even more pointed manner. "For who regards you as superior? What do you have that you did not receive? And if you did receive it, why do you boast as if you had not received it?" (4:7). Notice that nothing we have, including the most powerful gifts, provides any basis for spiritual boasting since they are gifts received by grace.

Before we proceed with our study of the gifts, let's make sure we understand the significance of the grace corrective. Whatever gift or gifts we possess, they offer no proof of spiritual greatness, nor do they provide any ground for boasting. Whatever ministry we might accomplish for God will be for His glory because it reflects His gracious redemption and empowering. But you can be encouraged because you have been graced by God. You are uniquely created and gifted for service to the King.

> *All ministries are grace empowered, and thus all praise must be God directed.*

The Variety of Gifts

While all believers are converted, incorporated into the body, and gifted by the Spirit, that does not mean all believers have the same gift. Even the casual reader of 1 Corinthians 12 will notice the emphasis on variety. "There are varieties of gifts" (v. 4), "varieties of ministries" (v. 5), and "varieties of effects" (v. 6). The three words *gifts*, *ministries*, and *effects* view gifts for ministry from three different perspectives. *Gifts* emphasizes the graciousness of the Spirit in the giving and thus excludes boasting. *Ministries* indicates that gifts cannot be regarded as spiritual privileges but must be viewed as God-given means for service to the King. Finally *effects* exalts God as the source and energizer of all activities of service accomplished within the body. These three words provide a crescendo that focuses all attention on God as the ultimate source of all gifts and the rightful recipient of all ministry.

The repetition of the word *varieties* contrasts with the repetition of the word *same* ("same Spirit . . . same Lord . . . same God"). Paul is laying the foundation for his insistence that variety and unity are not mutually exclusive. Unity and diversity are divinely given, and both are necessary for the proper functioning of the body. The spirituals had placed a premium on a few miraculous "sign" gifts. Their neglect of a more diverse palate of gifts had actually ignored the diversity of the body and had thus harmed its unity. The same thing can happen today if we allow those who are overzealous concerning a few visible or audible gifts to keep us from seeking to discover and employ our own gifts. We cannot allow the abuse of a few to create a "charisphobia" in the many.

Verse 7—"But to each one is given the manifestation of the Spirit for the common good"—serves as a bridge between the emphasis on "variety" and the first listing of gifts. Two points are made that we must pause to underline. First, Paul emphatically declares that "each" Christian has been given the manifestation of the Spirit. The phrase "manifestation of the Spirit" in this context means spiritual gift. Thus no one can argue that they themselves or any other believer is lacking in spiritual gifts. Second, no one is given the manifestation of the Spirit for personal gratification. Each gift is given for the "common good."

This final point has already been alluded to with the use of "varieties of ministries" in verse 5, but it is stated here in such a clear manner that no one can miss the implication. Gifts are not given to a *few* spiritually elite for *self-glorification* but to *each* for the *common good*. Both of these points will be illustrated by comparing the body of Christ to the human body.

In verses 8–10 we come to the first list of gifts. Since Paul's letters have several lists, we can be certain that this particular list was not intended to be comprehensive. Yet the deliberate nature of this list indicates that the gifts listed here were not chosen in a haphazard manner. When we look at the list as a whole, we will notice that several characteristics emerge.

- These gifts would have been prominent in the worship service.
- They are the gifts most frequently referred to by people as "miraculous."
- Many of the gifts are directly related to speech and revelation.
- We can see little continuity between these gifts and any ability possessed before one becomes a Christian.

Why does Paul include such a "miraculous" list of gifts at this point after arguing that diverse gifts are distributed by the Spirit for the good of the whole? Part of the problem in Corinth was caused by the fact that not all believers possessed such miraculous expressions of the Spirit as we find listed here. It may, therefore, seem that Paul has virtually retreated from his position that all are gifted and agrees with the spirituals.

This first gift list clearly reflects those gifts that were most eagerly sought by the spirituals in Corinth for their sign value. If you glance back at 1:5–7 and ahead to 13:1–3, you will find further evidence that the spirituals have placed an exaggerated interest on a *few* gifts. These gifts were visible or audible and dramatic, easy to display in the gathered assembly, and thus they provided "seemingly" incontrovertible proof of one's spiritual ascendancy. Their possession and arrogant use by the spirituals had caused doubts and confusion in the minds of those lacking such gifts.

While it may appear that this list is a concession to the position of the spirituals, it is in truth an important plank in Paul's corrective argument. Paul wanted to underline a truth that was obvious but widely ignored by the spirituals. *A variety of gifts were already being practiced in Corinth.* The spirituals hadn't observed that tongues, prophecy, miracle-working faith, and other gifts actually demonstrated a variety of gifts because they saw them only as a sign of spiritual greatness. I am not suggesting that the spirituals had drawn up a list of gifts like this. On the contrary they viewed these manifestations in a monolithic fashion as miraculous signs. The variety among the gifts already possessed had not registered on their radar screen because they had never thought about gifts in terms of service. They were only interested in gifts in terms of sign value.

Now having established the principle of *variety* even in their chosen but limited understanding of gifts, Paul expands the scope of his argument to introduce abilities and ministries not previously thought to be a work of the Spirit. Paul does this by his illustration taken from the human body and his second listing of gifts in 12:28–30. Second, by listing these gifts, Paul indicates that he does not oppose or rule out "miraculous" manifestations. However, he indicates that they are given by the Spirit for the common good and thus must be used for the edification of the body.

Before we turn our attention to the imagery taken from the human body, we should notice the impact of verse 11: "But one and the same Spirit works all these things, distributing to each one individually just as He wills." The emphasis here is on the sovereign activity of the Giver. First, this reminds the reader that the possession of any of the gifts cannot be used as an argument for spiritual ascendancy. Second, it indicates that God has gifted the body to accomplish His kingdom purpose on earth. We cannot claim that the task of discipling the nations is too large a task. We have been created, empowered, and gifted to accomplish nothing less.

The Illustration from the Human Body

The human body is a miraculous instrument, particularly when all the parts work in harmony. Yet when one part fails to perform, the entire body is affected. As a child, I had a knack for stumping my big toe. I can still remember the pain that shot through my body like a jolt of high-voltage electricity when I drove my toe into a raised section of the sidewalk. Yet my macho persona would cause me to choke back my tears and continue on my way. "After all, it's only one toe!" After a short time of my awkward gait, I would begin to notice that my hip was throbbing with pain. Then the pain began to crawl up my spine, and soon my whole body hurt. All because of one big toe!

Paul uses the inner working of the human body to illustrate the need for variety and unity, which together provide for mutual care. For churches to work effectively to advance the kingdom, all the body parts must work in harmony and demonstrate respect and care for one another. The picture of the body will help us understand not only the correctives needed in Corinth but also those needed in our churches today. Some analysts indicate that nearly 80 percent of all churches in America are plateaued or are declining. Could it be that internal dissension and the failure of many body members to function could be at the heart of our problem?

You will also notice that in this section containing the imagery of the body, Paul moves his argument for an expanded definition of gifts a step further. He establishes five critical points through this extended metaphor of the body. (1) There is one body, (2) with diversely functioning members, (3) sovereignly designed, (4) with no useless appendages, (5) enabling it to advance the kingdom and provide mutual care to all members.

All Believers Belong to the One Body

Paul first focuses on the unity of the body. He repeats the word "many" twice in verse 12 to draw attention to the diversity represented by the many members of the body. "For even as the body is one and yet has many members, and all the members of the body, though they are many, are one body, so also is Christ." Yet he concludes that the "many" members all belong to the one body. The conclusion to verse 12 seems abrupt—"so also is Christ." The jolt of this phrase was intended to direct the reader's attention from the human illustration to the spiritual truth concerning the Christian community. We might have expected Paul to say, "So also is the church." But he employs the more dramatic— "so also is Christ"—because the church is more than the mere assemblage of many members, it is the body of Christ. The sober reality of this truth makes disunity all the more heinous.

When you were saved, the Spirit immersed you into the body of Christ (v. 13). We express this reality by our relationship with the church, His earthly body. I sometimes hear people list their church membership as if it is simply another organization to which they belong, like a club or fraternal group. No other single community on earth has the eternal significance and impact as does the church. It alone has been given the keys to the kingdom (Matt. 16:19), and it alone as the bride of Christ will continue unabated for all eternity (Rev. 21:2). Does your commitment to and ministry through the church indicate that you grasp the eternal significance of its earthly task?[2]

The indication that the one Spirit baptizes or immerses all believers into the one body is the last mention of the Spirit in chapter 12. It is the pivotal point that enables Paul to move his teaching on gifts beyond the limited understanding of the spirituals. We have already noticed that Paul has focused throughout these first verses on the work of the Spirit that all believers share in common. The Spirit enabled every believer to confess "Jesus is Lord" (12:3), and He dispensed gifts to each as He willed (12:11). In this verse Paul takes the next logical step by insisting that the *one Spirit* had baptized *all* believers into a single body.

Notice that the emphasis shifts from the work of the Spirit in an individual's life to the work of the Spirit in unifying the many members of the body. This is wholly consistent with Paul's insistence that the manifestations of the Spirit were given to *each believer* for the good of the *whole body*. Paul first affirmed the individual's participation in the Spirit in order to move his readers to a deeper and more mature level of understanding of the Spirit's work in the community of believers. The spirituals had clamored for gifts in an immature *individualistic* fashion as a sign of spiritual achievement and had totally neglected their true purpose—to edify the whole body. While the Holy Spirit works in each of us individually, He does so for the good of the body.

We repeat the errors of Corinth today anytime we seek spiritual gifts without concern for how we may work in unity with other body members to enable the church to advance the kingdom. When people come to me wanting help in discovering their spiritual gift, I usually inquire first about motive. "Are you seeking a spiritual badge of honor to prove you are spiritual? Are you looking for spiritual prestige and power over others? Are you seeking gifts because you have been intimidated by a well-meaning friend who has suggested that you are lacking spiritually? Or do you want to find your area of service in the body of Christ?"

If your motive is other than kingdom centered and service oriented, then your desire for gifts will provide only a distorted view of spirituality and will harm the unity of the body. If your motives are pure, the discovery and employment of your gifts will enable you to discover your God-given purpose in His body. You will then use your gifts to advance His kingdom, by His power, and for His glory until His return.

The One Body Has Diverse Members

Christian unity is unique because it preserves individuality. Paul's reference to various national and social groups represented in the Christian community clearly illustrated diversity— "Jews or Greeks . . . slaves or free" (12:13). Yet all alike are baptized into one body and made to drink of one Spirit. The reference to the common experience of water baptism is not simply a nostalgic reminder of a past event but is intended

> *You will then use your gifts to advance His kingdom, by His power, and for His glory until His return.*

to impress upon the Corinthians the ability of the Spirit to bring unity in diversity. Ironically, by their zeal to possess only the spectacular gifts, the spirituals had ignored the God-given variety that was necessary for the unity of the one body.

To express his point visibly, Paul turns to an extended illustration of the working of the human body. Paul's use of a familiar image is striking because the examples often verge on the ridiculous and the humorous.

The phrase "for the body is not one member, but many" (v. 14) sets the tone of the passage and shows that Paul is concerned about the individualistic mind-set of many in Corinth. The zeal of the spirituals to be alike in possessing the spectacular gifts had resulted in the failure to appreciate the diversity demonstrated by the members possessing different but less visible gifts. Further, it had created a rampant individualism with everyone clamoring for their rights. This caused them to act or speak without considering the impact of their actions on the other members of the one body.

The foot and the ear are first pictured as complaining that they are not a part of the body because they are not the hand or the eye. We may think of the foot as less glamorous than our hand or our ear as less vital than our eye, but in truth all parts are equally important to the proper working of the body. The parts differ because the body demands diversity in function for unity in action.

The argument among body members reminds me of the childhood squabbles that occurred when we were going out for recess at our elementary school.

"If I can't pitch, I'm not going to play!" "That's not fair; she always plays the center position!" Childhood games are precisely that—childish. They were silly but they weren't dangerous. When we play such games in the church, they become dangerous and detrimental to the work of the church for the kingdom. Here's what they may sound like. "If I can't teach, I'll leave the church!" "Why does she get the solo part? She's only been a member a short time!" Statements like this demonstrate a failure to appreciate the purpose and function of the diverse gifts.

Ministry opportunities are not awards for longevity or faithful attendance. Because you don't have a "solo quality" voice doesn't mean you are less important to the ministry of the choir. We're not in competition with one another in the body of Christ. We are members of the same body, uniquely gifted by the Spirit so that we might work together with other body members for the good of the whole and the glory of the King. In the same way that the ear is no less vital to the human body than the eye, so the secretary is no less strategic than the soloist. The primary focus in spiritual gifts is on function and not status.

The Body Is Designed by the Master Architect

I have always admired the work of an architect who can design a building that has beauty, symmetry, and functionality. I have great news for you. Not only were you designed by the Master Architect; you were designed with the larger body of Christ in mind. You are by design an integral part of one of the most exciting communities on earth or in heaven.

In 1 Corinthians 12:17–19 Paul poses three questions that demonstrate the sovereign design of the body. When we link the three questions together, we can hear their impact. "If the whole body were an eye . . . if the whole were hearing . . . if they are all one member?" The thinking that all must be alike sounds childish. Equality of function would, in fact, destroy the body (v. 19), a danger which was all too real in Corinth. When I read these verses as a child, I would picture a huge eyeball rolling down the road. What a ludicrous and childish picture! A huge eye has neither value nor life when separated from the other members of the body.

Verse 18 is a key verse that should be underlined in your Bible and in your heart. "But now God has placed the members, each one of them, in the body, just as He desired." The denial of diversity, either in theory or practice, not only has practical consequences, but it contradicts the will of God. He has constructed the body just as He desired.

In case you are tempted to think this verse applies to everyone but you, notice that the emphatic "each one of them" actually interrupts the flow of the sentence. When we understand the principle of "master design," the discovery of our gift(s) for service cannot be ignored or left to chance. The Master Designer has constructed the body with you in mind. By God's grace you have been created to serve with other members of the body to advance His kingdom on earth.

Let this idea sink in. You have been placed in the body by design! You are exactly who God designed you to be! Your function is vital to the body because God made you just as He desired and with the body in mind. Without you the body would be lacking. Your goal in life is to please the One who created and designed you.

When someone completes a project, the essential question is whether the created object pleases and serves the purpose intended by the designer. Thus, when it comes to us as believers, the primary question concerning our giftedness is not our worth in the eyes of the world but in the eyes of God. Am I serving God's purpose and pleasing Him through my gifted service to His body?

Several years ago Greg Louganis was at the pinnacle of his athletic prowess and at the top of the diving world. Even though he was the best, there were times when he did not perform well. At one point in his career, he went through a serious diving slump. As a result he had a dangerous accident when his head hit the high diving platform. The reporters speculated about his ability to come back from a life-threatening accident. One reporter asked Greg what his last thought was as he stood motionless on the high platform. His response was simple but profound. "My last thought

> *Your gifts are grace expressions from the Father; you're not being graded for performance but empowered for service.*

is that whether I hit the dive correctly or not, Mom will still love me." Great perspective! Your gifts are grace expressions from the Father; you're not being graded for performance but empowered for service. Just please the Father and be assured that He will always love you.

While this verse rules out the attitude that I have no value, it also provides a correction for the arrogant assertion that as a believer, I don't need others. I am always saddened when I hear people talk about their independence. "I don't need anybody else to be a Christian; I can serve the Lord without being part of a local church." Such a statement ignores the design and desire of the Creator. We are not independent; we are interdependent. We need one another to function properly as a body. God has designed us for the body, and He has so designed the body to cause us to be fully interdependent with other members. Since no one can possess all gifts, we are all in need of others. "And the eye cannot say to the hand, 'I have no need of you'" (1 Cor. 12:21). In terms of function we are dependent in two ways. As one member of the body, I depend on the gifts of others to meet my spiritual needs. And any gift isolated from the remainder of the body will have no effect. Thus we depend on other gifted members to give meaning to the function of our gift.

No Useless Parts in God's Design

The imagery of the body is pressed even further with the Corinthian controversy clearly in view. The spirituals were behaving as if they had no need for other Christians, particularly those they deemed to be weaker or without honor. Some of the arrogant spirituals believed they were especially honored by God and thus viewed "inferior" members to be of little use, perhaps even a hindrance.

In order to appreciate what Paul means in this section, we must seek to understand who in the community is in view when words such as "weaker," "less presentable," or "less honorable" (vv. 22–23) are used. Several earlier passages in 1 Corinthians have already used similar terms to speak of certain members of the community. In 1 Corinthians 1:26–28 Paul reminds the Corinthians that when they came to Christ not many of them were "wise," "mighty," or "noble." This reference to their humble beginnings is necessary because some now believe they are mighty and noble. Paul concludes this section by reminding them that God chooses the weak to shame the strong. Thus they need to remember that whatever they are it is only because of God's grace and therefore the only appropriate boasting is in the Lord (1:31).

A more pointed passage is 4:8–13. The possession of certain spectacular gifts had caused the spirituals to feel superior to their fellow believers and even to the apostles. In their own distorted view they were "already filled," they were "rich," and they reigned like "kings." In contrast the apostles were last of all, like men condemned to death. "We are fools for Christ's sake, but ye are wise in Christ; we are weak, but ye are strong; ye are honourable, but we are despised" (v. 10 KJV). You don't have to read too carefully to hear the ironic edge to that verse. Did you notice the similarity with the description in 12:22–23?

The same type of irony present in 4:8–13 is also present in 12:21–26. Although the spirituals judged themselves to be most valuable and honored, the opposite is true. Those members they considered to be weaker are both necessary and honored. The parts of the body that we think to be less honorable by human standards are invested with greater honor and treated with greater modesty.

Commentators have different views about the meaning of "less presentable members." But if we remember that we are looking at the human body as a metaphor for the body of Christ, we can see the significance of this reference. Nearly everyone has some body part that they believe to be their least attractive feature. You may think your nose is too long, your hips too large, or your eyes too dull. When you choose clothes, comb your hair, or put on makeup, you actually pay greater attention to your least flattering body part. In your attempt to hide or decorate this unseemly member, you actually give it more abundant honor. Tongue-in-cheek, Paul suggests that the estimation of the spirituals has actually backfired.

Paul rejects the spirituals' criteria of the spectacular for evaluating which gifted members were most honorable. They had sought the most visible or audible gifts for selfish reasons. Since the purpose of the gifts was to build up the body of Christ, the true criterion for greatness of any gift would be its usefulness in edification of the body and glorification of the King. All members alike are vital to the body. There are no useless appendages and no unseemly members when all work together for the King.

When I was a child, my dad took me to nearly every local high school football game. He used these Friday night outings to teach me about football and about life. One year our team had a uniquely gifted quarterback. The only problem was that he knew he was gifted and constantly reminded others of that fact. He was cocky! You could see it in his disregard for other team members. It was apparent that he viewed the linemen as unskilled hulks who did little more than provide a stage for the display of his spectacular gifts.

What transpired over the course of the season was not commendable on anyone's part but may have taught the quarterback a lesson. My dad pointed out to me the linemen clustered on the sidelines in deep conversation as their quarterback strutted back and forth in view of the crowd. Apparently these meetings were used to devise their strategy. If the quarterback believed he could win by himself, they determined to let him try it. By prearranged agreement they all decided to miss their blocking assignment. This seemed to happen when the quarterback called a play designed to showcase his own talents. Needless to say the quarterback spent considerable time observing the stars from the flat of his back. Perhaps he learned the hard way that there are no useless appendages.

As I read this critical corrective in 12:21–26, I wonder if Paul had in mind the teachings of Jesus that radically reversed the world's estimation of greatness.

Jesus taught that the servant, the one deemed to be lowest, was, in truth, the highest in the kingdom. Those who desire true spiritual greatness must therefore choose to be servants. In any case Paul illustrates the reversal of human values by indicating that God Himself "composed" (v. 24) or "blended together" the body so as to give more abundant honor to that member who lacks.

Here's a little test to help us think about our motive for seeking to discover our gifts.

- Do I desire to discover my gifts so that I can find my proper place of service?
- Do I truly believe that servanthood is the highest form of leadership?
- Would I be disappointed if I were to discover that I am gifted to be a helper and not a leader?
- Am I infected with the disease of the spirituals that causes me to desire the more visible and honorable areas of ministry?
- Are my feelings hurt when no one gives me credit for my hard work?
- Am I willing to volunteer for an unheralded area of service?

Slam-dunking a basketball over Michael Jordan is a more appealing image than wrapping Michael's ankles. Which appeals to you the most? Gifts are designed to allow us to serve the body even when it is in a leadership position.

Please don't jump to any premature conclusions. Paul does not want to discredit the spirituals. He wants to redirect their zeal for gifts away from ego gratification and toward a more productive end. Gifts for them were signs of their heavenly status, not gifts of grace enabling them to care for the body and advance the kingdom.

The Design of the Body Mandates Mutual Care

The picture of the human body reminds us that all the members of the one body depend on one another. The proper working of the body demands unity, and therefore we must guard against discord. Division in the church is not simply wrong; it is disastrous because it inhibits the proper working of the body. Can you imagine the embarrassing results if your brain thought one thing and your mouth said another? What if one foot decided to go left while the other went right? Like the little boy with the stumped toe, the church without mutual care limps ineffectively from one task to the next. The advancement of the kingdom through the church is too important a mission for us to allow discord to creep into the body and siphon away our power.

When the body functions properly with all the gifted members working in harmonious relationship, mutual care (12:25) and total empathy (12:26) will permeate the church. When you read the first Corinthian letter, you will notice events where mutual care was conspicuously lacking. Some had, through their gift of knowledge, determined that idols were nothing; and therefore they were free to eat meat offered to idols (8:1). They had not, however, considered the effect their eating idol meat might have on a weaker brother. The celebration of the Lord's Supper was another prime example where mutual concern was lacking. The wealthy came early and ate to excess while the poor left hungry. Paul declares that they were not only shaming those who were poor; they were despising the church of God (11:21–22).

Here in chapter 12 Paul takes the theme of mutual care a step further. As members of the same body, we are so closely bound together that we share the same feelings. What causes joy for one member delights the whole body. Conversely, when one member suffers, the entire body hurts. We generally find it easier to empathize with those who suffer than to rejoice when another member is honored. How do you react when someone else gets the part in the musical event that you really wanted? When a fellow church member receives recognition and honor, do you ever feel a twinge of jealousy?

When we begin to deal honestly and seriously with the scriptural teaching that we are truly members of one family, it will change many of our attitudes about ourselves and others in our church. I know that I receive greater pleasure from seeing my children succeed than I do from my own achievements. Since we are family, why is it so difficult to see a brother or sister in Christ receive honor? Now you may be asking how this all relates to the issue of gifts. Glad you asked! Our desire for seeking gifts must never be to outshine other members of the body. And the employment of our unique gifts must always be measured by their edification of the whole body.

Paul will not allow us to ignore the vital importance of fully understanding the imagery of the church as a body. "Now you are Christ's body, and individually members of it" (12:27). The church body belongs to Christ and not to any one of us. When we harm the body, we are in essence harming Christ. Do you remember what the resurrected Lord said to Saul when he was persecuting the early Christians? "Saul, Saul, why are you persecuting Me?" (Acts 9:4).

Further, Paul underlines the fact that they were "individually" related to the entire body. Members of the body are not simply absorbed into the body, losing their own personal identity, but each member is placed in the body by God's design (v. 18), and thus has a distinct place and function by the grace of

God. A balanced understanding of spiritual gifts is one of the most affirming and challenging of all biblical doctrines. You are vital to the proper function of your church. Are you presently serving based on your giftedness?

The Second Gift List

As you have read this chapter, you may have wondered why Paul includes a second list of gifts in the span of a single chapter. Why does he include a few new gifts not mentioned in the first list (12:8–10) and then repeat several from that list? Why does he list the first three gifts in order?

In spite of all Paul has written about each individual being gifted, some in Corinth may not have been convinced. After all, they had not personally experienced any of the gifts Paul listed in verses 8–10. This is precisely the reason Paul includes a second listing of gifts that differs from the first list in several unique and meaningful ways.

The list begins with a note of sovereign design: "God has appointed in the church" (v. 28). Thus the imagery of the body continues but with an emphasis on God's organization of that body with kingdom purpose. It is unwise to read too much into the order of the entire list since Paul drops the numbering sequence after the first three gifts. Nonetheless, it is obvious that the numbering and the use of persons rather than gifts is intended to draw attention to the apostles, prophets, and teachers.

The listing of persons required the Corinthians to think concretely of the people who were carrying out these leadership functions in Corinth. Apostles, prophets, and teachers were involved in leadership functions from the beginning of the Christian community. They participated in the work of church planting, proclamation, and clarification of the gospel. Many of the difficulties in Corinth can be traced to the spirituals' willingness to criticize and disregard their God-given leaders and to press for their own rights.

Paul's apostolic authority had little meaning to the spirituals who believed that they already reigned. We can hear clear echoes of this sentiment in 1 Corinthians 4:8–13. With tongue in cheek Paul speaks of the apostles as "last of all" and a "spectacle to the world." They are "fools," "weak," and "without honor," "the scum of the world," and "the dregs of all things." Paul's apostolic authority seems to have had little meaning to the spirituals. They judged persons by their commanding presence and dramatic gifts, which Paul seemed to lack (2 Cor. 10:10–12:13).

First Corinthians 16:15–16 indicates that there were people, notably the "household of Stephanas," who were recognized as leaders of the Corinthian congregation. They too were likely being ignored by the spirituals. For that reason Paul writes, "That you also be in subjection to such men and to everyone who helps in the work and labor" (16:16).

In this second gift list—with its focus on apostles, prophets, and teachers—Paul is clearly saying that God has established a leadership structure in the church and that these people are also gifted by God to function as leaders. The more expansive breath of the Pauline concept of "gifts" is becoming more apparent. The abilities that enabled these men to lead are no less "spiritual" than those "seemingly spectacular" abilities proudly displayed by the spirituals. To ignore the gifted ministry of church leaders is tantamount to ignoring the divine structure provided by God for His body.

Paul is not through broadening the understanding of what might be considered to be a spiritual gift. After reiterating a few gifts mentioned in the first list—miracles, gifts of healing, and various kinds of tongues—Paul includes what we might call mundane service abilities. "Administrations" and "helps" translate two Greek words that occur only here in the entire New Testament. The ability to administrate or to do helpful tasks must have seemed pretty mundane and lacking in demonstrative spiritual power to the proud spirituals who loved to boast of their dramatic gifts. Yet Paul wanted to affirm those who thought their only value was to administrate or assist others in ministry, that these abilities presented in service to the Lord were spiritual gifts.

When I read this gift list with the mention of these "mundane" service gifts, I am reminded of the individuals who argue that they aren't gifted because they can't teach or sing a solo. They indicate they will be glad to keep the records or stuff envelopes as they sigh, "I guess I just don't have any spiritual gift." Good news if you sometimes feel like you were missing when the gifts were handed out: all are gifted. The ability to serve in these capacities is just as supernatural as any other gift enabling you to serve the King through His body. These sorts of functions were looked down on as being "less presentable" or "weaker" (vv. 22–23) by the powerful spirituals, but they had misunderstood both the purpose and the breadth of the gifts.

Now we can suggest why Paul included two gift lists in one chapter. The two lists are critical to establish a broadened understanding of spiritual gifts. The first list included only the prized gifts of the spirituals—the visibly miraculous gifts. In the second list Paul literally pulls the top and bottom out of the first list and expands the accepted definition of gifts by adding leadership and service abilities.

This should warn us when we are attempting to discover our own gifts that we need not treat any New Testament gift list as comprehensive. We do not gain anything by adding the two lists in chapter 12 together and then calculating the number of gifts available to the church. These lists were teaching tools, and therefore Paul selected gifts that would illustrate the point he wanted to make to the Corinthian community.

Paul follows this second list with a series of rhetorical questions that pointedly establishes the need for diversity in the body of Christ. "All are not apostles, are they? All are not prophets, are they? All are not teachers, are they? All are not workers of miracles, are they? All do not have gifts of healings, do they? All do not speak with tongues, do they? All do not interpret, do they?" (12:29–30).

Notice that all of the questions anticipate a negative response. Paul actually repeated the list of gifts from 12:28 with the conspicuous omission of "helps" and "administrations." Paul may have left these two out to draw particular attention to them. While simple observation makes clear that not all are leaders or possess "miraculous" abilities, it may not always be apparent that all are gifted for ministry even if their gifts may "appear" to be mundane.

Nothing God gives is mundane, nor should it be neglected. If you have been feeling left out when you read the gift lists or observe "more talented" people around you, this should provide strong encouragement for you to continue to seek your gift so that you may abound to the edification of the church (14:12).

Desire the Greater Gifts

When we first read 1 Corinthians 12:31, "But earnestly desire the greater gifts," we could be somewhat confused. How could Paul speak of "greater gifts"? We may think, *I thought he spent an entire chapter establishing the fact that all members are equally important since God designed the body as He chose.*

This verse may echo a slogan of the spirituals. If so, Paul is quoting it so that he can bring positive correction. At several places in this letter, Paul appears to quote a slogan and then immediately redefines it. For example, 10:23 contains a Corinthian boast and an immediate correction. "All things are lawful, but not all things are profitable. All things are lawful, but not all things edify." The Corinthians were declaring "all things are lawful," and Paul's corrective moves them to edification. Paul refers to the Corinthian zeal for gifts on four occasions (12:31; 14:1, 12, and 39). In each case he immediately qualifies the slogan by the discussion that follows.

Thus Paul is here appealing to their zeal for gifts to move them toward the "greater gifts." We still must answer the question concerning greater gifts. It cannot mean the ecstatic or miraculous gifts, for such an assertion would undo the flow of his argument in chapter 12. It cannot be "love," the topic of chapter 13, for love is not a spiritual gift but rather the substance of Christian life.

Here Paul again uses his favorite word for gifts, *charismata* (cp. 12:4), which he has employed to broaden the understanding of gifts. Thus the corrective "greater gifts" prepares us for the full discussion of the use of gifts in the assembly which follows in chapter 14. When we study that chapter together, we will see that the "greater gifts" are those most suited for the edification of the body and the conversion of the lost. Let's not make the mistake of the Corinthian spirituals and equate "gift" with "person." Paul is not suggesting that some persons are "greater" or "more important" to the kingdom than others. He is merely teaching that in the context of the gathered church gifts which edify the body are "greater" than those that simply edify the person exercising the gift.

This emphasis on "edification" was introduced in 12:7 where Paul insists that the gifts are given for the "common good." It was further suggested by the reversal of what is most valued in verses 21–24. While all gifts are expressions of God's grace and are thus necessary for the functioning of the

> *While all gifts are expressions of God's grace and are thus necessary for the functioning of the body, some gifts are more valuable in terms of their ability to contribute to the kingdom work of the church.*

body, some gifts are more valuable in terms of their ability to contribute to the kingdom work of the church. These gifts would be "greater" only in terms of edification.

Before Paul can move to the discussion of the edifying use of gifts in the assembly (chap. 14), he must first put gifts in the broader perspective of the total life of the community (chap. 13). The phrase "And I show you a still more excellent way" (12:31) causes the reader to look at the larger context of the Christian life. This phrase does not mean that love is a better way than gifts.

Love and gifts are not in conflict, nor is love the highest of the spiritual gifts. Such a suggestion might lead one to think, "I am not required to love the brethren since that is not my gift." Love is the character of the kingdom citizen and is thus the only sign for determining true spirituality! With that understanding, the truly spiritual person would seek gifts which enable him or her to express love and then use those gifts in a manner that edifies the body.

You can see that our study of the next two chapters will be an adventure.

A Brief Recap

Paul is responding to a question from the Corinthians related to spiritual gifts which suggests that some confusion about the matter of spiritual gifts, and persons had emerged since his departure.

> *The truly spiritual person would seek gifts which enable him or her to express love and then use those gifts in a manner that edifies the body.*

He establishes two fundamental correctives before he offers a broadened understanding of gifts. First, he declares that no believer can say "Jesus is Lord" apart from the work of the Holy Spirit. Thus at the most fundamental level all believers have received the Spirit. No particular gift or spiritual experience is necessary to "prove" the possession of the Spirit. The second corrective occurs with the substitution of the term *charismata* for *pneumatika*. Gifts thus are declared to be a "manifestation of grace" and therefore no grounds for boasting. They tell us nothing about the possessor but everything about the "Giver."

The first gift list (vv. 8–10) reflects those gifts most desired in Corinth. Paul uses their own gifts to establish that variety already exists among the gifts practiced in Corinth. This allows him to broaden further the accepted understanding of what constitutes a spiritual gift.

The use of the human body to illustrate the church enables Paul to make several key points. All members belong to the one body. This body has diverse members who have different but equally important functions. The members have been placed in the body by the Creator Himself, and thus the goal of each member is to accomplish the task assigned to it. There are no useless appendages; even those members who receive the least attention are equally important.

The second list follows the illustration of the body and stretches the accepted understanding of what qualifies as a spiritual gift. Leaders and those who possess service abilities are also gifted persons.

Paul ends this section by encouraging his readers to focus their attention on those gifts that have the "greater" ability to edify the body. Further, he prepares the reader for a "more excellent way" which will focus on the character of Christian living.

QUESTIONS FOR REFLECTION

1. Spiritual gifts are actually "grace gifts" and thus tell us nothing about the possessor and everything about the Giver. Have you ever been guilty of judging your worth by comparing yourself to someone you consider to be more gifted than yourself? Are you willing to trust God when His Word affirms that you are gifted? What are your reflections on this truth?
2. Since God designed the body, there are no useless appendages. The proper functioning of the body demands that each part serve its purpose and care for all other parts. Have you found where you fit in the body? Why do you sometimes think you are of no value to the body?
3. Calling any gift or gifted member "ordinary" loses sight of the fact that God always works in a supernatural way. What would change in your life today, if you really began to act upon the principles you have learned in this chapter?

4

The Spiritual Person Redefined

A Study of 1 Corinthians 13

How many weddings have you attended where 1 Corinthians 13 was read, recited, or sung? It would be difficult to determine the number and with good reason. If a couple is familiar with any text on love, it is this one. This passage is beautiful, and it describes love profoundly in both negative and positive statements.

But our familiarity with this text can cause us to miss its significance as Paul attempts to redirect the spiritual zeal of the Corinthians toward more edifying behavior. Having just heard 1 Corinthians 12 read, many in Corinth were facing a dilemma. If possessing certain gifts did not prove one to be spiritual, what sign should they seek, and what evidence could they produce? Paul has just clearly indicated that all believers alike share in the work of the Spirit in conversion, incorporation in the body, and the reception of gifts for service to the King. Was there any sure sign of growing spirituality? Can we know when we are serving empowered by the Holy Spirit?

A Word to the Wise

It is impossible to read 1 Corinthians 13 without being impressed by its beauty, style, and depth of teaching. These features have caused some commentators to call it a "hymn" and assign its authorship to someone other than Paul. Other people have suggested that Paul composed it on a separate occasion and inserted it here. In this light it becomes a polished gem inserted here by the author because of its relevance to the Corinthian situation. Yet some find its insertion at this point "unfortunate" and would place it next to chapter 8 or after chapter 14. These suggestions fail to appreciate the powerful polemical tone of this chapter and its centrality for Paul's corrective teaching.

It is not accidental that this chapter falls between Paul's broadened definition of spiritual gifts (chap. 12) and his explanation of how gifts could be used in an edifying manner in the assembly (chap. 14). This chapter is the peak of Paul's corrective teaching on gifts and thus must be fully understood before one is prepared to read and understand chapter 14.

Having said all that, I will readily admit that the style of chapter 13 does differ radically from its immediate context. Thus we must ask why Paul would make such a significant stylistic shift right in the middle of his discussion of gifts.

The style of this chapter shares certain similarities with "wisdom literature" of the period. Paul, under the guidance of the Holy Spirit, intentionally chooses to use the style of popular wisdom literature to meet the spirituals on their own ground.

We have already noticed that the spirituals boasted of their wisdom. They had attacked Paul because his preaching lacked persuasive words of wisdom. Thus it is both brilliant and ironic that Paul used "persuasive words of wisdom" in this chapter to express his most pointed correction. One might wonder if this passage elicited the remark recorded in 2 Corinthians 10:10: "His letters are weighty and strong, but his personal presence is unimpressive and his speech contemptible."

Love, the Only Authenticator of Spiritual Maturity

You might ask why Paul pauses in this section to move his argument to a higher and broader level, virtually interrupting his discussion of spiritual gifts. Paul needed to do so because the spirituals linked certain *gifts* with *persons* and saw the gifts as signs of that person's spirituality. Thus you will notice that this chapter is primarily about *persons* and only secondarily about *gifts*. Paul is thus offering a comprehensive and radical redefinition of the spiritual person. Love is the one authenticator of spiritual maturity.

Read the first three verses and you will see that Paul is concerned with the "perceived" worth of persons and not just with gifts themselves. Listen carefully! Paul is not placing love against gifts, implying that love renders gifts unimportant. Those who make such an assertion have a personal agenda and ignore the clear teaching of chapter 12. Why would someone dare call any work of the Holy Spirit "unimportant"? Neither is Paul describing the way all must walk whether they are gifted or not. Such a suggestion stands against the clear teaching of Scripture that constantly underlines the universal giftedness of believers with the use of words like "all persons" and "each one" to describe the work of the Spirit in distributing gifts.

You will recall that the spirituals zealously desired miraculous sign gifts to prove that they already reigned (4:8). The idea that one "already reigns" or has already experienced all the kingdom realities in this life is referred to as "over-realized eschatology." It is one of the central flaws of the "health and wealth" purveyors who suggest that God *always* blesses the faithful with health and wealth in this life. Perfect health and eternal riches will be ours when the kingdom comes in its fullness, but that is not yet.

In this chapter Paul provides a corrective to overrealized eschatology with its dependence on sign gifts by pointing to love as the one expression of the eternal, which is actually available in the present. Loving behavior then is the one present-day kingdom sign that one is an authentic spiritual person. The love Paul speaks of is neither emotional attachment nor mere human sentiment. Love is relational and thus finds its foundation in the reality of God's love that was given when undeserved (Eph. 2:4–5). Love is experienced in the cross and thus becomes the controlling motive of all Christian activity (1 Cor. 16:14; 2 Cor. 5:14). Thus the Christian is called to "walk in love" (Eph. 5:2).

> *Loving behavior then is the one present-day kingdom sign that one is an authentic spiritual person.*

The expression of love described by Paul is not produced by human effort but by the power of the Spirit who poured out God's love within the human heart (Rom. 5:5). Christian love will be the visible controlling element in the authentic spiritual person's relationship with others. Paul emphasizes this practical and visible expression of love and contrasts it with the egotistical individualism of the spirituals. Love will thus be the central determinative that guides the desire for and use of spiritual gifts.

We might look at a simple illustration to further explain Paul's point. I can tell you about my parents. I might even introduce them to you, but you have no real assurance they are actually my parents. The only authenticator I can provide is my birth certificate accompanied by my family resemblance. So I can boast to you about my advanced spirituality. I might even demonstrate my sign gifts, but the only authenticator I can offer is my spiritual birth certificate that will be seen as I express God's character through my loving actions.

The Transforming Power of Love

If love is the sure sign of the Holy Spirit's presence and the work of the Holy Spirit is to bring us into conformity to the image of God's Son, then we should not be surprised to discover that the description of love in this chapter bears striking similarities with the description of the fruit of the Spirit in Galatians 5:22–23. The fruit of the Spirit is the life of Christ produced in the believer by the indwelling Holy Spirit.

Let's not be confused about the work of the Spirit. The moment you received Christ, the Holy Spirit came to indwell in you (Rom. 8:9). We can rightly refer to this as the baptism of the Holy Spirit. The Holy Spirit immerses you into the body of Christ (1 Cor. 12:13) where your gifts find their locus for effective ministry. Further, He works in your life to produce the character of Christ in you, ensuring that you will desire to use your gifts to edify His body and bring Him glory.

Paul reflects further on this transformational work of the Spirit in 2 Corinthians 3:1–18. He compares and contrasts the work of the Spirit with the Ten Commandments. The commandments reflected the character and glory of God, but they produced a ministry of condemnation because no one could live up to them by the exertion of the human will. But now we can turn to Christ and receive the Spirit producing liberty. This does not mean we ignore God's law. On the contrary, it means that the Holy Spirit now indwells us, enabling us to obey the law and thus reflect the character of holy God. "But we all, with unveiled face, beholding as in a mirror the glory of the Lord, are being transformed into the same image from glory to glory, just as from the Lord, the Spirit" (2 Cor. 3:18).

The Holy Spirit who provides gifts for ministry produces the character necessary for life in community. These two themes are inextricably bound together. Paul makes that clear as he drives his corrective home with hammer-like blows by looking at a few of their prized "sign gifts" expressed to the n'th degree but devoid of love. Don't overlook the fact that the gifts mentioned here are the same ones that have been a priority since chapter 1. Nothing about this passage is generic. Too much is at stake in the advance of the kingdom for the Corinthians to miss the corrective that gifts are given for God's kingdom work and His glory and not the advancement of people and their esteem.

The Tongues of Men and Angels

"Speaking in tongues" held a prominent, though not exclusive, place as a sign of one's present reign in the kingdom. The mysterious nature of such a gift would have commanded great attention when practiced in the gathered assembly. The extensive treatment of this particular gift in chapter 14 indicates both its importance and abuse in Corinth. This gift is at the heart of much confusion over spiritual gifts. So we will find this section relevant for evaluating present-day concerns.

What does Paul mean when he speaks of "the tongues of men and angels" (13:1)? Did Paul really believe that when a person spoke with tongues he communicated with angels? Many commentators argue that this phrase is symbolic for every possible type of speech in heaven and on earth. If you read the first three verses, you will note that every gift listed is spoken of in an exaggerated manner. For example, Paul mentions knowing all mysteries and having all knowledge, a concept that he clearly refutes throughout this letter. Thus, Paul's reference to "tongues of men and angels" may be a similar exaggeration that would cover all forms of speech here and in the coming kingdom. If that is Paul's point, he is simply arguing that none of these languages would prove one's spirituality.

Some commentators, who disagree with the suggestion that this phrase be taken in a comprehensive and symbolic fashion, insist that Paul himself believed that glossolalia was the tongues of angels. The English word *glossolalia* is derived from two Greek words, *glossa* and *laleo,* and means literally "to speak tongues." We must then ask if any evidence exists that Paul thought the individual "speaking in tongues" was speaking to angels?

Those who take this view point to 1 Corinthians 14:2 and 2 Corinthians 12:4 for support. The first passage simply asserts that men do not understand tongue speech since the individual speaks "mysteries" and the audience is God not man. We will return to this passage when we look at chapter 14, but at this point we should only note that this passage does not support the notion that Paul believed tongue speech was addressed to the angels.

The passage in 2 Corinthians is more relevant. Paul speaks of a visionary experience where he "was caught up into Paradise and heard inexpressible words, which a man is not permitted to speak." Notice, however, that Paul makes clear that what he heard in paradise was "inexpressible" and that man "is not permitted to speak" these words. Since the revelation in the vision could not be spoken, it could not be a reference to tongues since that gift relies on speech.

Later in chapter 13:10 Paul indicates that tongues will cease "when the perfect comes." *Perfect* most likely refers to the fullness of God's kingdom in heaven. If that is the case, we must ask why tongues would cease just when they would prove to be particularly useful in talking with the angels in person. We can safely conclude that Paul did not think people on earth could communicate with the angels through tongue speech.

The spirituals themselves, however, may have believed that their tongue speech enabled them to communicate with the angels. What better evidence could one offer that he or she already reigns in the heavenlies than angelic tongues? If this is an accurate reconstruction, then 2 Corinthians 12:4 is a pointed corrective to the mistaken idea of the spirituals. Paul asserts that man is neither able nor permitted to speak what he hears in paradise.

Paul's corrective to the arrogant spirituals is sharp indeed. Paul argues that even if people were able to speak with the tongues of men and angels and yet lacked love, they would become like a noisy gong or clanging symbol. At this point Paul is not concerned about the ability of any of the gifts mentioned here to edify; he is simply describing the effect of any gift practiced to its utmost degree but devoid of love.

Some commentators suggest that the words "noisy" and "clanging" may allude to sounds present in pagan worship. If that is accurate, Paul's corrective is even more sharply defined. Tongues practiced by the person lacking love have much the same effect as the clanging symbols of pagan worship. This would certainly be a blow to the pride of the spirituals. Their worship, rather than glorifying the King and drawing the lost, had much the same effect of "clanging" pagan worship. For example, in chapter 14 Paul gives a positive assessment of prophecy in terms of its capacity to edify and convict the lost.

The main point of the corrective is abundantly clear; tongues do not prove that a person is spiritual!

Prophecy, Mysteries, and Knowledge

Prophecy, mysteries, and knowledge are closely related because they all demand special revelation and involve verbal declaration in the assembly. It is difficult for us, reading this text centuries later, to reconstruct what might have been the subtle distinctions between these gifts as practiced in Corinth. Paul may have had in mind some distinctions (see 14:6), but any subtle distinctions likely were irrelevant to the spirituals since they claimed to abound "in all speech and all knowledge" (1:5). Paul again draws our attention to the arrogant boasting of the spirituals concerning the abundance or "completeness" of their gifts with the fourfold repetition of "all" in 13:2–3: "all mysteries," "all knowledge," "all faith," "all possessions."

We can actually trace several of the problems in Corinth to the spirituals' claim to possess special knowledge. We have already drawn attention to the example in chapter 8. The spirituals had freely partaken of the meat offered to idols on the basis of their knowledge. Paul's corrective was twofold. The results of their "supposed" knowledge were spiritual arrogance (8:1) and "a stumbling block to the weak" (8:9). In stark contrast love would lead to edification. Paul informs them that their knowledge was not full but partial (8:2). This point will be clarified and specifically applied in 13:12, a passage we will look at in a few pages.

Miracle-Working Faith

Miracle-working faith is next in this short listing of gifts. We don't have any specific mention of miracle-working faith in the Corinthian letters, but some among the spirituals may have pointed to the ability to work miracles as evidence of their spiritual status. The phrase "faith, so as to remove mountains" (1 Cor. 13:2) actually echoes a saying of the Lord (Matt. 17:20; 21:21; and Mark 11:23). Some of the Corinthians may have misused sayings of the Lord to defend their insistence on sign gifts to verify one's spirituality. Notice that once again Paul reproduces the boast of the spirituals only to refute and redirect it.

Second Corinthians 10–13 indicates that some of the Corinthians were impressed with signs and wonders and the "most eminent apostles" (2 Cor. 11:5) who manifested them. In that section Paul reluctantly enters their game of boasting, but he turns the tables by boasting about his weaknesses. "If I have to boast, I will boast of what pertains to my weakness" (11:30). Paul finally speaks of a visionary experience that was so profound that what he experienced was inexpressible, and thus he was not permitted to speak of it (12:4). With some hesitation and profound humility, Paul noted that his own ministry had indeed been accompanied by the signs of a true apostle (12:12).

The Gospels make abundantly clear that signs and wonders were evidenced throughout Jesus' ministry. This is made more understandable when we remember that during the three years of Jesus' earthly ministry the spiritual battle, which is normally waged in the "heavenly places" (Eph. 6:12), was conducted on an earthly stage for all to witness. When the King came in human flesh, Satan concentrated his evil forces on earth to do battle with God's only begotten Son. Satan's ultimate defeat was sealed on this earthly platform when

Jesus rose triumphantly from the dead. With the exaltation of Jesus, the spiritual battlefield was once again located primarily in the heavenly places. Satan, the conquered adversary uses deception and accusation to wage war against the saints today.

A simple reading of the book of Acts makes clear that similar "signs and wonders" accompanied the first-century ministry of the early apostles. Paul chose to focus on the sign of conversion as the primary evidence of effective apostolic ministry. When Paul mentions "signs and wonders" in Romans 15:19, he couples it with the power of his preaching. "In the power of signs and wonders, in the power of the Spirit; so that from Jerusalem and round about as far as Illyricum I have fully preached the gospel of Christ."

Today we most often hear of the occurrence of supernatural signs as the gospel is first presented in areas where the written and verbal witness has been lacking. Missionaries regularly tell of Muslim converts having visions of Christ, which prepare them for a verbal witness. Several stories of such supernatural signs have been included in the book *Muslims, Magic and the Kingdom of God* by Rick Love.[1] Another good reference is the book edited by Cynthia A. Strong and Meg Page titled *Ministry Among Muslim Women*.[2] Caution is always advisable when we feel led to put God in a box and make categorical statements about what the Holy Spirit is not able to do in our day. We must be careful not to grieve the Spirit.

In the Corinthian letter Paul makes a concerted attempt to redirect their zeal for gifts toward ministry gifts. These gifts are given to the church and must be discovered and used for the edification and advancement of the church in each generation for the sake of the kingdom. The ministry gifts will be necessary until the present order is brought to a close by the return of the King.

We shouldn't become overly concerned with trying to specify the actual operation of the various gifts mentioned in the first few verses of chapter 13. We need to focus on Paul's pointed correction. Any and all of these gifts, exercised to their fullest extent but devoid of love, renders the same spiritual assessment: "I am nothing." In other words, they have no sign value!

All My Possessions to Feed the Poor

First Corinthians 12:3 actually presents the reader with several difficulties. There is nothing in here to suggest that the Corinthians were zealous to feed the poor. In fact, the opposite seems to be the case. Paul devotes three chapters (1 Cor. 16 and 2 Cor. 8–9) to discuss the offering he was collecting for the saints in Jerusalem who were suffering great need due to a famine. Paul expresses concern that his boasting about the readiness of the Corinthians to participate in the offering for the saints in Jerusalem may actually prove to be in vain. The two chapters of 2 Corinthians are a stern reminder of their responsibility to participate fully in this offering. He exhorts them to bring their offering to a successful completion (8:11). In chapter 9 he indicates that he has sent the brethren to complete the offering "in order that our boasting about you may not be made empty in this case" (9:3). I can find no evidence that the Corinthian believers were overzealous in their giving to the poor.

A textual variant in some of the earliest manuscripts reads "boast" rather than "burn" in the next statement: "If I surrender my body to be burned." The arrogant attitude of the Corinthians may seem to recommend the reading "that I may boast," and the manuscript evidence is nearly equally divided on this matter.

Both of these problems are resolved if we simply focus on the immediate and historical context of 1 Corinthians 13. In verses 1–3 Paul takes several of their most prized gifts, places them in the most positive context, and indicates that they may be practiced to the most abundant degree, and still they would not indicate spiritual superiority. Thus, in this instance, Paul is not concerned about sacrificial self-giving but is actually alluding to the spirituals' disregard for their physical bodies. Tragically, their disregard for their body was not being expressed positively but arrogantly in numerous ways, incest (chap. 5) and sexual asceticism (chap. 7) being two.

The spirituals' disregard for the physical body issued from their conviction that as spirituals they lived above the laws that govern ordinary people. Tragically we have seen this same aberrant view of spirituality in some of the cults where sexual relationships with the cult leader are seen as a spiritual act. Paul, however, takes the most positive expression of disregard for bodily existence possible—"If I give all my possessions to feed the poor" (1 Cor. 13:3)—and indicates that such a noble act, devoid of love "profits me nothing." Once again, if one's goal in seeking and displaying a particular gift is to prove spirituality, this display offers no proof of spiritual maturity because it issues out of selfish self-love. By using a positive expression of disregard for the body, the contrast with the selfish and arrogant Corinthians is made even more vivid.

I would paraphrase this verse as follows: "You disregard the physical body for selfish reasons such as sexual indulgence, and you are proud because you think that proves you are spiritual. Even if I were to disregard my body for the most noble reason possible—to benefit others—and I lack love, it is of no spiritual benefit to me." The bottom line of the first three verses is obvious and pointed. No spiritual gift is evidence of one's spirituality!

Further, Paul's use of himself as a hypothetical case—"If I surrender my body"—would have made this point an intensely personal one. While few of the Corinthians had been called on to live sacrificially for the gospel, Paul had done so on numerous occasions. Paul had "suffered the loss of all things" (Phil. 3:8) and bore the "brand-marks of Jesus" on his body (Gal. 6:17). When Paul is forced into boasting about his visionary experience (2 Cor. 12), he turns the table and declares, "Most gladly, therefore, I will rather boast about my weaknesses, so that the power of Christ may dwell in me" (v. 9). He then proceeds to list insults, distresses, and persecutions (v. 10). For Paul physical suffering was a part of his apostolic calling and a continuation of the sufferings of Christ (Col. 1:24). Yet, if all of this had not been motivated by love, then Paul would gain nothing.[3]

Love Contrasted with the Behavior of the Spirituals

Paul is aware that the arrogant spirituals might miss the point of his corrective. They might glibly think they already excel in love. For this reason Paul contrasts love with the actual behavior of the spirituals. To do this Paul carefully selected eight negative statements to define what love is not so that he might demonstrate conclusively that the spirituals lack the only true sign of spirituality.

Paul begins with two positive statements, "Love is patient, love is kind" (1 Cor. 13:4). Both patience and kindness emphasize one's behavior in relation to others. Patience is foundational to the proper functioning of the gifted community (cp. 1 Thess. 5:14) since it is the basis of unity. Kindness reflects one's tender care for the needs and feelings of another. Neither of these characteristics of love has been widely demonstrated in Corinth as believers have asserted their own rights.

Is Not Jealous

Love, which is patient and kind, will not be jealous of another. The word translated *jealous* is the same Greek word Paul uses to describe the "zeal" of the spirituals for gifts. Spiritual zeal can be praiseworthy if its focus is on the kingdom of God and the glory of God. But in Corinth, zeal for gifts had degenerated into jealousy and self-striving. Their zeal for various wise leaders had divided the community and had demonstrated that they were babes and not spiritual persons (3:1–4). They were zealous to possess spiritual gifts (14:12) but for all the wrong reasons. Zeal, untamed by love, exhibits itself in self-seeking jealousy. Love, however, does not act this way.

This might be a good time to pause and ask about our own motives for wanting to discover our gifts. Is your zeal motivated by the desire to serve the King and advance His kingdom? Are you willing to serve in any capacity the King desires? Do you have any jealous motivation that desires a gift that will gain attention or the admiration of others? Gifts sought for the wrong reason can be disruptive to the work of the King through His community.

Love Does Not Brag and Is Not Arrogant

Even a cursory reading of 1 Corinthians reveals that Paul constantly rebukes the spirituals for their arrogance and the resulting boasting. The Greek word translated *brag* occurs only here in the New Testament. It contains a word picture of a windbag or, in our jargon, one who is puffed up like a toad. It is not a very pretty picture, but unfortunately it is an accurate one when it comes to the spirituals. "Is not arrogant" is a particularly pointed correction of the spirituals, since the same word is frequently employed by Paul to characterize the behavior of the spirituals (4:6 ff.; 4:18 ff.; 5:2 ff.; 8:1 ff.).

They had become inflated over their perceived wisdom and oratorical ability (1:5). They boasted about the abundance of their gifts. They boasted about their freedom from the law and traditions of the church in matters of behavior and decorum (5:2). Paul intentionally drew attention to his previous discussions concerning spiritual pride to warn them that arrogant boasting is contrary to love, which is the only sign of spiritual maturity.

It is so easy for us to fall into the trap of spiritual pride that we can't afford to neglect Paul's warning. We can become arrogant about how much we do for the Lord and forget that our ability to serve is but a gift of grace. We can swell with pride when someone tells us how great we are. We believe them and become so enamored with ourselves that we lose our servant spirit.

Love Does Not Act Unbecomingly

The word "unbecoming" occurs on one other occasion earlier in this letter. In chapter 7 Paul speaks of improper behavior toward a virgin. The context indicates that Paul was referring to the danger of unseemly sexual behavior between a man and his fiancé. Apparently some of the spirituals were unduly extending their engagement period in order to boast about their spiritual ability to withstand sexual temptation. Some had overestimated their self-control and had behaved in an unacceptable manner prior to marriage.

In chapter 14 Paul deals with proper behavior during gathered worship. The spirituals saw the worship service as an ideal forum for displaying their gifts to prove their spirituality. This had led to confusion and discord. Paul insists that God is not a God of confusion, and thus he demands that there be clear guidelines for control and decency in the public use of gifts. Verse 40—"But all things must be done properly and in an orderly manner"—is not an appeal based on what works, but it is an appeal based on the standard of love. Love does not act unbecomingly, and therefore the truly gifted person will exercise his gift in an orderly manner precisely because he is controlled by love.

Unseemly behavior was nowhere more evident than in the celebration of the Lord's Supper where division, revelry, and a lack of concern for the poor was the order of the day (11:18–22). Earlier in the same chapter Paul declared that women who insisted on praying and prophesying with their heads uncovered had disregarded the traditions of the church and thus had behaved in an unseemly manner (11:1–16). The possession of spiritual gifts does not elevate the believer above concern for orderly community function. Love demands that spiritual persons employ their gifts in such a manner that they will enhance community relations.

Love Does Not Seek Its Own

With the use of this negative descriptor, Paul touched the nerve center of the Corinthian problem. For example, the controversy concerning the eating of meat offered to idols was selfish to the core. There were two closely related problems. Some Corinthians were buying meat in the market that had been previously used in pagan worship. Other persons, however, were participating in social events held in the pagan temple. Events such as weddings were frequently held in the temple halls. Paul warns those persons who were participating in events held in pagan temples that they might become sharers in demons. Yet the overriding principle that he appeals to in both cases is that of responsible behavior toward others rather than asserting one's own rights (8:13 and 10:23–33).

Paul illustrates his corrective teaching by alluding to his right as an apostle to receive financial support from his communities. He had chosen to forego this right of an apostle in order to remove all possible hindrances to the gospel (9:12). The sentiment of 1 Corinthians 10:24 is identical to that of 13:5: "Let no one seek his own good, but that of his neighbor." The principle of love, which seeks the good of the brethren, is the controlling principle of the Christian life and therefore for the use of one's gifts. Love demands that we seek gifts with the good of the body in mind. The individual who seeks gifts for ego gratification rather than edification of the community demonstrates spiritual immaturity.

Is Not Provoked, Does Not Take into Account a Wrong Suffered

These two phrases are closely related and thus should be taken together. "Is not provoked" is defined by "does not take into account a wrong suffered." Love is not embittered by injuries, real or supposed. The loving person refuses to make a mental scoreboard of wrongs suffered. The Corinthians, however, had hauled one another before secular judges. Paul pointedly asks, "Why not rather be wronged? Why not rather be defrauded?" Then Paul ponders, "Is it so, that there is not among you one wise man who will be able to decide between his brethren?" (6:5). Don't miss the pointed correction in this verse. The spirituals were arrogant about their wisdom, and yet they weren't sufficiently wise to settle simple disputes among themselves.

Their concern for the unity of the body should have been so great that they would not "take into account a wrong suffered." The brutal facts were that the Corinthians were easily provoked with one another, and instead of bearing the wrong, they wanted retribution.

This comes too close to home for us to be comfortable. How often have we been guilty of demanding our own rights when we think we have been injured by another? Do you ever find yourself keeping a mental scorecard? Have you ever thought, *I'll get you back for that one*? The process of keeping count of wrongs suffered can invade the privacy of our homes. A wife is hurt by her husband's actions. She declares that she will forgive him this time. Yet she marks it in her scorecard and readily brings it back to the table when needed. Love is so prepared to forgive that it doesn't bother to mark the score.

Does Not Rejoice in Unrighteousness, but Rejoices in the Truth

Simply stated, love finds no joy in sin! We have already looked briefly at the account of a man living with his stepmother (chap. 5). Paul is not only grieved by the deed; he is staggered by the reaction of the spirituals. Instead of being grieved and taking appropriate disciplinary action, they had become arrogant (vv. 2–6). For this reason Paul does not simply say, "Love does not practice unrighteousness"; he says that love "does not rejoice in unrighteousness" (13:6).

Love, unlike the spirituals, rejoices in truth. The word *truth* in this context means the opposite of unrighteousness. Paul was asserting that love rejoices in righteous, obedient, ethical behavior. Love reflects the character of God who is righteous. The authentically spiritual person can never be indifferent when it comes to issues of moral concern. The spirituals in Corinth wanted the appearance of spirituality, but they used it as a cover for unrighteous behavior.

We are shocked when we hear of a local pastor or televangelist who has used his position for sinful gain. Rightly so! Spiritual maturity should be evidenced in ethical behavior in every sphere of life. But we must apply this principle of "rejoicing in the truth" to all believers. We are all gifted and called by God for ministry as we advance His kingdom. It is always wrong when we use a claim to spirituality as a cloak for sin. Neither the possession of any gift nor the holding of any office places us above the standard of God's law. Rather the possession of God's grace expressed in our giftedness should make us more acutely aware of our responsibility to "rejoice in the truth."

A Positive Summary of Love

"Love bears all things, believes all things, hopes all things, endures all things." Now that Paul has finished his contrast of love with the behavior of the spirituals, he begins a positive presentation of the superiority of love. Love not only avoids all the exaggerated behavior patterns of the spirituals, but love "bears . . . believes . . . hopes . . . endures" (1 Cor. 13:7). Paul declares that love has a self-giving nature that refuses to give up.

The verb translated *bears* has the basic idea of "cover," "hide by covering," or "endure." Love has the power to cover over that which is displeasing in another. This stands in stark contrast to those who would "rejoice in unrighteousness." Love does not conceal in the sense of ignoring moral wrong; it seeks to cover over and heal that which is evil in another. Love does not easily give up, and thus it has an enduring quality.

> *"Love bears all things, believes all things, hopes all things, endures all things."*

When Paul states that love "believes all things," he is referring to the capacity of love to believe the best of others. It seems to be human nature to expect and believe the worst, but love has a faith quality that enables it to consider the circumstances and look for, anticipate, and believe the best. This does not suggest that love is either naïve or easily deceived. It is modeled after God's love, which looks beyond our sin with forgiveness and sees our greatest potential. We can easily see how such love is necessary for the unity and ministry of the body.

"Hopes all things" looks positively toward the future. There seems to be a progression in these three statements. How does love respond when all the evidence has been gathered and our "bearing" and our "believing" encounter a harsh dose of reality? The persons we have "believed the best" about are actually found to be guilty. Love does not ignore the evil in another; it simply refuses to believe that any failure is final, and thus it hopes for the best. Love anticipates the ultimate victory of God's redeeming grace and stands by the brother, suffering when he suffers and rejoicing when he rejoices. In this sense love "endures all things." It is the endurance of the athlete who simply refuses to stop short of the ultimate goal. Love never quits!

When I was in elementary school, one of my teachers wrote on my report card that I was tenacious. That is a big word for a little kid. When my dad helped me look it up in the dictionary, I settled on a simple definition: "has an attitude like a bulldog." When I asked Dad what the teacher meant when she referred to me as tenacious, he indicated that like a bulldog, I refused to quit. I would stay with any problem until I solved it. Christian love that binds us together has the same quality of tenacity.

Do we manifest this love in our relationship with others in the Christian community? Do we think the best or assume the worst? Do we cling to one another with tenacity?

Express the Eternal in the Now

We have already discussed the spirituals' conviction that they already possessed the fullness of the kingdom, an aberrant view which Bible teachers called "over-realized eschatology." Earlier Paul declares, with no small amount of irony, "You are already filled, you have already become rich, you have become kings without us; and indeed, I wish that you had become kings so that we also might reign with you" (4:8). If you think this earlier corrective was pointed, prepare for Paul's most radical surgery on this mistaken view.

Paul proceeds now to destroy the framework on which their arrogant spirituality had been constructed. Paul again accepts on face value their boast to abound in all gifts, but now his correction takes an unexpected turn. He argues that their possession of spiritual gifts actually disproves their claim to reign spiritually. Prophecy, tongues, and other such gifts are manifestations of grace provided to enable believers to serve the King and advance His kingdom on earth. Thus if gifts are signs in any sense, they are signs of earthly, not heavenly, existence. Someday, when believers enter into the fullness of the kingdom, their earthly gifts will have no purpose. Thus the spirituals' boasting to abound in spiritual gifts has literally invalidated their argument that they "already reign." The possession of any spiritual gift proves beyond question that the possessor still belongs to this age.

Love, which Paul has demonstrated that they do not display, is the greatest expression of the eternal in the present age!

The earthly and transient nature of all spiritual gifts is made explicit in 13:8 with the repetition of "done away . . . cease . . . done away." Prophecy, tongues, and knowledge are mentioned because of their prominence in Corinth, but the truth presented is valid for all gifts. All gifts for earthly ministry are destined to pass away when the perfect comes. Obviously the gifts do not have the eternal sign value assigned to them by the spirituals.

Paul makes a second critical corrective in this short section. The repetition of "in part" in verse 9 and the stark contrast between "perfect" and "partial" in verse 10 are a pointed part of Paul's argument. At their best the present manifestations of prophecy and knowledge so desired by the spirituals are imperfect and partial. This must have been a shock to those who boasted to possess *all knowledge.*

Now we must ask what Paul means by his reference to the "perfect." Let's allow the text to speak for itself. We know that "when the perfect comes" gifts like prophecy, tongues, and knowledge "will be done away" (vv. 8–10). With the coming of the "perfect," seeing dimly will be replaced with face-to-face knowledge (v. 12). When the "perfect" comes, believers will actually know as fully as we have been fully known by God (v. 12). Thus we can conclude that Paul is not simply talking about the Christian's coming to maturity but about the "perfect" replacing the "partial" in all avenues of life.

Some have suggested that the "perfect" refers to the end of the apostolic age and the closing of the canon of Scripture. They then argue for the cessation of certain of the sign gifts with the end of the foundational period of church history. However appealing such an argument may be to some, the end of the apostolic age was not a time when the "partial" was replaced by face-to-face knowledge. Believers did not come into full knowledge. No, it is clear that we still live in the time of the partial and the incomplete.

For this reason Paul will proceed to give detailed explanation of how gifts such as tongues and prophecy must be used and controlled in the gathered assembly (chap. 14). Chapter 14 would be largely irrelevant if Paul believed that gifts such as prophecy and tongues were at the point of cessation. This conclusion, however, does not mean that the exercise of any gift will add to the completed and full revelation of God that came in Christ (Heb. 1:1–3). Gifts that might appear to add to revelation and thus claim to have the authority of Scripture came to an end when God spoke His final word in His Son. For this reason Paul defines prophecy in terms of speaking to men for "edification and exhortation and consolation" (1 Cor. 14:3). The prophet now interprets and applies the Word as completed in Christ.

The term *perfect* refers to the end of time as we know it and the return of the King. When Christ returns, gifts such as prophecy and knowledge will be rendered obsolete since we will be in the presence of the King and know as fully as we are known by God. Our service to the King in our glorified body will be of a wholly different order, and thus we will move beyond earthly gifts in the same way that a child discards childish toys.

Spiritual gifts have value, but because their purpose and value are defined by this present age, they must be sought and appraised in terms of their role in edifying the church and advancing the kingdom until the return of the King. Simply put, gifts are manifestations of the *now* and thus are limited to and by the present age. When the Lord returns, there will be *full* participation in the kingdom, but ironically this will mean the demise of the gifts as they are now experienced. Spiritual gifts are not "signs" that we "already reign." They are precisely the opposite. They are "signs" that we still serve the King in anticipation of His return and visible reign.

The illustration of childhood should be taken at its face value. Speaking, thinking, and reasoning refer to normal functions of man. Childish thinking and speaking are not evil; they are simply inadequate in comparison with mature speaking and thinking. The mature person sets aside childish thinking precisely because it has been surpassed by maturity. The implication is obvious! The spiritual manifestations of this age, no matter how magnificent they may seem now, will seem childish imitations in comparison to serving God in His presence when the kingdom is fully realized.

> *Manifestations of God's grace in the present age enable the believer to participate in kingdom activity.*

Paul does not want the Corinthians to abandon their desire for gifts (cp. 14:12). That suggestion would negate the extended discussion of the appropriate operation of gifts here in 1 Corinthians 12–14 and the subsequent discussions in Romans 12 and Ephesians 4. He does, however, want them to view, seek, and use gifts in their proper perspective. Manifestations of God's grace in the present age enable the believer to participate in kingdom activity.

The illustration of the mirror provides a pointed contrast between the nature of gifts experienced in the now and the fullness of the coming of the kingdom. The spirituals claim to possess "all knowledge" (1:5 and 13:2). They further believe that this full knowledge was evidence that they "already reigned." Paul counters by asserting that present knowledge is like a dim image in a mirror, whereas knowing when the kingdom is fully experienced will be like seeing face-to-face.

The mirrors of Paul's time were not as refined as present-day mirrors. They were often made of metal and the reflected image was dim or distorted. Knowing dimly is not a fault. Present knowledge, by its very nature, is partial. At its best it will be obscure when contrasted with perfect knowledge. Paul uses this illustration to make two points. First, he demonstrates that possessing gifts actually proves that a person is still of this earth since gifts have value and meaning for the present age. Second, any and all earthly gifts are partial and not perfect.

The Superiority of Love

Paul concludes the chapter with an exclamation on the superiority of love. "But now," in contrast with spiritual gifts, there remain faith, hope, and love. Faith or "trust" in the Lord begins in this present age the moment we receive Christ. That relationship will continue into eternity, but there faith will become sight. Our conversion thus gives us a sure hope that will not disappoint. In eternity, when we dwell in the presence of the Lord, hope will find its total fulfillment. Thus faith and hope are exceeded by love. Love is the one eternal reality we can express both now and for all eternity. Love is superior to faith and hope in that both faith and hope focus on our own relationship with the King, while love enables us to look beyond ourselves and edify others both now and in eternity.

> *Love is the one eternal reality we can express both now and for all eternity.*

Our spiritual gifts enable us to express the "eternal" love in the present by using them to edify the body of Christ, the church. Later in Ephesians 3:21

Paul links the church and Christ as the places where God receives glory. When we use our gifts to edify the "bride," we glorify Christ and please the Father.

The claim to spirituality based on miraculous gifts is not valid because they are earthly manifestations of grace enabling us to serve the King for His glory alone. The greatest eternal reality that man can experience in the now has been found to be conspicuously lacking in the behavior of those claiming to be spirituals. While chapter 13 clearly denies any sign value to gifts, it does not render them worthless. On the contrary, gifts can now be seen in their proper perspective. Gifts are expressions of God's grace in the now, and therefore their real meaning is discovered only when "spiritual persons," as defined in chapter 13, employ them to express the eschatological reality of love in the now.

> *Spiritual gifts have meaning only when they are used to edify the body and advance the kingdom.*

Let me make that last statement in a simpler way. Spiritual gifts have meaning only when they are used to edify the body and advance the kingdom. With the broadened understanding of what qualifies as a spiritual gift (chap. 12) and with the redefinition of the spiritual person (chap. 13), Paul is now prepared to explain how the mature spiritual person can use gifts in the community of believers.

A Brief Recap

Paul establishes "love" as the only authenticator of spiritual maturity. Love is described against the arrogant behavior of the spirituals. Love is the work of the Holy Spirit as He produces the character of Christ in the life of believers.

Paul contrasts love with the "vaunted" gifts of the Corinthians to demonstrate that the selfish display of any gift to its ultimate degree, devoid of love, is of no profit to the individual. It has no "sign" value.

The negative descriptions of love are intentional correctives aimed at the arrogant behavior of the spirituals.

Paul uses their boast to an abundance of gifts to prove that they are "earthly" and not "spiritual." The gifts are given for earthly ministry and thus will have no value when the "perfect" comes. *Perfect* refers to the return of the King and the inauguration of the kingdom. All spiritual gifts are therefore "partial" and are designed for earthly ministry not given as signs of spiritual ascendancy.

Spiritual gifts do have value, but it is determined by their use in the present age. Thus they must be sought, appraised, and used for the edification of the church and the advance of the kingdom until the return of the King.

Love is the one eternal reality we can express both now and for all eternity. Gifts are the grace gifts that enable us to express love to the King through His bride the church.

QUESTIONS FOR REFLECTION

1. Love should be the controlling factor in our desire for and use of spiritual gifts. If love motivates our desire for gifts, what sort of gifts would we most desire?

2. Love enables the body to have the unity necessary for the function of the gifts. Do you respond in a loving manner when you are wronged? Do you have a mental scoreboard of wrongs suffered that needs to be erased? What steps are you willing to take to ensure the unity of your church?

3. Gifts are given in this age to express love through the edification of the body. What gifts do you see demonstrated in your church that clearly reflect the love of Christ? What are you presently doing that manifests the love of Christ?

4. In what areas of ministry do you think God has gifted you to demonstrate His love and advance His kingdom?

5. We still have a tendency to "evaluate" spiritual maturity based on gifts and abilities. If other persons were to evaluate your maturity based on the love you have shown to others this week, how would they rate you?

5 Guidelines for Gifts in the Gathered Assembly

A Study of 1 Corinthians 14

The Corinthian community has provided for us a wonderful setting to learn more about the meaning and purpose of spiritual gifts. We have had to look at each text carefully to understand which elements of Paul's teaching are corrective and which provide new information not previously understood by the Corinthians.

We have seen that Paul first redefines spiritual gifts to include leadership and service functions thus broadening the "accepted" understanding of gifts. Further he demonstrates that gifts prove nothing about anyone's spirituality. They don't provide a sign that the believer has been baptized in the Holy Spirit or has achieved advanced spiritual status. They simply prove that God is gracious and that He will empower and gift His church to accomplish His kingdom purpose in every generation.

In chapter 13 Paul establishes love as the sign or evidence that one is filled with the Spirit. Paul's definition of love is not only based on the character of Christ; it is contrasted with the behavior of the spirituals. Their self-seeking, ego-centered desire for gifts that would draw attention to themselves was a sure sign that they lacked spiritual maturity.

Paul brings his discussion of gifts to a close in chapter 14 by answering several questions related to a spiritually mature desire for and use of gifts. Paul's clear preference is that they would seek gifts that would build up the church. Verse 12 is a key verse for our understanding of chapter 14. "So also you, since you are zealous of spiritual gifts, seek to abound for the edification of the church." Paul does not want to dampen their zeal for gifts; he simply wants to redirect it toward more productive ends.

Further, Paul's instructions would be incomplete if he did not deal with questions concerning the use of such miraculous gifts as "tongues" in the assembly. How is a church to avoid the potential confusion created by the desire of several "gifted" members to employ their gifts in the assembled church? The issue of gifted women is also addressed. These same questions are being asked by the church today. Thus we need to understand the directions given by Paul in chapter 14 and then ask how we can apply them in our present-day context.

What Is the Purpose of the Gifts?

This question may seem to you to be too obvious to ask. Yet the study of 1 Corinthians and my many years of pastoral ministry have caused me to conclude that it is a critical question and must be both asked and answered. I have counseled numerous people who attended seminars on spiritual gifts and wanted to discover their gifts. I was excited that they would desire the things of the Spirit but wanted them to understand why God chose to give them good gifts.

I ask a simple but pointed question, "Why do you want to discover your gift?" If you are simply curious about your gift, God is not interested in curing your curiosity. If you want to boast about your gift to impress, God is not interested in that either. God is interested in you and wants you to experience His abundance and join Him in His earthly work.

God gifts members of the church to accomplish His kingdom purpose. Thus the goal for seeking gifts and the subsequent employment of gifts must correspond with God's purpose in the giving of the gifts.

The first verse of chapter 14 links the priority of love with the pursuit of gifts. "Pursue love, yet desire earnestly spiritual gifts, but especially that you may prophesy." This introductory statement raises the question, "How would the spiritually mature person respond to the goal of kingdom advance and the needs of the church in seeking and using gifts?"

When you read chapter 14, the word *edification* stands out in bold relief. Paul uses edification to bring the heavenly minded spirituals back to earth. Believers can and must use their gifts to build up the body of Christ and thus enable the church to advance God's kingdom. Ironically, the responsible use of gifts in the now will enable the believer to have eternal impact. The spiritual man can use spiritual gifts, which have meaning in the now, to express the eternal reality of love through ministry to and through the church. When gifts are used properly to express love, the end result will be the building up of the church. Our spiritual gifts are but one example of how God enables us to use our *temporal* possession to have an *eternal* impact.

As we continue our study of gifts, we must diligently ask about our motivation to understand our giftedness. Would you be happy to discover that your gift enables you to serve in an unheralded support capacity? Or are you seeking a gift that draws attention to you?

If you are apathetic about discovering your gift, could it be that you are afraid someone will expect you to get involved in the ministries of the church? Tragically, some studies indicate that fewer than 25 percent of church members ever do anything in their church to advance the kingdom. The New Testament knows nothing of a member of the body (church) who does not function for the good of the body. There are no spiritual spectators in the body of Christ.

Why Prophecy and Tongues?

If you take a moment to read through 1 Corinthians 14, you will notice that Paul devotes a great deal of attention to two gifts—prophecy and tongues. We can reasonably conclude that these two gifts were popular with the spirituals in Corinth. Whenever I teach on spiritual gifts, the first question asked usually relates to tongues. When I wrote my first book on spiritual gifts, a woman from the newspaper spent several hours in an interview to prepare for an article on the book. On several occasions I pointed out that the issue of tongues was a minor issue in the full discussion of gifts and that I did not want her to emphasize tongues in her article. When the article appeared, the headlines screamed, "Baptist Pastor Has New Interpretation of Tongues."

Why might Paul have given such focus to only two of the many gifts practiced in Corinth? There may have been several reasons. First, these two gifts were not only popular; they were being abused by the spirituals as proof of their advanced spirituality. Thus Paul wants to challenge the Corinthians to use these gifts for the common good. Second, these two gifts share similarities and differences that easily allow Paul to contrast the two in terms of edification. Both require an act of speech, would be most frequently used in the gathered assembly, and would by their nature draw attention to the speaker. For example, it would be more difficult to compare and contrast prophecy and administration since they are so dissimilar and the context of their use is different. Third, it would have been cumbersome for Paul to deal with a large number of gifts in this final section, and thus he selects only two.

While Paul is concerned about the use and abuse of these two gifts, in a greater sense these two gifts are actually used in a representative fashion. The conclusions reached in relation to these two gifts can be applied to all gifts. The bottom line is that we should earnestly desire gifts that allow us to build up the body of Christ and advance God's kingdom on earth.

Contrasting Prophecy and Tongues

Tongues create the same fascination for believers today that they created in the first century. They have a miraculous and mysterious quality that can create such interest that we can read chapter 14 and actually miss Paul's primary point about the value and purpose of gifts. Since Paul uses tongues and prophecy to provide the backdrop for his teaching on the purpose of all gifts, we must deal with questions about tongues. What are they? Do they have a purpose? Are they still valid today?

> *We should earnestly desire gifts that allow us to build up the body of Christ and advance God's kingdom on earth.*

Yet I would implore you not to allow the discussion of tongues to cause you to miss the central message: spiritual gifts are manifestations of God's grace, which enable every member of the body to participate in kingdom advance.

The phrase "especially that you may prophesy" in 14:1 serves to direct the reader's thought back to 12:31 and Paul's insistence that the believer should "earnestly desire the greater gifts." "The greater gifts," simply stated, are those best suited for edification. Don't forget that the spirituals evaluated "greater" in terms of sign value.

Paul is not saying that prophecy is the greatest gift of all the gifts available to the church; he is simply saying that when you compare prophecy and tongues, prophecy is the

> *Spiritual gifts are manifestations of God's grace, which enable every member of the body to participate in kingdom advance.*

"greater gift" in terms of its ability to edify because it is intelligible to all. Once again we must point out that Paul's primary context in this section is the church assembled for worship, and his major concern is building up the body of Christ and advancing God's kingdom.

Do not forget the larger context where Paul has already demonstrated that the gifts are given by sovereign design and thus body members should not argue about which body part is most important (12:14–26). Each member of the body must play its given role for the good of the body and the glory of the King.

The controlling thought of the first twenty-five verses of chapter 14 is the intelligibility of prophecy and the corresponding unintelligibility of tongues. Thus the first reference to tongues in verse 2 must be interpreted in light of Paul's overarching preference for intelligible speech in the gathered assembly. The statement that one speaking in a tongue speaks to God and not to man provides a stark contrast to the prophet who speaks to men for edification (v. 3). Keep in mind that Paul's goal is to establish the priority of prophecy in the gathered assembly in terms of intelligibility and thus ability to edify.

Read verses 2–4 as a single paragraph, and you will notice that Paul first contrasts tongues and prophecy in terms of *who is addressed.* He specifically indicates that tongues are not addressed to people but to God since "no one understands." The prophet speaks to people with the result of edification, exhortation, and consolation. Thus the comparison concludes by indicating that the person speaking in the tongue edifies himself, whereas the one who prophesies edifies the church.

The emphasis in verse 2 falls on the statement "no one understands." Tongues are inferior to prophecy in the gathered assembly when it comes to the edification of the body precisely because men do not understand them. The phrase "in his spirit he speaks mysteries" must be interpreted in light of the context. It explains why other people do not understand tongue speech. They are "mysteries" spoken "in the spirit" or "by the Spirit." The Greek text allows for either interpretation.

The last phrase of verse 2 may be translated either as "in his spirit" or as "by the Spirit." If we translate it as "in his spirit," Paul is referring to the human spirit. Paul would thus be indicating the person speaking in tongues was speaking in a state of ecstasy where the mind is unfruitful. This idea is given some support by verse 14 where Paul discusses tongues in greater detail. "For if I pray in a tongue, my spirit prays, but my mind is unfruitful."

If we translate this phrase as "by the Spirit," it would mean that "tongue speech" is produced by the power of the Holy Spirit. This interpretation is supported by the listing of tongues in 12:10 as a work of the Spirit. We will look at this issue again when we study verses 14–15. It is likely that both ideas are actually implied and therefore Paul is referring to a state of ecstasy prompted by the Holy Spirit.

Could Tongues Be Known Languages?

A few interpreters have attempted to argue that "one who speaks in a tongue" should be understood to mean that one is speaking a known language which he does not understand. This interpretation is based on the assumption that the tongues spoken in Corinth are the same as those heard on the day of Pentecost (Acts 2:1–13). In that case each man heard the gospel in his own tongue. We must, however, be careful to allow each text to speak for itself.

There is no question that Acts 2 refers to known languages: "Each one of them was hearing them speak in his own language" (2:6). Interpreters debate whether the miracle at Pentecost was one of hearing or speaking, but they do not debate that what was heard were known languages.

However, the suggestion that Paul believed the Corinthians were speaking in known languages finds no support from the text or the context. First, Paul clearly indicates that the speaker does not address man but God. If the tongue speaker was speaking a known language, he would have the possibility of addressing both God and man. Second, Paul indicates that "no man understands." If "no man understands" the mysteries spoken in the tongue, then Paul cannot be referring to known speech. If the tongues in Corinth were a known language, someone, somewhere in the known universe could understand it.

Third, Paul speaks about known languages later in Acts 14:10–11. In that case he uses a different Greek word (*phone*) than he does in any other reference where he mentions speaking or praying in a tongue (*glossa*). In fact the combination of "speak" (*laleo*) and "tongue" (*glossa*) is the basis for the English word *glossolalia*. In other words, the Greek vocabulary has terminology that would allow Paul to make clear that tongues were actually known languages.

Fourth, Paul's comparison of Corinthian tongues to indistinct sounds produced by musical instruments (1 Cor. 14:7–9) implies that the sounds being produced by those speaking in tongues are indistinct and may be either annoying (flute or harp) or dangerous (bugle). He concludes that if they do not utter speech that is clear they will be speaking into the air. He then compares the Corinthian tongues to known languages (vv. 10–11). It would be unusual, if not nonsensical, to compare a thing to itself.

Fifth, the impact of the tongues spoken in Corinth on unbelievers who might be present is opposite of the impact of the languages spoken on the day of Pentecost. "Therefore if the whole church assembles together and all speak in tongues, and ungifted men or unbelievers enter, will they not say that you are mad?" (1 Cor. 14:23).

If we could somehow interpret tongues in this section to mean "foreign languages," charismatics and evangelicals alike should pray that God would pour out this ability on His church again for the ministry of those who are taking the gospel to the ends of the earth. It would be a powerful boost for global evangelism if missionaries could speak the native language without spending years in language school. Paul does not see tongues as an evangelistic tool, nor does he understand *tongues* to mean "known languages." The tongues speaker utters mysteries that lie outside the understanding of both the speaker and the hearer and thus have little value in the assembly.

We will encounter other passages that refer to tongue speech as we study this chapter, and we will examine each in turn. Paul was referring to some form of "prayer or praise" that has value as a personal prayer language, "one who speaks in a tongue edifies himself" (14:4), but which has little value in the gathered assembly, precisely because "no man understands" (v. 2).

Greater Is the One Who Edifies

The contrast between the one who speaks in a tongue and the one who prophesies is strengthened by the use of three words to express the outcome of prophecy—"edification and exhortation and consolation." Having described the differences between prophecy and tongues, Paul compares the edifying value of each. "One who speaks in a tongue edifies himself; but one who prophesies edifies the church" (14:4). The contrast between "edifies himself" and "edifies the church" leads to the conclusion of verse 5, "Greater is one who prophesies than one who speaks in tongues, unless he interprets." Paul's clear preference for prophecy in the gathered assembly is based on the intelligibility of prophecy and therefore its ability to edify.

If we read other statements in this chapter about the value of tongues (vv. 17 and 28), it can hardly be denied that Paul indicates that the greatest benefit of tongues is personal and not corporate; their value is in private prayer and praise. You may wonder how a language that cannot be understood by the speaker could have any positive value for the speaker. That view may expose our Western bias for the rational over and beyond the contemplative. The Spirit can minister to us in ways that do not require words and may thus communicate directly to the heart and not the head. You may experience this work of the Spirit by contemplating the beauty of the fall leaves or the majesty of the ocean.

Some persons hear God speak to them through a symphonic presentation of the great Christian classics. God can speak in diverse ways to His diverse body. We can trust the Spirit to act in harmony with the character of the Father.

Yet the phrase "edifies himself" in verse 4 is primarily intended to contrast tongue speech with prophecy which "edifies the church." In light of the Corinthian problems and the present context, we cannot ignore earlier injunctions such as "let no one seek his own good, but that of his neighbor" (10:24) and "[love] does not seek its own" (13:5). Edifying oneself is admittedly pale in contrast to the opportunity of edifying the church. Paul's primary concern in these opening verses is contrasting the relative value of these two gifts in the *gathered community* and not their value for *personal* devotional life. Paul wants to redirect the selfish desire of the spirituals to *exhibit* their spirituality to a more productive desire to *edify* the church.

Prophecy—Prediction or Proclamation?

Let's look at the description of prophecy in 14:3 and seek to understand its content. Sometimes we hear people talk about prophecy in terms of prediction, as if the primary role of the prophet was to predict future events. There are certainly instances in the Old Testament where prophets spoke of events that were future in terms of their ultimate fulfillment. At least one instance recorded in the book of Acts speaks of a prophet's foretelling an event "by the Spirit," which is still in the future (Acts 11:27–28).

We should be more than cautious about modern-day prophets who make "prophetic claims" that add content to completed revelation. The book of Hebrews contrasts the revelation of God through the Old Testament prophets and the revelation of God through His Son (chap. 1). The conviction of the early church was that revelation came to its ultimate culmination when God spoke fully in His Son. For this reason the Scriptures were canonized and thus considered to be complete. We can thus reject any predictive prophecy that attempts to claim the authority of Scripture or add to Scripture in any way.

The description of prophecy in 1 Corinthians would be more in line with what we call proclamation of God's revealed Word. The prophet speaks to men for edification, exhortation, and consolation. These three words do not suggest three different kinds of inspired speech but the threefold impact of authentic prophecy. Both mystery and miracle are at work when a pastor speaks with prophetic power. All those who hear with ears of understanding will be edified; some however will receive consolation while others receive exhortation. The

Spirit is at work in the speaker and the hearer, and the actual results will often differ according to the need of the individual.

I always stand amazed at the power of God when the Word is proclaimed or taught in the power of the Holy Spirit. We may study and outline and illustrate, but the Spirit brings the edification, consolation, and exhortation. We search for words to define the mystery that occurs when we preach or teach with the empowering of the Spirit. We use words like *unction, authority,* or *inspiration* to define the event when God's Holy Spirit enlivens the preaching and teaching of His Word. While we often define this event in terms of preparation and ability, it is no less miraculous and mysterious than any other work of the Spirit.

I Wish You All Spoke in Tongues!

Since Paul's primary concern in this section is for edification in the gathered assembly, the statement "Now I wish that you all spoke in tongues" (14:5) is not a concession to those who desire tongues for their sign value, nor is it straightforward praise of tongues. The emphasis in this verse is on the phrase "even more" (Paul uses the same Greek word as in 14:1), and therefore the contrast of the preceding verse is still being advanced.

Paul's statement cannot be taken to mean that Paul desires a universal practice of tongues. For that matter, Paul would not desire that everyone prophesy. Such an interpretation would contradict Paul's earlier statement that all do not speak with tongues, nor do all have the gift of prophecy (12:29–30). It would run counter to the earlier emphasis on unity in diversity established by the body imagery in chapter 12. Paul was simply underlining their zeal for the dramatic gifts (like tongues) and redirecting it toward seeking and using gifts in the assembly that are better suited to edification (like prophecy). Remember these gifts are used in a representative fashion so that the truths taught can be applied to any and all gifts.

The prophet is greater than the tongue speaker only in terms of his ability to edify the congregation. Here again Paul is not contravening his earlier teaching that various body members should not argue about their relative importance (12:14–17). Paul does add the option that the tongue speaker could speak for edification if "he interprets, so that the church may receive edifying" (14:5). Paul suggested that the speaker in tongues, if he desired to edify other believers, could pray for and receive the ability to interpret his own speech, rendering it intelligible.

You may be wondering, *Where did I get the idea that the interpreter was a person other than the individual speaking in tongues?* That's a good question. The answer seems to be traditional practice rather than biblical exegesis. The listing of interpretation as a gift distinct from tongues in 12:10 would allow for the interpreter to be different from the speaker, but it does not demand it. If you will carefully follow the text as it unfolds, it will become clear that Paul expected the tongue speaker to interpret for himself and give only the interpretation so that the congregation could be edified without running the risk that the unbeliever will be offended by hearing tongues spoken audibly (14:23).

Now I would grant you that few of the "spirituals" in Corinth had any interest in interpreting their tongue for the sake of the body. Such a practice would render them less mysterious and thus negate their perceived sign value. Thus Paul's insistence upon interpretation accomplishes three objectives: it removes any possible sign value, protects the body from confusion, and avoids offending the unbeliever.

The Significance of Intelligibility

In 1 Corinthians 14:6–8 Paul introduces a rhetorical question using himself as the example to underline the importance of intelligibility in the assembly. Paul first asks how he could benefit the Corinthians if he had come to them speaking in tongues that were unintelligible to them. This is likely not only a hypothetical argument but one which accurately portrays his ministry in Corinth. Later in verses 18–19 he will boast that he speaks in tongues more than all of them, and yet he prefers to speak intelligibly in the gathered assembly that he might instruct others.

The impact of this statement relies on the fact that they were unaware of Paul's practice of speaking in tongues. Paul rejects the sign value of any gift and therefore refuses to play the spirituals' game by impressing them with tongues or visions (2 Cor. 12:1–6). The fact that Paul ministered in Corinth for more than a year without audibly speaking in tongues is further evidence that he found this gift ill-suited to the gathered assembly.

Paul insists on intelligible speech because it is profitable to all. He then illustrates intelligible speech with the listing of revelation, knowledge, prophecy, and teaching. The listing of prophecy in the third position is another demonstration that the preceding argument has not been about prophecy and tongues per se but about intelligibility versus unintelligibility in the context of gathered worship. Commentators can reach no consensus about the subtle distinctions between the four forms of speech mentioned. There would be little value in attempting to do so. Paul is simply illustrating the value of intelligibility in the assembly. You might compare this fourfold listing of forms of intelligible speech with the threefold content of prophecy in 1 Corinthians 14:3. The use of multiples in both cases is intended to underline forcibly the importance of clear and intelligible speech and contrast intelligible speech with tongue speech.

Paul now uses two practical illustrations to emphasize further the importance of intelligibility. The first (14:7) is that of a musical instrument played without a clear distinction of notes. Most parents have suffered through the torturous weeks when their child first attempted to play a musical instrument. Dad's Sunday afternoon nap is rudely interrupted when strange screeching noises erupt from the adjoining room. He leaps from his chair, fearing his child has met with calamity, only to find him proudly holding up a tiny violin he has just begun to play. An instrument like a flute or a harp (v. 7), or a violin for that matter, played with unclear notes is not dangerous, but it can be annoying.

Paul's second illustration is the bugle that is intended to prepare one for battle. In the case of the bugle played with notes that make its message unclear, the results are far different. The results of unintelligibility in this case will be dangerous confusion and possible defeat. Paul may have in mind the two concerns uniquely related to tongues spoken in the public assembly: (1) The person unversed in the gift of tongues is simply not edified; that is annoying. (2) The far greater concern is the impact of tongues on the unsaved: "Will they not say you are mad?" (v. 23). In this case the unintelligible tongues are dangerous because they are a barrier to evangelism.

The phrase "so also you" (v. 9) specifically applies the preceding illustrations to the situation in Corinth. Unless one uses his human tongue for intelligible communication, his speaking will be as futile as speaking into the air. Paul's argument proceeds from lesser to greater. If it is important for lifeless instruments to produce intelligible sounds, how much more important is it for believers to use their tongues for intelligible speech?

Paul uses one final illustration that may have anticipated an objection from the spirituals: "You can't compare our speech in tongues with indistinct notes of an instrument; they are the language of the angels." Paul concedes that no language is without meaning when uttered in the proper context (v. 10). Yet he insists that any valid language will have no meaning if the hearer cannot understand what is being said. The speaker and the hearer will be like barbarians to each other. If you have ever traveled abroad, you will immediately understand the logic of his argument.

The unintelligible tongues, the source of pride for many of the spirituals, would have precisely the opposite effect than they anticipated. Instead of praising them as "spiritual" persons, the hearers would regard them as barbarians. The goal of any and all gifts is to edify the church and to glorify the Giver. Whenever any gift draws attention away from the Giver and His kingdom purpose, it is being abused.

What Then Should We Do?

Paul may have anticipated that the Holy Spirit would have used these words to bring such depth of conviction that some might now want to know what to do. "Should we just avoid gifts altogether since they can be abused and bring confusion in the church?" No, that would deprive the body of the ministry of the Spirit in the gifting and empowering of the church for kingdom advance.

Paul's solution is simple but profound. "So also you, since you are zealous of spiritual gifts, seek to abound for the edification of the church" (14:12). Paul first alludes to their zeal and then attaches his corrective. Once again we can see that Paul's primary concern was not to exalt prophecy as the gift *par excellence* but to redirect the Corinthian zeal for gifts toward more productive ends, the edification of the church.

Zeal for gifts is commendable when gifts are properly understood as God's gracious manifestations given for the building up of the church. In fact, the truly spiritual person will desire to abound in gifts with the goal of edifying the church. Even today we must test our motives by asking, "Do I desire a particular gift for selfish reasons, or do I desire to have the gift that would best equip me to serve the King in and through His church?" Paul's desire was not to dampen their enthusiasm but to redirect it toward *edifying behavior* rather than *emotional showmanship*.

This leads to another important conclusion and concern. Paul argues that spiritually mature persons will be zealous for the gifts of the Spirit. Some Christians have allowed the abuse of gifts to have such a profound negative impact that they want to avoid the topic of gifts altogether. This reaction is as childish as is the desire of the spirituals to have the showy sign gifts. In both cases the body is made weaker.

Some believers apparently avoid the topic of gifts because they have no desire to become involved in the life of the church. They behave like spectators who would rather pay others to play than to put on the uniform and get in the game. Scripture teaches that the true kingdom citizen will manifest zeal to abound in gifts that will enable them to edify the body and advance the kingdom. I have been involved in sports most of my life, and I have never met a true athlete who didn't want to get into the game. If you have no desire to get into the game and serve the King, you should ask yourself whether you are certain that you have a genuine personal relationship with the King.

The command to "seek to abound for the edification of the church" (1 Cor. 14:12) raises another question: If the gifts are distributed by the Spirit as He wills, how can Paul suggest that believers should seek gifts better suited to edification? The fact that gifts are a manifestation of God's grace does not mean that they cannot be sought. The principle here is similar to the whole issue of prayer. In Matthew 6:8 Jesus told His disciples that the Father knew their needs even before they asked. Yet in the same context He gave them specific instructions for asking. The sovereign activity of God works in concert with human responsibility. We can and we should seek gifts that edify the church. We can do so with the absolute confidence that God desires to give them in abundance.

Do Tongues Have a Place in the Assembly?

You have probably heard someone say, "Anytime you find a 'therefore' in Scripture, you need to determine what it is 'there for.'" The "therefore" that introduces 1 Corinthians 14:13 ties the next section to the principle stated in verse 12. Paul now explores the question of whether tongues have any place in the gathered assembly since they are unintelligible to man. Can tongues be used for the edification of the body?

In verse 5 Paul indicates that the person with the gift of tongues can speak for edification if "he" interprets. Paul now returns to that point with greater specificity. Notice that the assumption here is precisely the same as verse 5: the speaker prays that "he may interpret." Verse 13 indicates that the individual prays in a normal manner asking God to give him the ability to understand the mystery uttered in a tongue so that he may edify the church.

Some scholars object to this explanation of verse 13, claiming that the tongue speaker and the interpreter are different persons. They point to the separate listing of tongues and interpretation in 12:10. The separate listing will allow for another to interpret but does not demand it. Further, all of the passages explaining the process of interpretation suggest that the same person should be the interpreter. We will return to this matter when we look at verses 27–28. Others base their objection on the observation of modern-day use of tongues. In many churches where tongues are practiced, the individual is not required to interpret their own speech. However, we cannot let observation or experience dictate our interpretation of Scripture. The reverse must be true. Our experience and practice must be governed by proper interpretation of Scripture.

I agree that it is highly unlikely that few, if any, tongue speakers in Corinth interpreted their own speech. They believed tongues were the language of the angels and thus signs of advanced spirituality. Therefore to render them intelligible would lessen the sign value. For that reason Paul actually *commands* the tongue speaker to pray that he may interpret. The verb is a third-person imperative. This gift, if it is to have any meaning in the assembly, must be rendered intelligible.

The impact of Paul's command is simple but profound. A person who possesses the gift of tongues and desires to use it authentically to edify the church should pray for the ability to interpret. Conversely tongue speakers who continue to exercise their gifts with no view to edification would demonstrate their lack of spiritual maturity. They have no right to speak in the assembly.

How Does Interpretation Work?

In 1 Corinthians 14:14–17 Paul gives practical instructions for the use of tongues accompanied by interpretation. The instructions are elementary, suggesting that Paul had not given the Corinthians any previous instructions for employing tongues in the assembly. The fundamental nature of these instructions suggests that Paul's revelation of his own private practice of tongues (v. 18) was a surprise to the Corinthians. This may suggest that Paul did not publicly speak in tongues while in Corinth, nor did he promote the use of this gift in the assembly since it is ill-suited to edification of the church. We can easily see that Paul would not agree with tongues being the sign that one is filled with the Spirit.

Verse 14 seems to give a straightforward appraisal of what takes place when one prays in a tongue. "For if I pray in a tongue, my spirit prays, but my mind is unfruitful." The contrast is between two states of consciousness—ecstatic and rational. "My spirit" refers to the human spirit moved to ecstasy by the Holy Spirit.

Once again we must be careful not to read our own thoughts into the text. Paul is not indicating that tongues are a work of the Spirit whereas prophecy or teaching or administrative ability, for that matter, is a rational exercise of the human mind and skill. The believer can do nothing to advance God's kingdom apart from the empowering of the Spirit.

On the other side of the coin, we must conclude that Paul was not demeaning religious ecstasy when authentically produced by the Spirit. Paul, however, does subordinate ecstatic experience to the rational when the edification of the body is in view.

In the ecstatic experience of tongues, Paul maintains that the mind of the individual remains unfruitful. That is, the words or sounds uttered have no rational content for the person uttering them (cp. 14:2). Thus the believer who desires to use this gift for the common good will first pray or sing in the tongue and then interpret the prayer or the song by praying or singing with the mind (v. 15). Singing or praying with the mind is the rational interpretation of what is uttered in the unintelligible tongue. He cautions that if one "bless[es] in the spirit only" (v. 16) the ungifted person could not say "Amen," signifying both comprehension and agreement. "Ungifted" refers to any Christian who is unskilled in tongues and interpretation. Paul then concludes, "For you are giving thanks well enough, but the other person is not edified" (v. 17).

Paul concludes these basic instructions on tongues plus interpretation with an unexpected boast intended as a sharp corrective for those who demand to speak in tongues in the assembly to demonstrate their own spiritual ascendancy. "I thank God, I speak in tongues more than you all; however, in the church I desire to speak five words with my mind so that I may instruct others also, rather than ten thousand words in a tongue" (vv. 18–19).

What are we to make of this boast? First, we must allow that Paul is giving a truthful confession about his own experience. Second, the entire context indicates that this was not a well-known fact to the Corinthians. Third, Paul likely knew that some of the spirituals would object that he was minimizing ecstatic gifts like tongues because he lacked them. The boast that he practices tongues in greater abundance than they do closely parallels his boast to visionary experience in 2 Corinthians 12. Their founder, who some regarded as unimpressive and contemptible in speech (2 Cor. 10:1), had experienced both tongues and visions. Yet, because of his concern for the church, he chose not to parade tongues and visions as signs of spiritual greatness.

Paul, who possessed their highly valued spiritual manifestations, voluntarily refrained from displaying them so that he might seek "the profit of the many" (1 Cor. 10:33). Paul had sacrificed what the spirituals considered to be their right—a public display of dramatic gifts—for the good of the community.

The impact of this confession depends on the fact that they were unaware of Paul's practice of tongues or his experience of visions. He had ministered among them for eighteen months and had not told them about his gift of tongues because he viewed it as a personal experience of ecstasy given by the Spirit and not a gift easily used to edify the congregation. Paul's preference for intelligible speech "in the church" is based on his desire to edify the whole. The contrast between five words of intelligible speech and "ten thousand words in a tongue" could not be more striking. The Greek word translated "ten thousand" is *murious* from which we get "myriad." It is the largest numerical designation in the Greek. As an adjective it can mean "countless" or "innumerable." Five words spoken for edification are better than a myriad of words spoken to draw attention to oneself.

A Brief Word on Ecstasy

In the West we are more reticent to talk about the mysterious or mystical element of our faith. Religious ecstasy has been experienced in different ways by different individuals throughout the history of the church. We need to be cautious not to force our experience on another and not to be judgmental concerning the experience of another. Paul subordinates the ecstatic experience to the rational in the context of the gathered assembly. Paul reiterates this point in 2 Corinthians 5:13, "For if we are beside ourselves, it is for God; if we are of sound mind, it is for you." Religious ecstasy has a place in Christian experience; but it is, by its character, more individual and personal. For that reason it is not suited for instruction in the assembly of believers.

Every believer has experienced the mystical side of faith at one time or another. Some people are moved by music, others through prayer, and still others by great religious art or nature's grandeur. Genuine ecstasy is given by God for the edification of the individual. The experience and results of ecstasy are such that they are not easily shared or understood by others.

The attempt to share the results of ecstasy reminds me of the attempt to tell someone about a beautiful vista encountered on a vacation. You recount the moment and describe the scene with all the excitement you can muster, but you know by the placid look on your friend's face that he or she cannot fully comprehend the depth of your experience. In frustration you reply, "I guess you had to be there." That is precisely the point of religious ecstasy. You have to be there! It is a personal gift. Its contents and impact are not easily shared. Ecstasy has a place, but it is not the focal point of worship or the basis for our teaching.

Paul gives personal testimony to a powerful visionary experience (2 Cor. 12). He does so only as a last resort to verify his own ministry to the immature Corinthians who were impressed by the visionary experiences of the so-called "super apostles." He explains that he is reluctant to talk about his experience because what he saw and heard is inexpressible. He concludes that his visionary experience was given him for his own edification.

We can welcome spiritual ecstasy when it is a gift of the Spirit. The Holy Spirit like our heavenly Father will not give us gifts that harm us. However, we must be aware of three potential dangers inherent in ecstasy. First, some people base their teaching on an ecstatic experience. When a person does this, there is neither room for discussion nor opposition. What does one say when an individual claims to have a word from the Lord given in vision or a moment of ecstasy? We must base our teaching on the inerrant Word of God. We should also require that those we listen to base their teaching on solid exposition of the Scripture.

Second, we must be careful not to become dependent on or addicted to ecstatic experiences. Ecstasy has an addictive quality and thus the individual requires a larger dose to achieve the same spiritual experience. This dependency can become idolatrous. We begin to desire and demand the spiritual high of ecstasy and neglect the spiritual disciplines that enable us to grow in our daily walk. Some people choose a church based on the excitement generated in the worship service rather than looking at issues of doctrinal integrity, the commitment to the disciplines of the Christian life, and the passion and strategy to reach the nations.

Third, we must not make our experience the norm for others. We cannot demand that other people must have the same experiences we have had to authenticate their walk with God. God works with each of us in an individual and personal way.

In my pastoral ministry I had the privilege of working with fine worship leaders. Some Sunday mornings a particular hymn or anthem would send spiritual chills up my spine. We lack words to explain what occurs at moments like this. We talk about the entire service being "anointed." My temptation as pastor was to tell our worship leader to replicate the service the next week. That strategy never works. We can sing all the same songs in the same way, but the results will not be the same. We can even turn up the amps and sing them louder and longer to no avail. We cannot manipulate the Holy Spirit.

We have all been guilty of trying to recreate the ecstatic moment that had a profound impact on our spiritual life. We think if we can just return to that retreat center or to our home church, the feeling we once had will be restored. If we pray long enough or sing loud enough, ecstasy will surely come. We're like Elijah of old who thought God could only speak in fire, wind, and earthquake. Remember, he had just witnessed the Baal prophets on Mount Carmel who attempted to gain the attention of their god through frenzied dancing. Elijah was surprised to discover that God could speak just as loudly in the "sound of a gentle blowing" (1 Kings 19:12). Ecstatic experience is the sovereign act of God, given for personal edification.

One more word of caution! Don't confuse ecstasy with spiritual gifts. The discovery and use of gifts does not necessarily entail ecstasy. If you have been reluctant to talk about the Holy Spirit or seek to discover your gifts because you fear you may be swept away in uncontrolled ecstasy, you can relax. These are two different experiences. Each has its place. Gifts are given to serve the body while ecstasy is for personal enrichment. Gifts can be sought, developed, and employed while ecstasy is a serendipitous experience given by the Father.

What Happens When an Unbeliever Is Present?

Paul now looks at another critical issue related to the use of prophecy and tongues in the gathered assembly. What happens when an unbeliever happens to be present? So far Paul has only discussed the impact of prophecy and tongues on the believers who are present. A cursory reading of 1 Corinthians 14:20–25 will reveal that Paul is primarily concerned about the impact of tongues on the unbeliever.

Verse 20 must have had the impact of a sledge hammer as it reverses the view the spirituals held concerning themselves. "Brethren, do not be children in your thinking; yet in evil be infants, but in your thinking be mature." In a single stroke Paul attacks their understanding of themselves as mature spirituals and counters their claim to excel in wisdom and knowledge (thinking). Earlier in chapter 3 Paul had indicated his inability to address them as spirituals because of their childish tendency to exalt one leader over another. In this case the issue of immaturity is shown in their desire to possess and display the ecstatic gifts rather than those that are most appropriate for the gathered assembly. This was not an evil decision, just a childish one. Their judgment concerning the relative value of manifestations of the Spirit had demonstrated that they were spiritual children.

When I was a child, my dad gave me money to buy gifts for my parents and my siblings. When I had children of my own, I carried on the tradition. When they were very young, I would accompany them as they made their gift selections. Innocently they would select the shiniest item replete with lights, bells, and whistles. Their choice was often accompanied by the innocent, "Won't Mom be surprised!" When I tried to intervene and suggest a more appropriate gift, my girls would object; "Oh, Dad, that's boring!" I could only smile since I did the same as a child. The affection for the showy and the shiny is a natural part of our childish enthusiasm.

Paul was confronting a similar childlike enthusiasm among the Corinthians for the gifts that were spectacular and showy. The edifying gifts might be more practical, but they could look and sound downright boring in comparison to the mysterious quality of tongues. Now here's the question. Are we interested in the showy or the useful?

To reinforce his argument that tongues have no "sign value" for the believer, Paul cites Isaiah 28:11 in a form slightly different from the Old Testament text. This verse is employed by Paul as a direct refutation of the argument that tongues are a sign of the fullness of the Spirit and thus of one's spirituality. The passage from Isaiah attracted Paul's attention because of the reference to men of other tongues. In its original context it refers to Israel's being taken into captivity by a people who spoke through "stammering lips and a foreign tongue."

Paul uses this Old Testament citation to make a single point—*tongues are not a sign for believers.* Paul balances this negative appraisal of the sign value of tongues by adding that prophecy is a sign for believers because of its value for the life of the church. Prophecy does not prove that an individual has achieved some "exalted spiritual status"; prophecy is a sign for believers only in the sense that it has value for edification of the church, the central purpose for all gifts of the Spirit. The practical illustration given in 1 Corinthians 14:23–25 confirms this simple explanation of a somewhat complex text.

Paul suggests a hypothetical situation in which the church family comes together and speaking in tongues occurs. The use of "all" in verses 23 and 24 is intended to give vivid impact to the illustration. Paul does not mean to convey the idea that everyone would be speaking in tongues at the same time. In truth, all prophesying (v. 24) at the same time would be just as confusing as all speaking in tongues. Nor do these verses suggest that Paul envisioned the possibility that everyone in the church might possess either the gift of prophecy or of tongues. Paul has already resolved that issue in 12:29–30. Paul is simply pressing his argument to the ultimate degree to make his point with absolute clarity.

The reader is now reminded of the negative response of the "ungifted" (14:16) and shown the impact of tongues on the "unbeliever." If the brother in Christ, who is ungifted in tongues has a negative response, what will be the response of the unbeliever? Their response is dramatically cast by a single question: "Will they not say that you are mad?" (v. 23). The word "mad" provides the most striking contrast possible between the potential results of prophecy and tongues.

The impact of the public display of dramatic gifts such as tongues would be exactly the opposite of what the spirituals had envisioned. Paul's primary concern about the public display of tongues, even when interpreted, is that the outsider would respond with such distaste that they would react against Christianity. In other words, the public display of tongues would be antievangelistic. This is quite a contrast to the response to the known languages of Acts 2. The ecstatic tongues so highly valued by the Corinthian spirituals would actually harden unbelievers in their unbelief.

The results of prophecy and tongues pictured here repeats the points made in Paul's illustration of musical instruments played without a clear distinction of the proper notes. In the case of the flute and the harp, indistinct sounds are merely unpleasant. In reference to the bugle, indistinct sounds are dangerous. Tongues spoken audible in the assembly are merely an unedifying noise to "ungifted" believers, but they are a dangerous stumbling block to the unsaved.

In 1 Corinthians 14:24 Paul plays out the same scenario in relationship to prophecy, and here the response in both cases is positive. Notice that Paul reverses the order and considers first the effect of prophecy on the unbeliever, his major concern in this section. The three positive phrases—"he is convicted by all," "he is called to account by all," and "the secrets of his heart are disclosed" (vv. 24–25)—are placed on the scale against the single phrase, "Will they not say that you are mad?" If the effect of prophecy on the unbeliever is so profound, it will have an equal impact on the believer who may not himself possess this particular gift. Prophecy, being clearly intelligible, would bring both the conviction of sin and the distinct awareness of the presence of God. Both the unbeliever and the believer will fall on their face and worship God, "declaring that God is certainly among you."

Once again we notice that Paul treats tongues, spoken in the assembly, with great reserve because of their potential negative impact. Tongues spoken followed by interpretation can resolve the issue of the edification of believers but will do little to resolve the antievangelistic impact of tongues. Once the tongue is verbalized, the unbeliever responds negatively to the tongue. With no further knowledge of the function of spiritual gifts, the interpretation of tongue speech would not counteract the original negative appraisal. Would the mature spiritual person be willing to risk the hardening of an unbeliever? I can only conclude that Paul viewed ecstatic experiences such as tongues and visions as having value for the individual but little if any value for the gathered church.

We have seen that Paul provisionally, and with some difficulty, makes a place for tongues in the worship service in Corinth. In our next section we will look at the controls he places on the use of tongues and prophecy. Paul does not ban tongues outright in the service because that would serve only to alienate the spirituals. Paul wants to redirect their zeal not to crush their enthusiasm for the things of the Spirit. Second, Paul was sensitive to the working of the Spirit and therefore cautious lest he be guilty of grieving the Spirit or hindering His work.

What Then Should We Do?

This next section of instruction anticipates a logical question about how the various gifted members could participate in the worship service in a meaningful way. With the question, "What is the outcome then, brethren?" (1 Cor. 14:26), Paul begins a much needed discussion of practical applications for the Corinthian worship service. This section is clearly concerned about issues unique to the Corinthian community, and therefore we must be careful not to insist that the exact pattern be followed in the church today. In other words, Paul is not suggesting that there must be two or three prophets or tongue speakers for the service to be complete. However, the principles learned here will be relevant in every generation.

This section suggests three overarching concerns: (1) Each gifted person may participate as time allows. (2) Each participant must exhibit the desire to edify the body. (3) The use of gifts must promote peace and not confusion. The spirituals' primary interest had been to use the worship service as a platform to display their sign gifts. Their behavior and the resulting confusion may have caused others in Corinth to shy away from participating fully in the service. Paul's primary corrective is to make the exercise of all gifts *answerable* to the assembly of believers and thus *serviceable* to the body.

We have come full circle in our discussion of gifts. At the beginning of his discussion on gifts, Paul establishes that gifts are given to each person for the common good (12:7). The instructions in this section clearly reflect that foundational principle. All believers have the right to contribute to the worship service according to their giftedness as long as this aim is to edify. Those whose primary goal is the arrogant display of sign gifts have no right to speak. This section is framed by the call to edification ("Let all things be done for edification," 14:26) and the call for order ("for God is not a God of confusion but of peace," v. 33). These twin standards provide both the individual and corporate control for the use of gifts in the worship service.

Each One

Notice that the context is the gathered worship service, "when you assemble." In the context of worship, those gifted to participate have the freedom to do so if they have the proper motive. The gift list in 14:26 is intended to be illustrative and not comprehensive. It is not intended to be an order of worship, and thus the order is not significant. It is simply an ad hoc listing of some abilities one might expect in gathered worship. All the gifts mentioned here focus on teaching and thus would lead to edification. The only new item is "psalm," which may refer to the ability to compose songs for worship. Paul further elaborates on this ability in Colossians 3:16: "Let the word of Christ richly dwell within you, with all wisdom teaching and admonishing one another with psalms and hymns and spiritual songs, singing with thankfulness in your hearts to God."

The range of abilities discussed under "gifted ministry" is impressively broad. Yet the center of attention once again is on tongues and prophecy. Remember that these two gifts are used in a representative fashion to illustrate the priority of intelligibility in the worship service. While they are used in a representative fashion, Paul apparently is concerned to give clear directions concerning their use and potential abuse.

If Anyone Speaks in a Tongue

The use of the indefinite "if anyone speaks in a tongue" leads once again to the conclusion that the public use of tongues was for Paul the exception and not the rule. His concern is twofold, the difficulty with which tongues can be used to edify the body and the effect on the unbeliever. Paul first limits the number of participants to two or three speakers in any one session of the assembled church. They must speak in turn, and their speech must be accompanied by interpretation. In other words, there would be no wholesale speaking in tongues that would only serve to add further to the confusion of tongues spoken aloud.

Our understanding of this passage is somewhat limited by our inability to reconstruct the practice of tongues plus interpretation in the first century. This is the only passage in the Bible that addresses the issue. Thus we have only our understanding of the larger Corinthian situation and the full context of this chapter to inform us on this controversial topic. We have already established that some individuals in Corinth valued tongues for their "sign" value. Further, we have noted that it is highly unlikely that the spirituals were concerned about control or interpretation since that would undermine the "sign" value. Paul now addresses the manner in which one might use this gift to edify others.

The phrase translated "one must interpret" is the key to understanding this section. When it is interpreted emphatically, as in the NASB, it appears to suggest that Paul anticipates that one person would interpret the message of several persons who may speak in tongues. Are we to assume that a single person with the gift of interpretation could interpret anyone's tongues speech? Nothing in this chapter supports such a conclusion.

This problem is alleviated when one translates the phrase in an indefinite sense "someone must interpret" as in the HCSB, which allows the immediate context to define the "someone" Paul has in mind. Bible teachers have struggled to understand how the tongues speaker could know in advance that an interpreter was present when he began to speak. Was the interpreter well-known to the church and thus conspicuous by his presence or absence? Could the person speaking in tongues know in advance that the interpreter could interpret his particular tongue?

"Let someone interpret" is the better translation of this Greek construction. The identity of the "someone" must be determined by what Paul has taught in his previous references to tongues plus interpretation (14:5, 13–16). Earlier texts make clear that Paul expects any tongues speaker who desires to edify the body to pray for and receive the gift of interpretation. In verse 5 Paul compares the tongues speaker with the prophet when "he interprets." Verse 13 is not a subtle suggestion but an imperative: "Let one who speaks in a tongue pray that he may interpret."

In light of these earlier texts, Paul does not likely expect someone other than the tongues speaker to provide the interpretation. The understanding that the speaker and the interpreter are the same person is not only consistent with the context, but it resolves several critical issues. Now we know how the tongues speaker could know that an interpreter was present since he was prepared to offer the interpretation. Further, the speaker who has the companion gift of interpretation has immediate confidence that he has a message that would edify the church since he would now understand that which was formerly a mystery (14:2).

Based on this interpretation, verse 28 would indicate that the tongues speaker who is not an interpreter should remain silent in the church. Paul's prohibitions in this section are not aimed at keeping anyone from speaking who desires to contribute to the edification of the body; they are directed at the spirituals who are seeking arrogantly to display a sign gift. The individual who has neither the desire nor the ability to interpret is instructed, "Let him speak to himself and to God" (v. 28). He could practice his gift at home or perhaps silently in a moment of meditation during the worship service. He is simply prohibited from speaking audibly.

What about the Impact on the Unbeliever?

Interpretation of tongues resolves the problem of the "ungifted" being able to say the "Amen" (v. 16), but we are still left with the potential effect of tongues on the unbeliever. If we take the directions given in verse 15 at face value, Paul anticipates that the tongue speaker would receive the message as he prayed silently in his spirit and then deliver his interpreted speech audibly through rational and understandable speech. In other words, the actual tongues would never be spoken audibly. This is the obvious implication of this passage and is fortified by Paul's own example (v. 19). The risk of offending an unbeliever would lead the mature Christian to forfeit the right to speak audibly in tongues. Delivering the edifying message is the goal, not revealing how one received the message. This forfeiture of "one's right to speak in a tongue" would correspond to Paul's example of forfeiting many of his apostolic rights to "win more" (9:19 and cp. v. 22).

As I have taught on this passage, I have had people object based on current practice in charismatic communities. We cannot allow tradition, charismatic or evangelical, to determine our interpretation of Scripture. Others argue that such a practice would not give the tongue speaker full freedom to practice his gift. No one in the church has unrestricted freedom to practice any gift. The prophets, too, face restrictions. Our freedom must always be understood in the context of

> *No one in the church has unrestricted freedom to practice any gift.*

the lordship of Christ as expressed in the community of believers. The mature believer will gladly forfeit the right to speak in order to edify the body. Paul employs the same argument earlier concerning the eating of idol meat. "All things are lawful, but not all things are profitable. All things are lawful, but not all things edify. Let no one seek his own good, but that of his neighbor" (10:23–24). The mere possession of a gift does not grant one a divine right to exercise that gift without due consideration for the body of believers.

Perhaps you are wondering whether it would be acceptable for the tongue speaker to indicate that he received the message while praying in tongues. What would be the purpose? Does it edify the church, or does it draw attention to the speaker and the gift possessed? Gifts have one purpose and value when used in the assembly: the good of the body. I can see no way that a statement concerning the source of the message would serve the common good given the controversy that surrounds this gift.

Let me illustrate this point in a different manner. Suppose each Sunday your preacher would begin his sermon with a detailed description of how much time he spent studying the Greek and reading the commentaries in preparation for his message. Would this knowledge help you hear God's message? I suspect your attention would be directed to the messenger and away from the message. Anything that draws attention to the speaker and away from the message is irrelevant and must be discarded as spiritual egotism.

Let Two or Three Prophets Speak

Paul's treatment of prophecy is once again more positive than his treatment of tongues because prophecy is intelligible and thus more suited for edification of the body. Nonetheless, Paul's teaching indicates that his understanding of prophecy may have differed substantially from that of the spirituals. Prophecy too had been abused, and therefore Paul limits the number of prophetic utterances at any one service to two or three. A prophet can exercise volitional control over the use of his gift (see 14:32), and therefore a prophet may need to leave without having an opportunity to speak.

Once a prophet has spoken, the "others" are given the right to pass judgment. Some evaluation of the source and content of prophetic utterance is suggested in this passage. But we must ask who "others" refers to? It could refer to other prophets, other believers, or other persons who have the gift of "distinguishing of spirits" (12:10). If we recall 1 Thessalonians 5:19, we might be led to conclude that Paul was once again referring to "other believers." Several passages indicate that all believers have the capacity and responsibility for evaluating prophetic utterance and determining whether they are authentic (cp. 1 Cor. 2:12–16, and cp. 1 John 4:1).

Other commentators argue that Paul was thinking of the function of those who had the gift for "distinguishing of spirits."[1] Bible scholars could be led to see such a gift in practice in this passage. Yet we are surprised that Paul would not simply say, "The others with the gift for distinguishing spirits," if he had that in mind.

Thus our decision on "the others" must be based on the present context. The flow of the argument makes clear that Paul turned his attention from those who speak in tongues to the prophets in 1 Corinthians 14:29. In this context "the others" would most naturally refer to other prophets, perhaps those who were not able to speak. The word "another" in verse 30 is clearly a reference to "another prophet," and "another" translates the same Greek word used here. It therefore seems likely that Paul is referring to other prophets. That does not, however, mean that each hearer should not exercise caution and discernment when listening to anyone who proclaims God's Word.

Now we must answer the question as to how the prophets pass judgment. Verse 30 likely provides the explanation. "But if a revelation is made to another who is seated, the first one must keep silent." Why did Paul instruct the first prophet to be silent when interrupted, rather than asking the second speaker to wait until the first had completed his message?[2] This regulation is surprising to the modern-day reader who was raised with the injunction that you don't interrupt when someone else is speaking.

The interruption by the second prophet indicates that the first prophet has failed to exercise self-restraint and has therefore exceeded his inspiration. The Holy Spirit, by means of the interruption by the second prophet, judges that the first prophet is no longer speaking under inspiration. Since "God is not a God of confusion but of peace" (v. 33), the Holy Spirit would not inspire two prophets to speak at the same time.

Two elements of control should always be at work in the assembly. First there is volition control. The truly spiritual person will control his impulse to speak or to exceed his revelation. But if he fails to do so, divine control can be exercised by others who have authority to silence the speaker. One suspects that this regulation was directed at the spirituals who desired only to exhibit their prophetic gifts, not to edify the body.

We can draw a similar parallel from the life of the church today. Perhaps you have attended a service where the microphones were placed in the aisle allowing anyone to give a word of testimony. Generally such a service moves along without a hitch. There may be moments of a deep stirring of the Spirit as people testify to the working of God in their lives. Yet occasionally some people will become so enamored with the sounds of their own voices that they seize the occasion to lecture the church concerning some failing. As I have observed the faces of listeners from the platform, I could see the uneasiness grow when the speaker exceeded his inspiration. There have been times when I had to intervene and interrupt the speaker. This is not dissimilar to the control being placed on the prophets in Corinth.

In verse 31 Paul describes the orderly use of the prophetic gift. All those with a prophetic gift could employ their gift "one by one" so that the whole body may learn and be encouraged. Notice once again the overarching concern for edification.

Paul may have anticipated that someone might reply, "But I can't control my inspiration. I must speak when the Spirit prompts!" Paul replies, "And the spirits of the prophets are subject to prophets" (v. 32). The phrase "the spirits of the prophets" has elicited much discussion. Two major lines of understanding are put forth. First this phrase has been taken to refer to the rational and volitional control that can be exercised by the prophet. The plural term "spirits" has been variously taken to mean "prophetic gifts," "revelations and inspirations," or "human spirits." "Human spirits" would correspond to a similar use of spirit in 14:2 and thus may be preferable. In any of these cases, Paul would be dealing with volitional control. As noted previously, volitional control would be necessary for the prophet to obey the regulations concerning the number of speakers and the orderly sequence of those who speak. The ability to control one's inspiration, whether tongues or prophecy, is assumed throughout chapter 12.

A second group of interpreters take "spirits" as a reference to the other prophets who may be allowed to interrupt. As we have seen, Paul does allow for outside control by another person when the rational or volitional control is ignored and unseemly behavior results. Since both of these ideas find support from the present context, we might suggest that Paul used the plural "spirits" in a manner which would allow for both internal and external control.

God Is Not a God of Confusion but of Peace

This section on the necessity for order and decorum in gathered worship is sealed by an appeal to the nature of God. One suspects that an observer of worship in Corinth, with its uncontrolled exercise of gifts, might not have surmised that the God these people worshipped was orderly. The proper exercise of spiritual gifts will always bear witness to the presence of God (v. 25) and to the character of God (v. 33). The unbridled use of gifts to display one's spirituality had not borne testimony to an orderly God.

> *The proper exercise of spiritual gifts will always bear witness to the presence of God (v. 25) and to the character of God (v. 33).*

People who argue that they cannot control their urge to speak or to burst forth in tongues or prophecy will find neither support nor encouragement from this passage. First, God places the gift under the volitional control of the believer. If however, the individual fails to exercise proper control, others in the assembly may call him to silence. The possession of gifts does not elevate the possessor above the order of the church established by the Author of the gifts.

Do You Have a Word for Gifted Women?

Not many phrases have created more interest than: "The women are to keep silent in the churches." Does this mean women are never allowed to speak in the assembly? If so, we must ask how we reconcile this text with 1 Corinthians 11:2–16 where Paul allows women to pray and prophesy if they conform to the custom held by all the churches concerning the covering of the head.

Can we reconcile the approval of 11:5 with the prohibition of 14:34? Some scholars have seen the problem of reconciliation so difficult that they call this one of Paul's worst moments where he has forgotten the implications of Galatians 3:28.[3] It is difficult to imagine that Paul, who has been so careful in his argument up to this point, would blatantly contradict himself. It also strikes at one's view of the inspiration of Scripture to suggest that an author would contradict himself writing under the direction of the Holy Spirit.

Several suggestions have been put forward by various commentators to reconcile the teaching in these two chapters: (1) Some argue that the prohibition in chapter 14 relates to women speaking in tongues. Such an interpretation is not evident from 14:34–35 and would thus have to be read into this text. The context immediately prior to this discussion concerns prophecy not tongues. (2) Others suggest Paul is prohibiting the women from participating in the judging of the male prophets. This prohibition is said to be based on the divinely ordained structure of authority.[4] This fits better with the context but is not fully satisfactory. Could a woman respond to the prophecy uttered by another woman? Remember that Paul has already allowed for women to prophesy if they did so in the right spirit (chap. 11). (3) A few commentators have attempted to resolve the tension between chapters 11 and 14 by arguing that chapter 11 pictures a prayer meeting in a home and not in the gathered assembly of the church. Thus the permission to speak in chapter 11 involves a small group setting whereas the prohibition in chapter 14 involves the gathered assembly. We would do well to recall that the early church had no official buildings and met regularly from house to house. Further, the instructions about women speaking in chapter 11 are followed by instructions on the Lord's Supper, an event that assumes the gathered church.

A better solution to this problem can be found by paying close attention to both the historical and textual context of both passages. First we should notice that the command to keep silent is repeated three times in our present context (1 Cor. 14) using the same Greek word (*sigato*). The tongue speaker who cannot interpret (v. 28) and the prophet who is interrupted (v. 30) are given the same call to silence as are the women. We have seen that in each instance Paul is concerned with silencing the spirituals who demonstrate no concern for the edification of others.

The instruction—"the women are to keep silent"—has in view silencing female "spirituals" who desire to speak in the service without regard to traditions of the church or concern for edifying others. Their desire is to demonstrate their freedom and prove their spirituality. Thus the contentious behavior Paul has in mind is that of women who demand their right to speak without any regard for the agreed-upon tradition of the church. Paul does not intend to rescind the permission to speak given in chapter 11. He desires only to silence the women who behave shamefully. They had thrown off all restrictions of decency and order under the banner of freedom because of their desire to prove their spirituality. These women, like the tongues speaker who has no regard for interpretation or the interrupted prophet, must be silent.

You might object that in the case of the women there is nothing in the present text that provides any exceptions, whereas the exceptions are stated in regard to the tongues speakers and the prophets. This concern overlooks a central point. The tongues speaker and prophet are dealt with only in chapter 14, whereas the participation of the women in the assembly is dealt with in two separate chapters. In the case of the women, the exception allowing them to speak is seen clearly when chapters 11 and 14 are taken together.

If you are thinking that Paul should have made the connection to chapter 11 obvious, I would respond that he did. Paul introduces this final section with the phrase, "as in all the churches of the saints" (v. 33). That phrase is intended to call to mind his final instructions for women in 11:16: "But if one is inclined to be contentious, we have no other practice, nor have the churches of God." These two verses on church tradition are the key that links the two sections. Rather than repeating the complex explanation from chapter 11, Paul simply calls them to mind with a similar phrase concerning church practice.

The verse divisions in our English text were not in the original Greek. The phrase "as in all the churches of the saints" makes better sense when viewed as an introduction to the issue of women speaking rather than as a conclusion to the statement about God's being a God of peace and not confusion. We might paraphrase the meaning as follows: "You recall that I gave you permission to speak if you did so with the proper attitude as we expect in all the churches of God. However, if you arrogantly ignore what is proper in all the churches, then you must be silent. If you need further instruction you may ask your husband at home."

Paul widens the scope of discussion concerning worship to the context of "all the churches." The larger context of the "body of Christ" is a third element of control concerning the abusive and confusing use of gifts for the wrong purposes. The spirituals in Corinth tended to act as if Christianity originated with them and therefore they could write their own rules. Paul asks, with no small irony, "Was it from you that the word of God first went forth? Or has it come to you only?" (v. 36). The arrogant display of gifts in Corinth suggests that some believe they can behave as they please without attention to the larger Christian community. The spirituals are behaving as if the gospel originated with them; as if they alone are Christians. Paul reminds the arrogant spirituals that they are not alone in the Christian faith. Not only must they demonstrate concern for the brethren in Corinth, but they must consider the wider fellowship of believers.

We, like the Corinthians, are sometimes so parochial in our thinking that we ignore the practices of the global body of Christ.

We tend to study a letter like 1 Corinthians over a period of weeks, and thus we forget what has already been said when we interpret a challenging section like this. The original recipients would have heard this letter in a single reading, and therefore the discussion of women from chapter 11 would have been fresh in their minds.

Since we may not have read chapter 11 recently, we must look at that chapter to understand the contentious behavior of some women who demanded their right to prophesy without any regard for edification, order, or tradition. The actual situation in chapter 11 is difficult to reconstruct because of the uncertainty about the role of head coverings in the time of Jesus. Most likely the covering of the head involved the styling of one's hair to be worn as a covering. The Jewish woman would wear her hair tightly braided on top of her head. When a Jewish woman of the first century let her hair down in public, she was making a sexual statement. You may recall the reaction of the Pharisees when the woman wiped Jesus' feet with her hair. "If this man were a prophet He would know who and what sort of person this woman is who is touching Him, that she is a sinner" (Luke 7:39). Her unfettered hair branded her as a harlot.

With that in mind, let's attempt to reconstruct the scene. The early Jewish Christians must have experienced considerable angst when women were allowed to engage in worship with men. In the temple women were relegated to the court of women, while in the synagogue they stood outside. The simple act of worshipping together would have been a substantial hurdle for most Jewish men. Now these men learn that women are allowed to pray and prophesy in the public assembly. Just when they are getting comfortable with this new concept, a woman stands to pray or prophesy and pulls the combs from her long hair, and it falls seductively about her shoulders and down her back. You can see the problem!

Paul declares that this woman has brought dishonor to her head (11:5). In chapter 11 there is a play on the word "head." The woman who lets her hair down in public disgraces her own head by wearing her hair like a prostitute. Paul concludes that if she wanted to look like a harlot, she should have her head shaved—the punishment for an adulterer (11:6). But her dramatic action also brought dishonor upon her husband (also her head). By releasing her hair, she declares her sexual availability and thus disgraces him. When Paul gives His final instructions in 14:34–35, he subjects the woman to her husband's authority. She must learn from him! Finally, the woman dishonors her head who is Christ, the head of the church, by flaunting all church tradition and decorum.

Admittedly both passages are difficult. We can, however, conclude that Paul is not teaching that a woman should not participate in discussion that has the goal of Christian instruction, nor is he banning her from ever speaking in the assembly. Paul would not contradict his earlier teaching that was inspired by the Spirit. We must then conclude that Paul allowed women to pray and prophesy when done with the right spirit and according to the tradition of the churches. But he also indicates that under certain conditions they must remain silent. The issue that requires "silence" in all three cases is the attitude of the spirituals, male and female alike, who desired only to *display* their gifts and not to *edify* the body.

These Are the Lord's Commands

The concluding verses of chapter 14 serve as a summary statement and underline the seriousness with which these corrections must be taken. Paul is aware that the arrogant spirituals might be tempted to disregard his teaching as one man's opinion, and one who in their thinking lacked miraculous sign gifts. Therefore, Paul left no opportunity for counterattack and no room for disobedience. "If anyone thinks he is a prophet or spiritual, let him recognize that the things which I write to you are the Lord's commandment" (v. 37). This verse has a not so subtle barb to it. The spirituals entertained no doubt about their elevated status. But in these three chapters Paul has attacked the basis of their claims and established a new criterion for proving oneself to be a spiritual person—love and its control upon gifts both sought and used.

Paul declares that all who accept his teaching as having the same authority as a command of the Lord would thereby demonstrate that they are truly spiritual. Paul is not likely appealing to any specific teaching of Jesus on the matter of gifts. He is simply bringing to bear the full weight of his own apostolic authority (cp. Rom. 15:15). Paul insists that these directions are to be obeyed with the same fidelity one would obey a command of Christ. Once again Paul confronts the Corinthians with the two criteria that have been at the heart of the entire Corinthian correspondence: (1) the ability to discern the graciousness of all Christian existence, and (2) behavior characterized by love.

Don't miss the severity of 1 Corinthians 14:38: "But if anyone does not recognize this, he is not recognized." We began this section on gifts with Paul's statement that he did not want them to be "ignorant" (*agnoeo*) concerning spiritual gifts (12:1). Now they have been fully informed about their breadth, value, and use of gifts by one who speaks with the authority of the Lord. If they chose to ignore Paul's teaching and use their gifts in an arrogant and destructive manner, they would not be "recognized" (*agnoeo*). To put it in another way, they would prove themselves to be spiritual imposters.

Paul concludes with a brief but positive summary: "Therefore, my brethren, desire earnestly to prophesy, and do not forbid to speak in tongues" (v. 39). The contrast between Paul's enthusiasm for prophecy and his provisional acceptance of tongues relates to his desire for believers to seek gifts with the edification of the body and the kingdom of God in mind. Yet those who are from the evangelical tradition must be cautious to remember that "do not forbid" is an imperative. We have no authority to ignore any command of Scripture.

Whatever gift you possess or desire to possess, one thing is certain: "But all things must be done properly and in an orderly manner" (v. 40).

A Brief Recap

This has been a long and complex chapter, and I applaud you for your diligence in working your way through the text. Let's take a moment and look back at some of the insights we have gleaned while studying the Corinthian correspondence, with particular attention to chapter 14.

Spiritual manifestations (*pneumatika*) sought immaturely and individual-istically for their sign value were at the heart of the Corinthian difficulties. The spirituals were primarily interested in miraculous speech and knowledge gifts.

The term *charismata* was selected as a more appropriate designation for spiritual gifts since it contains the corrective of grace, which is a consistent theme of the entire letter. The emphasis is on God as the ultimate source of all gifts and thus rules out all human boasting.

All believers are spiritual in the most fundamental sense of that word since the confession "Jesus is Lord" is possible only through the ministry of the Spirit. Further, all believers are baptized into the body (church) by the one Spirit. Since God equips each member for service, all believers possess some gift.

The body imagery and the two separate gift lists in chapter 12 are intended to broaden the understanding of spiritual gifts and to illustrate the unity and diversity of the body. The inclusion of leadership functions in the second list illustrates that, while all are gifted, some are gifted for leadership roles.

Chapter 13 establishes love as the only authenticator of spirituality. Love is the character of Christ produced in the life of the believer by the Holy Spirit. Gifts and behavior are closely related in 1 Corinthians because the two have been largely divorced from one another by the spirituals. Love is the greatest expression of the eternal in the now and gifts provide the "truly" spiritual person with a means for expressing love by using gifts for the edification of the body.

The redefined spiritual person, whose concern is for the body of Christ, will seek gifts that edify the body. Further they will use any gift already pos-sessed in such a manner that it edifies the church and shows sensitivity to the unbeliever who may be present in worship.

Prophecy and tongues are used in a representative fashion in chapter 14, and thus the principles learned here must be applied to all gifts. Paul's prefer-ence for prophecy over tongues in the assembly is based on intelligibility and thus the ability to edify.

The tongues being practiced in Corinth were of a different nature alto-gether from the tongues of fire and known languages evidenced at Pentecost. The person speaking in tongues speaks mysteries that no man understands. The tongues of Pentecost were evangelistic whereas those of Corinth were not. Paul explains how the tongue speaker might seek and practice interpretation in order to use his gift to edify the body. Interpretation of a tongue will enable the speaker to edify the believer. Nonetheless, tongues spoken audibly will have an antievangelistic impact. Thus the tongue speaker would forgo the right to speak audibly in the assembly, giving only the interpretation unaccompanied by the tongue.

The directions for the control of the gifts were made necessary by the Corinthian abuses. The control of the gifts has three distinct elements. The spiritual person, whose desire is edification, can exercise volitional control. If he fails to do so, the Spirit can prompt someone else to bring control. Finally, the tradition or customs shared by the larger Christian community must be taken into consideration.

Paul calls to silence all persons who want a platform for the demonstration of any gift. Among those called to silence are the tongue speaker who cannot interpret, the prophet who is interrupted, and the woman who ignores the traditions of the church.

Paul did not deny the value of ecstatic religious experiences, but he greatly preferred that intelligible gifts be used in the assembly. Paul tentatively and diplomatically makes a place for tongues but preferred that tongues, owing to their inherent limitations, be practiced in private.

Paul's final comments speak to his preference for the intelligible in the assembly, but indicates his sensitivity to any and all work of the Spirit (v. 39). The bottom line then and now is that everything must be done in an orderly manner. God has gifted his church of every generation to join Him in advancing the kingdom. We must seek and employ gifts with His purpose in mind.

QUESTIONS FOR REFLECTION

1. Paul's primary concern in chapter 14 is to motivate the zealous Corinthians to seek gifts that most readily edify the body. He compares prophecy and tongues to illustrate the priority of intelligible gifts over ecstatic ones in the context of the assembly. Ecstatic experiences may have personal value, but they do not contribute easily to the church service. Do you seek a church home based on the inspiration provided by the worship service or based on the opportunity to use your gifts in service? Is there evidence that you desire to abound for the edification of the church? Explain.

2. The use of tongues in the assembly creates two distinct problems. The person "ungifted" in tongues is not edified, and the unbeliever is confused and may conclude that Christians are mad. For this reason Paul anticipates that the mature Christian, concerned for

edification and evangelism, will forego the right to speak audibly in tongues. While the issue of tongues may not specifically concern you, are there areas where you are claiming your rights to the detriment of the church? It could be related to preferences in worship style or when your class meets. What is the Spirit saying to you?

3. All gifts may be controlled by the possessor and by the community. Neither gifts nor status in the church elevate us beyond the need for accountability or control. Are there issues where you avoid accountability, and if so, what are you willing to do for the sake of the body?

4. Do you desire to abound for the edification of the church? If so what gifts are most needed in your church? What ministries remain undone or are presently understaffed? Could God be speaking to you about a gift that would enable you to serve in this particular area? Are you willing to accept this gift even if it is not what you expected?

6 Five Principles of Spiritual Giftedness

A Study of Romans 12

Science was never my strong suit during my high school or college years, but I did learn a few things about conducting an experiment. In order to determine what actually occurs in an experiment, you need a control situation with which to compare your results.

You have seen the television commercials that promise a certain product gives results that are measurably different. Various toothpaste companies claim that using their product will reduce cavities by some specified percentage. In order to verify such a claim, those conducting the test must have a control group who used a similar toothpaste but without the key ingredient. Once the results are documented, they can advertise that people using our brand had 20 percent fewer cavities. I have often wondered how those people who functioned as the control group felt about their rotten teeth.

In our attempt to discover the essential elements in Paul's understanding of the purpose, scope, and function of the spiritual gifts, it would be good to have a control situation. If we could find a community that Paul had not visited and thus had not given previous instruction about gifts, we could discover the principles Paul considered to be fundamental.

In our study of 1 Thessalonians, we discovered an early, less developed, and thus incomplete look at the function of the gifts in the life of the early church. The materials we were able to examine and the principles we learned in that context were valuable but limited. In 1 Corinthians we were inundated with material. We were challenged to sift through three lengthy chapters, attempting to separate the "zealous claims" of the Corinthians from those things Paul would consider to be basic. But I have good news. The book of Romans provides us with the control situation we need at this point in our study.

Rome: The Control Situation

Most Bible commentators agree that Paul wrote Romans after he wrote 1 Corinthians, probably from Corinth during the three-month period described in Acts 20:2ff. Several interrelated concerns prompted Paul to write the Roman letter. This letter is unique because Paul did not plant the church in Rome. His other letters (other than the Pastoral letters) are addressed to churches he established.

Why then did Paul write to a community which he did not establish? First, Paul indicates that he has a desire to visit the Roman believers and to encourage them in their faith. In Romans 1:10–15 Paul shares that he has been praying for the Roman believers. The passion of his prayer has been that God would allow him to visit them and encourage them in their faith. "For I long to see you so that I may impart some spiritual gift to you, that you may be established" (v. 11). He writes that he has planned to come on several occasions but has been prevented from doing so. Further, he tells of his desire to "obtain some fruit among you also" (1:13). He then speaks of his obligation to preach the gospel to those in Rome. Thus we can determine that Paul wants both to encourage the believers in Rome and to expand the church through evangelistic preaching.

> *I pray that believers today would be filled with the boldness to believe that we are gifted and empowered to complete the Acts 1:8 mandate in our generation.*

Second, Paul likely has a missionary motive in writing this letter. Paul wants to solicit the help of the Roman believers for the spread of the gospel into Spain. I have always admired Paul, who was bold enough to believe that he must be obedient to the full scope of the Great Commission. I pray that believers today would be filled with the boldness to believe that we are gifted and empowered to complete the Acts 1:8 mandate in our generation.

Antioch had provided the base for Paul's initial missionary journeys, but if he was to broaden the scope of his ministry, Rome would provide a wonderful platform for the further expansion of the gospel. "But now, with no further place for me in these regions, and since I have had for many years a longing to come to you whenever I go to Spain—for I hope to see you in passing, and to be helped on my way there by you, when I have first enjoyed your company for a while" (15:23–24). Paul's missionary motivation helps us understand the detailed and systematic theological teaching in Romans 1–11. If you were a missionary and wanted to gain the support of a church, you would certainly be expected to express your theological convictions.

The two suggestions mentioned above certainly explain the expanded theological teaching in the first eleven chapters, but they do not fully account for the specific nature of the teaching of chapters 12 and 13 or the direct admonitions in chapters 14 and 15. Paul likely had knowledge of the state of the church in Rome. It is not unreasonable to think that Paul would have gathered information about a church he intended to visit in the near future. Paul actually knew several members of the Roman community, such as Priscilla and Aquila who could have provided detailed information. Thus, we can see that Paul had a genuine pastoral concern both in his writing and in his upcoming visit.

Here's how Paul expressed it in his own words: "And concerning you, my brethren, I myself also am convinced that you yourselves are full of goodness, filled with all knowledge and able also to admonish one another. But I have written very boldly to you on some points so as to remind you again, because of the grace that was given me from God" (15:14–15). Notice that Paul based his authority to write this pastoral letter on his "grace empowering."

If we assume that Paul had some knowledge of the Roman community, we would be curious to know if this church was also struggling with problems related to spiritual gifts. We can answer this question with an unqualified no for at least three reasons: (1) The tone of the gift section, unlike 1 Corinthians, does not suggest any critical issues. (2) The brevity of the passage would be surprising if there were serious problems or misunderstandings. (3) The content of the passage takes the form of general principles rather than corrective teaching. Thus this passage provides a "neutral setting" for us to grasp the most important principles related to spiritual gifts.

The Foundation for Gifted Service

Before we look at the five principles of giftedness, we must first establish the foundation for all gifted ministry. As indicated earlier, the division between theological teaching (1–11) and practical application (12–15) in the letter to the Romans is more pronounced than in many of the Pauline letters. Yet careful study will indicate that the teaching material is both related to and dependent on the theological foundation laid in the first eleven chapters. The content of these two sections is inextricably knit together by the phrase, "Therefore I urge you, brethren, by the mercies of God" (12:1). Thus the admonitions that follow are based on the profound truth that believers have been the recipients of God's mercies as described in chapters 1–11.

Romans 12:1–2 thus forms both a prelude to and a foundation for all that follows. The presentation of the body and the transformation of the mind are the twin foundations upon which the exercise of gifted service must be constructed. You may recall that Paul precedes his discussion of gifts in the Corinthian letter with the affirmation of the ability of the believer to discern spiritual things and thus understand the gracious quality of all of life. "Now we have received, not the spirit of the world, but the Spirit who is from God, so that we may know the things freely given to us by God" (1 Cor. 2:12). Christian conversion and the gift of the Spirit enable the believer to see himself in a wholly new perspective as the recipient of grace.

> *The presentation of the body and the transformation of the mind are the twin foundations upon which the exercise of gifted service must be constructed.*

Gifts are never an independent item of Christian living as if they are a "premium upgrade" option available for a select few for their personal esteem. They are part and parcel of the life of grace and have meaning only when presented to the King for His service and glory. The presentation of ourselves and our gifts relies upon our Spirit-enlightened understanding of the graciousness of all of life.

Note the progression of thought in Romans 12 that is not unlike 1 Corinthians 12–13. Verses 3–8 deal with ministry in and through the community while verses 9–21 deal with living in community. Again, you should recall that 1 Corinthians 12 dealt with gifts for ministry while chapter 13 dealt with loving relationships that define community. We are thus reminded that gifts find their appropriate context in service for the King to and through His church.

The Presentation of the Body

Since Romans 12:1–2 serve as a bridge between teaching and application and a prelude to Paul's instructions on gifts, we would be well served to give it our attention. The last phrase of verse 1 defines the thrust of the first section, "your spiritual service of worship." The phrase is difficult to translate. The Greek word is *logikos* and can be translated as "spiritual" or "reasonable." The phrase modifies the command "present your bodies . . . to God," making clear that the fundamental act of worship is the presentation of our body. We sometimes think of worship only in terms of what we do when gathered with other believers on Sunday, but the Bible presents worship as an ongoing, everyday activity that requires the presentation of our bodies and thus our gifted service.

I prefer the translation "reasonable" or "rational." Paul means that the presentation of our total being to God is "logical," "appropriate to," or "normative" when we consider what God has done to redeem us. "Reasonable worship" thus recalls the truth that God has made our bodies alive from the dead through the gift of His Son (Rom. 6:4–6). What God has made alive from the dead is all that He desires and all that He will receive.

The mention of "living sacrifice" would have brought to mind the sacrificial system of the Old Testament. In contrast to "dead" animal sacrifices, Christians are expected to present their bodies as living sacrifice. In other words we must present ourselves—our physical body, all that makes us who we are—to God for His use. What else could we offer Him other than the body He has made alive. Paul has already stated this same truth in the negative and the positive: "Do not go on presenting the members of your body to sin as instruments of unrighteousness; but present yourselves to God as those alive from the dead, and your members as instruments of righteousness to God" (Rom. 6:13). Paul uses the same argument with the Corinthians to call them to holy living: "For you have been bought with a price: therefore glorify God in your body" (1 Cor. 6:20).

The service, which is appropriate to the nature of Christian existence as described in Romans 1–11, is the presentation of the body in service to the King. Those who have received mercy are now empowered to express that mercy through bodies that have been made alive by the resurrection and gifted by God's Spirit!

Thus it is not an oversimplification to say that the remainder of chapter 12 is the practical application of "normative" Christian worship based on the premise of the call for living sacrifice. Paul applies this principle of normative worship to the functioning of the gifted community. We commonly make the mistake of believing that we have completed our worship duties for the week when we have gathered to sing hymns or choruses, give our offering, and listen to a message. Authentic worship is seen when believers present themselves—their very bodies—to the King for His use and for His glory. This presentation is a continual act of worship that is required 24-7-365 for our entire lifetime.

Living, Holy, and Acceptable

The three qualifying words "living," "holy," and "acceptable" are of equal value and thus define the presentation of our bodies. "Living" not only provides a contrast to dead animal sacrifices of the Old Testament, but it has meaning in a broader theological sense. The believer has been raised from the dead and granted newness of life (Rom. 6:4) and thus has a body which now has the potential of producing righteous acts for God. "Living" also signifies that the sacrifice of our bodies is a "daily" and "ongoing" gift. An animal offered as a burnt offering has but one act of service, but the redeemed and "living" body of the believer can be offered continually to God. God has Himself redeemed our body so that we may offer it to Him continually.

You may have already made the obvious connection that the physical body is where the spiritual gifts reside. Thus when we offer ourselves, our giftedness is part of the package. The gifts all operate in the context of our physical bodies, and thus, without the gifts that enable us to serve, we would have nothing to offer the King.

"Holy" underlines both the totality of the sacrifice and its ethical character. As Christians our bodies are separated unto the Lord, and we no longer make claims as to how or when or where we serve. These issues are no longer significant because we serve to advance His kingdom, by His power, and for His glory. It is about Him, not us! As living sacrifice we can no longer ignore the desires of the King with the excuse that "my time" is precious to me. All that we are is placed at His disposal.

> *We serve to advance His kingdom, by His power, and for His glory.*

The sacrifice is "holy" in an ethical sense because God who indwells us is holy. Throughout the Old Testament God echoes His desire that His people embody His name, which means reflect His character. The same is true for those who have been rightly related to God through His Son. Our gifted service to the King should be such that it reveals the holiness of God, pointing to Him and not to the gifted servant. Hear that last phrase again! Authentic gifted service will draw attention to the King and not to the servant!

The presentation of our body is "acceptable" in the sense that it is what God requires and only that which He will accept. Anything less is insufficient and inappropriate. Have you ever been guilty of giving less than your whole self; offering God a portion and not the whole? Have you ever waited until the last minute to prepare to teach God's Word? Have you ever failed to show up for a team meeting at your church?

Are you appalled that churches are forced to beg people to become involved in ministry? With such a demonstration of apathy, is it surprising that healthy evangelistic growth is declining in virtually every denomination? Is it surprising that we seem to be losing the cultural war? When those who claim to be the recipients of mercy place conditions of time and convenience on our service to the one living God, we hamper the advance of the kingdom through us and through our churches.

Understanding the principle of living sacrifice would solve the problems we confront in the church today related to the lack of commitment. It would put an instant end to apathy and casual Christianity. A living sacrifice no longer has any claim over time, money, use of gifts, or influence. Once we give ourselves bodily to God, we will no longer struggle with "uncommitted areas" of our lives. There are no uncommitted areas of living sacrifice.

Another truth is declared in the word "acceptable." God has already declared your service "acceptable" or "pleasing." God desires you and what you have to offer Him. He has made you for Himself, redeemed you by His grace, and gifted you by His Spirit to join Him in the earthly advance of His kingdom. No matter what you discover your gifted service to be, God accepts it with great pleasure.

Many Christians remain on the sidelines because they don't think they have anything worth offering to the King. Good news—He has already declared your gifted service acceptable!

My five grandchildren are the joy of my life. They often present their "Papa" with pictures they have drawn. These childlike drawings bring me great pleasure, and I quickly and proudly display them on my refrigerator. I humorously like to think that God has a refrigerator

> *He has made you for Himself, redeemed you by His grace, and gifted you by His Spirit to join Him in the earthly advance of His kingdom.*

door as big as all of heaven, and He proudly displays our gifted service to Him. One day we can stroll through the heavenly gallery and gaze with wonder on all our "drawings" that have been lovingly displayed by our heavenly Father. These "childlike drawings" may have been our fumbling attempt to present the gospel to a friend or a solo that sounded like a disaster to our ears. Another picture in the gallery shows us teaching a youth class that had left us in tears. Only the King can evaluate the eternal impact of our gifted service, and He has already indicated that our offerings are acceptable to Him. What other affirmation do you need? Get your crayons and start drawing for the King.

Transformation through the Renewing of the Mind

Christian worship/service takes place in the real world, and therefore the Christian must guard against being conformed to the values of the present age. The mind-set of the present age tells us that life is really about us. It convinces us that we are number one and that the present life is all that counts. It assures us that true value in this life is found in financial attainment, power, awards, or physical looks.

We can easily be tempted to buy into this false value system and allow the world to squeeze us into its mold. But we are kingdom citizens, and we know that this present order has already been shaken and will be shaken again with the return of the rightful King. "Therefore, since we receive a kingdom which cannot be shaken, let us show gratitude, by which we may offer to God an acceptable service with reverence and awe" (Heb. 12:28). How then do we escape the power and pressure of the present world values?

The only solution to the constant pressure to conform to the world is to be "transformed by the renewing of your mind" (Rom. 12:2). The incredible good news is that the believer can have victory over the tyrannizing forces of this age by submitting himself to the transforming power of God that occurs through the constant renewal of the mind.

The thought of continual transformation permeates Paul's teaching in the Roman letter. "Therefore do not let sin reign in your mortal body . . .; but present yourselves to God as those alive from the dead, and your members as instruments of righteousness to God" (Rom. 6:12–13; cp. 6:17–18). As we come to comprehend who we are in Christ and the kingdom potential provided through the process of redemption, our passion to serve the King is born and intensified. Many Christians stop halfway in this equation; they are made alive through grace but never submit themselves to God for service. This lack of kingdom activity allows them to be sucked back into the tyrannizing power of the flesh and the world. If you ever wonder why the transformation process in your own life seems so slow, ask these questions.

- Do I view myself from God's perspective as gifted and empowered?
- Have I offered Him my all in service?
- Do I know my gift, and am I employing it to advance His kingdom?
- Am I experiencing transformation of the mind because I am involved in service?

In Romans 8, where Paul discusses the work of the Spirit, he pays particular attention to the transforming work of the Spirit and role of the mind in that transformation. "For those who are according to the flesh set their minds on the things of the flesh, but those who are according to the Spirit, the things of the Spirit. For the mind set on the flesh is death, but the mind set on the Spirit is life and peace" (8:5–6).

Paul speaks of transformation in similar terms in 2 Corinthians 3:12–18. He writes of those whose minds are hardened by the veil of unbelief, which can only be removed in Christ. He then explains the process of transformation: "But whenever a person turns to the Lord, the veil is taken away. Now the Lord is the Spirit, and where the Spirit of the Lord is, there is liberty. But we all, with unveiled face, beholding as in a mirror the glory of the Lord, are being transformed into the same image from glory to glory, just as from the Lord, the Spirit" (2 Cor. 3:16–18).

"Mind" denotes the inner part of the human constitution where feeling, thinking, and willing take place. It is not an issue of becoming more intelligent; it is an issue of the reorientation of both thought and deed to align with the truth experienced in Christ. The non-Christian mind is reprobate, issuing in a futile lifestyle. "And just as they did not see fit to acknowledge God any longer, God gave them over to a depraved mind, to do those things which are not proper" (Rom. 1:28). But the believer's mind, made alive through conversion, is to be constantly renewed, enabling the believer to "prove what the will of God is" (Rom. 12:2).

We know that our thinking impacts our behavior. The golfer who gazes at the pond and concludes he can't possibly avoid the hazard is most often going to baptize another ball. The athlete who sees the opponent as too large to beat has already sown the seeds of defeat. We must, however, be careful that we don't fall into the deception of "positive thinking," with its promise that what your mind can conceive you can achieve. While positive thinking has an element of biblical truth, it is fundamentally flawed. It is simply not true that we can accomplish anything the mind conceives.

I may think I can hit a drive like Tiger Woods, but it isn't likely to happen in this lifetime. One of my favorite childhood books was *The Little Engine That Could*. It is the story of a little engine that was faced with the seemingly impossible task of pulling a heavy load over the mountain. The little train's huffing and puffing were translated into the repeated phrase, "I think I can; I think I can." Did that positive inner thought propel the train over the mountain? No! Truth is, if the train did not have the horsepower to climb the mountain, all the positive thinking he could muster would not have enabled him to accomplish the task. Positive thinking may allow us to tap unused potential, but it will not provide any additional resources.

Now here's the difference for the believer! The renewal of the mind allows us to see ourselves from God's vantage point. It enables us to discern the gracious character of all of life and thus to discern the work of the Holy Spirit in our physical bodies. The indwelling Holy Spirit can provide the supernatural resources that you need to serve the King effectively, thus proving the will of God. The Spirit then empowers us to "prove the will of God."

The word *prove* includes the ability to discern or discover the will of God, the will to embrace it, and the power to accomplish or carry out the will of God in concrete activity. Paul gives the ability to prove the will of God ethical content by indicating that it is "good and acceptable and perfect." The renewal of mind and life that the Spirit inaugurates in the believer will always be evident in both behavior and service (cp. Eph. 4:17–19, 22–24; 5:8–10; Phil. 1:9–10; and especially Col. 3).

> *We must discover and employ our gifts, for they enable us to offer God a life of service that He has already declared good, acceptable, and perfect. In turn, service through our gifts accelerates the process of transformation.*

The reader might expect that the phrase "that which is good and acceptable and perfect" would be followed immediately by teaching on ethical behavior. Note, however, that it is followed by a call to sober evaluation of one's life and the proper use of one's gifts in service to the King through His body the church. The understanding and employment of gifts is not a minor note for kingdom citizens but a major one. We must discover and employ our gifts, for they enable us to offer God a life of service that He has already declared good, acceptable, and perfect. In turn, service through our gifts accelerates the process of transformation.

The Principle of Sound Judgment

Listen as Paul introduces the topic of spiritual gifts in this control situation: "For through the grace given to me I say to everyone among you not to think more highly of himself than he ought to think; but to think so as to have sound judgment, as God has allotted to each a measure of faith" (Rom. 12:3). It isn't difficult to understand why Paul first cautions against thinking more highly than one ought to think. Spiritual gifts often create spiritual pride, as was the case with the spirituals in Corinth. When anyone sees his or her gift as a sign of advanced spirituality, it leads to arrogant destructive behavior that hinders the body of Christ.

I played football throughout high school and college. I was a linebacker and as such was assigned certain defensive responsibilities based on what the offensive lineman in front of me did. For example, when the lineman pulled down the line, I was supposed to mirror his actions and flow with him. Yet when the lineman pulled down the line, he left a gapping hole. I was always tempted to dart through the hole and make the tackle on the quarterback. Such a play made you look good to the fans and got your name announced on the public-address system. In one game I ignored my given responsibility and darted continually into the backfield. I was having a field day, and the fans were recognizing my awesome play.

But there was one little catch with this strategy. The opposing coaches saw the arrogant showboat playing out of position. In the second half they adjusted their strategy and ran a counterplay that took advantage of a foolish linebacker who was constantly out of position. My arrogant overevaluation of my importance had actually put our entire team in jeopardy.

Gifts tell us nothing about the possessor but everything about the Giver.

When someone in the church thinks more highly of himself than he ought to think, he impacts the church's ability to accomplish its kingdom assignments. By definition our gifts are manifestations of God's grace and thus offer no basis for boasting. Gifts tell us nothing about the possessor but everything about the Giver.

God Has Allotted to Each a Measure of Faith

Paul not only cautions about overevaluation; he insists that everyone should practice sound judgment based on the fundamental truth that "God has allotted to each a measure of faith." Paul is aware that a second and equally devastating problem is under evaluation. This occurs when people argue that they have no gifts to offer, and thus they become *consumers* of grace without ever becoming *contributors* to the church in its kingdom enterprise.

I have dubbed this the Eeyore syndrome. If you have read the popular Winnie the Pooh books, you remember the little flop-eared donkey named Eeyore. He slumped around with head between his legs complaining that he had no particular value. Individuals who claim they have no gifts may sound piously humble, but they are behaving in a manner that is contrary to the plain teaching of Scripture and one that is harmful to the ministry of the church. Perhaps our confusion about gifts can account in part for the fact that a large percentage of those who claim to belong to Christ and His church never participate in the ministries of the church. Take God's Word for it: you are gifted!

Did you notice that Paul addresses the believers in Rome "through the grace given to me" (Rom. 12:3; cp. 15:15). This phrase is not intended to give apostolic authority to Paul's appeal but rather to underline Paul's dependence on God's grace and the Spirit's empowering for ministry, the same grace and empowering available to every believer.

Paul consistently underlines his dependence on grace for his ministry. In Galatians 2:8–9 Paul defends his ministry to the Gentiles by comparing his ministry to Peter's. "For He who effectually worked for Peter in his apostleship to the circumcised effectually worked for me also to the Gentiles, and recognizing the grace that had been given to me." The same idea is taught in 1 Corinthians 3:10 where Paul addresses his role in church planting. "According to the grace of God which was given to me, like a wise master builder." In 1 Corinthians 15:10 Paul describes his apostolic labors and declares: "But by the grace of God I am what I am." Paul begins this letter by linking grace and his apostolic ministry, "through whom we have received grace and apostleship to bring about the obedience of faith among all the Gentiles for His name's sake" (Rom. 1:5).

Paul's ability and authority to write this letter to the Romans was a gift of grace. Thus we can say that Paul had received grace (*charis*), God's special energizing for his ministry to the churches, and the corresponding gift or ability (*charismata*) to accomplish his work. Notice that grace takes on a sense beyond that of "God's goodness in the forgiveness of our sins," it also refers to the "empowering for ministry."

But this grace for ministry is not simply reserved for "apostles" or professional seminary-trained pastors and staff; it is available to every believer. Paul uses nearly identical phrases in the description of his own ministry and that of his readers, "through the grace given to me" (Rom. 12:3) and "according to the grace given to us" (v. 6). Paul thus uses his own ministry to introduce and illustrate the concept of *charismata* as gifting for service ("since we have gifts").

How could Paul have better addressed this church unknown to him than to assert that his authority and ability for writing to them were of the same nature as the abilities that enabled them to fulfill their particular tasks in the community? What better way to introduce a new concept of giftedness than to illustrate personally what he planned to describe! Let's offer a paraphrase of Paul's intent: "I can write to you because God has gifted and empowered me to do so, but that simply illustrates the good news I want to share with you. You too are gifted for service!"

Please note the close link between the truth of verse 2, transformation by the renewal of the mind, and the request of verse 3, think with sound judgment. The believer, who has been transformed by the renewal of the mind, is now capable of evaluating his or her gifted potential based on the understanding of the graciousness of all of life (cp. 1 Cor. 2:12).

Another link that we shouldn't miss is in Romans 12:2 where Paul indicates that the transforming of the mind enables the believer to prove (discern and accomplish) the will of God. That truth is now applied to one's giftedness. The believer has the ability to discern his or her gifted potential (v. 3) and the power to employ that gift for the good of the body (v. 6).

Sound Judgment Based on the Measure of Faith

Sound judgment of oneself is based on the truth that "God has allotted to each a measure of faith" (12:3). Several truths must be underlined. The emphatic use of "each" indicates that "a measure of faith" has been "allotted" to each and every member of the body. Since the "measure" is distributed to each, it is likely that this word should be translated "portion" or "measured part." The emphasis is on the individuality and uniqueness of each portion and not on the quantity of the gift. The same idea is taught in 1 Corinthians 12:18 where Paul asserts that each member of the body has been placed there by God's unique design. Thus when one soberly evaluates himself with the awareness that God Himself has given each person a measure of faith, he discovers his appropriate place in the body where every believer has a unique and assigned task to perform.

You may be wondering why Paul uses the phrase "measure of faith" rather than the simpler expression, "spiritual gift." This has troubled numerous Bible teachers, but a simple explanation is found by paying careful attention to the context. Paul is concerned to link the renewal of the mind and the accompanying ability to prove the will of God to the discovery and use of one's gift. Notice that Paul uses "sound judgment" with the phrase "measure of faith" in Romans 12:3 to discuss the *ability to discern* one's giftedness. In verse 6 he links "according to the proportion of his faith" and the understood verb "each of us is to exercise them accordingly" to discuss the proper use of one's gift.

The word *faith* is not used here in the sense of one's ability to trust God. If that were the case, someone could then say, "I have the gift of prophecy, and you have the gift of mercy because I have greater faith than you have." Such an understanding would lead to spiritual arrogance that would demonstrate a lack of understanding of the goal of the gifts. "Measure of faith" means the comprehension of one's charismatic potential and the accompanying understanding of the role of gifts in the advance of the kingdom.

Using the prophet as an example, we might describe the process as follows. The prophet soundly evaluates himself and becomes aware of his gift or charismatic potential. But this "transformed mind" understanding is more than simply knowing that one is gifted. I have been acquainted with many people who could tell me what they believed their gift to be, but they weren't engaged in kingdom pursuits through the use of their gift. This person does not demonstrate a proper understanding of the purpose of the gifts. Thus sober evaluation includes a proper understanding of the nature, goal, and boundaries of one's gift. The renewed mind enables us to see that gifts are individualized expressions of God's grace given us for the edification of the body. Such knowledge will keep us from overevaluation, which leads to arrogant boasting and from underevaluation, which leads to apathetic uselessness.

When spiritual gifts are rightly understood in terms of their purpose, nature, and boundaries, control is inherent within the gifts themselves. In other words the truly spiritual person who thinks with the renewed mind would never employ gifts in any manner that would be showy or disruptive to the fellowship. Each individual would understand that he has been graciously gifted to function within the community according to God's own design. Thus he is compelled to service based on a simple truth—"since we have gifts that differ according to the grace given to us" (12:6). Based on this understanding, he desires to exercise his gifts "according to the proportion of his faith" (12:6).

In other words, we serve based on our gifted potential, understanding both the purpose and limitations of our unique gift.

Do you truly believe that God has given you a unique and personalized measure of faith that will enable you to understand your gifted potential and serve for the good of the body? What is your gift? Are you using it for the good of the body and the advance of the kingdom? Still not sure that you are gifted? Can't find yourself on any gift list? Keep reading; the next section is just for you.

The Principle of Universal Giftedness

This entire passage is based on the understanding that every believer is gifted for service. Romans 12:6 is the key: "Since we have gifts that differ according to the grace given to us, each of us is to exercise them accordingly." The fact that "each" person has gifts that "differ according to grace" is the basis upon which one is to evaluate his or her gifted potential and participate in kingdom service. This idea of "universal giftedness" is not a new one. This concept is central to the entire body of Pauline teaching related to gifts. When the Corinthians wanted to emphasize a few gifts desired for their sign value, Paul responded with no uncertainty: "But to each one . . . to one . . . to another (8 times) . . . But one and the same Spirit works all these things distributing to each one individually just as He wills" (1 Cor. 12:7–11).

You were never intended to be a spectator in the family of God. You were uniquely created and gifted by God for a special role that will enable you to advance His kingdom on earth and thus live with eternal impact. That thought should challenge and encourage you. You were created and redeemed with purpose. Here's how Paul states this truth in Ephesians 2:10: "For we are His workmanship, created in Christ Jesus for good works, which God prepared beforehand so that we would walk in them." Do you know that you are gifted to participate in kingdom activity prepared specifically for you by God before you were born? Pretty exciting, don't you think?

Perhaps you are thinking, *I would like to believe what you're saying, but I just can't find myself on any of the gift lists in the New Testament.* That's OK! There are four specific lists—two in 1 Corinthians 12; Romans 12; and Ephesians 4—and each is unique based on the specific context of the particular letter. The lists were never intended to be *comprehensive* but only *illustrative* of the sort of abilities God might give an individual that would enable him or her to serve the King of kings acceptably.

If you recall the two gift lists in 1 Corinthians 12, you will remember that the second list (12:28) repeats a few of the gifts included in the first list (12:8–10) before it adds new gifts such as teaching, helps, and administrations. Paul includes two different but similar lists in the same chapter to broaden the understanding of the Corinthians who were only interested in spectacular gifts. Notice that the list in Romans 12:6–8 is intentionally broad in its scope and includes gifts not mentioned in either list in 1 Corinthians. Further, it omits many of the gifts listed in that letter. If Paul had in mind any complete listing of all available spiritual gifts, why not repeat them on each occasion that he writes about gifts? He had no such list in mind and thus provides only a few possible options to illustrate the principle that all are gifted and that gifts differ according to God's intentional design.

Look at the uniqueness of this particular list. It includes gifts we might expect to find such as prophecy and teaching. Service, leading, and exhorting are new but not surprising since many of those abilities are included in earlier gifts such as prophecy and administration. Giving and showing mercy, however, are unexpected. While these may sound like unusual spiritual gifts, they demonstrate the breadth of Paul's understanding of what might qualify as a spiritual gift.

The one with the gift to give is instructed to do so "with liberality." This qualification refers not only to generosity but also to the compassion of the person gifted to give. One would naturally assume that Paul is referring to giving that goes beyond the tithe, which is expected of every believer. Paul explores this gift of giving in 2 Corinthians 8 where he discusses the giving of the churches of Macedonia to the offering for the saints in Jerusalem who were suffering due to a severe famine. Paul refers to capability to give beyond their natural ability (8:3) as a "gracious work" (8:7; cp. 8:1, 6). Verse 7 is most instructive since Paul compares their gracious giving with the abundance of "faith and utterance and knowledge" manifest by the Corinthians. Perhaps the giving of the Macedonian believers prompted Paul to include giving as a spiritual gift in our present context.

On one occasion when I was preaching on this text, a young wife came to me with a huge smile on her face. "That explains it," she exclaimed. She then told me about her husband's passion for giving. The opportunity and ability to give generously beyond the tithe gave purpose to his hard labor to earn money. All of us are called to be good stewards in the giving of tithes and offerings, but some people are given the unique ability to earn and give with liberality. I have been fortunate to know many of these people throughout my ministry both at the local church and at the seminary. They saw their ability to give generously as both a gift and a privilege. They often spoke of "investing" in kingdom activity rather than giving.

"Showing mercy" may have suggested such functions as tending the sick, relieving the poor, or caring for the aged and disabled. Notice that these benevolent tasks must be accompanied with an attitude of cheerfulness. When showing mercy is one's gift, functioning in such a seemingly menial way does not seem like a duty or imposition. Rather it is seen as a calling and a privilege. The gifted individual understands that giving a cup of cold water to the "least of the brethren" is the same as giving it to the King. The attitude of cheerfulness accompanies the service and thus enables the recipient to receive the act of mercy with cheerfulness. There is never a sense that the gift of mercy is a handout to an unfortunate; it is a service offered the King.

Prophecy and teaching were both found in 1 Corinthians 12:28. Service (*diakonia*), because of its location between prophecy and teaching, may merit a translation more specific than "service." It may be that *diakonia* points to a "recognized" ministry, existing in some if not all early congregations. Paul gives specific greetings to "the overseers and deacons" in the church in Philippi (Phil. 1:1). Thus we could conclude that our deacons like our prophets (preachers?) and our teachers should be gifted by God to serve the congregation. One must then ask whether churches today seek out and elect persons who are gifted to serve before they elect them to be deacons of the church.

Did you notice that this gift list lacks the enthusiastic or miraculous gifts such as tongues and miracle-working faith? The gifts listed here fall into two broad categories—service gifts and leadership gifts. We are once again reminded that Paul's discussion in 1 Corinthians 14 demonstrated a preference for the more edifying gifts rather than the dramatic ones when it came to the edification of the body. The gifts listed in Romans 12:6–8 give us no information about the actual makeup of the church in Rome but rather give us an insight into Paul's passion to stress the gifts of leadership, proclamation, and service.

The freedom with which Paul refers to persons or abilities is clearly evidenced in this passage. In 1 Corinthians 12:28–30 Paul begins with persons (apostles and prophets) and moves to abilities (miracles and healings). In Romans he begins with abilities and moves to persons. In other words, Paul felt the complete freedom to speak of prophets in one list and prophecy in another. The relationship between the individual and the gift possessed was so integral that individuals could be referred to in terms of their gifted service.

If, for example, you have the gift of teaching, it would be appropriate to refer to you as "he who teaches."

Why is this list so unusually broad? It illustrates the broad spectrum of abilities where people might discover their unique giftedness. Don't despair if you have struggled to find yourself on any gift list or inventory. The lists in the Pauline letters were intended only to represent the sort of gifted activity the Spirit might give to individuals to enable them to serve the King by advancing His kingdom.

The Principle of Unity through Diversity

The statement, "For just as we have many members in one body and all the members do not have the same function, so we, who are many, are one body in Christ" (Rom. 12:4–5), indicates that diversity is the key to unity. In a manner reminiscent of 1 Corinthians 12, Paul employs the picture of the human body to illustrate the proper functioning of the gifted community.

The human body functions as a unified whole precisely because it is made up of a variety of members, each with a unique and yet indispensable function. Each member of the body has a specific role to play, and therefore all members are equally necessary to the proper functioning of the body. When any one member fails to serve in his or her given role, the entire body is impeded in its mission faithfully to advance God's kingdom. Conversely no one member or group of members, no matter how powerful, can fulfill all the functions of the body.

Even though the entire creation clearly illustrates the principle of unity through diversity, we still struggle to believe it applies to us specifically and to our church. We can watch any successful sports team, and we see that each player has a unique and differing role, but each player must faithfully fulfill the role assigned if the team is to succeed. We may notice the skills of the quarterback or the running back, but if the linemen up front fail to block, we would quickly discern that those players whose roles are most visible are having a difficult day. Players whose roles are often unnoticed are equally vital to the success of the team. The same is true in the church. Many of the functions of the body of Christ often appear unremarkable and insignificant, but they are indispensable because they are part of the King's design.

When I lived in England, I decided to take up a new sport—rowing. Our boat had eight oarsmen and a coxswain. The task of the oarsmen is pretty obvious. They provide the energy to move the boat. I doubted the value of the cox.

He sat comfortably in the rear of the boat, never once breaking a sweat. All he did was shout orders to the hardworking oarsmen. I wondered why we needed him and often dreamed about dumping him out of the boat to lighten our load.

The races in the narrow and winding Cam River were called the "bumps" because the object of the race was physically to bump the boat in front of you before the boat behind you bumped you. Since all the oarsmen are looking backward, the only one who can see the boat in front of you is the cox. During practice each team creates a system of elaborate signals that will help the oarsmen know precisely how close they are to the boat ahead. The signals work well in practice when you are alone on the river, but they are useless in the cacophonous noise created by the crowds on race day.

The races last four days, and the objective is to get consecutive bumps on each day. We had achieved our goal on days one and two and were looking good to earn our oar. On the third day we quickly pulled up on the boat ahead of us. We were leaning on the oars in a concerted effort to make our third bump. We felt the thump and heard the grating sound that seemed to assure victory. When we turned to look, our thrill of victory was turned to the agony of defeat. Our cox had momentarily lost his concentration by looking back to see the boat behind us. In that split second we approached a sharp bend in the river—and the rest is history. No oar! For the first time it dawned on me that the cox was vital to the success of our boat.

Maybe you think that your gift and your role in the body of Christ are insignificant and no harm will be done if you fail to function. Nothing could be farther from the truth. All members are equally important, and the body is impaired in its ministry when any one member fails to function according to his or her gift. You are vital to the work of your church; you have been placed in the body by the design of the King Himself.

We sometimes dream about having a more visible role. We want uniformity rather than unity. We think, *If I could only sing like her, or if I could only teach like him.* The body could not function if everyone had the same gift. For you to compare your role with anyone else's role isn't necessary or helpful. Your role is to fulfill the purpose for which God created and gifted you. You were created by God with intentionality, redeemed by Christ for service, and gifted by the Spirit for effectiveness. You will find a new dimension of Christian living when you discover and employ your gifts in the service of the King.

When we think about the implications of this important principle related to spiritual gifts, we can see why many churches are ineffective in their quest to fulfill the Acts 1:8 mandate. When members of the body fail to function according to their gifted role, the body is rendered ineffective. When members think their gift is insignificant and thus remain on the sidelines of kingdom activity, they are essentially saying that the King made a mistake when He created, redeemed, and gifted them. Our King makes no mistakes. You are created, redeemed, and gifted with intentionality so that your life and service can have an eternal impact. What could be more exciting than that?

> *You were created by God with intentionality, redeemed by Christ for service, and gifted by the Spirit for effectiveness.*

The Principle of Interdependence

The phrase "individually members one of another" (Rom. 12:5) breaks the parallelism with verse 4 and thus stands out in bold relief. Gifts should never lead to spiritual pride and isolation, for they actually cause us to be interdependent.

A part of our fallen human nature drives us to independence. We can watch the preschooler who pulls away from the parent's grasp to declare, "I can do it myself." We later hear our young adult child defiantly assert, "I don't need you or anyone else!" We struggle with the issue of independence. In some regards we must cut the umbilical cord of dependence and become responsible adults. But we were created by God as relational beings, and therefore we will always need to be a part of community, which in turn makes us interdependent.

The idea of being interdependent not only conflicts with our desire for independence; it also runs counter to the climate of our day. The world around us tells us that life is about us. We are encouraged to focus on building our own image and our own career. We are told that we must look out after number one since everyone else is looking out for their own self-interests. This philosophy caters to the desire for independence and ignores the need for fellowship in community.

The biblical pattern offers a more balanced perspective on life. Discovering our own unique gifted identity does not lead us to arrogant isolation but rather to responsible community living. When we discover who we are in Christ, we no longer have to be all things to all people. The compulsion to prove ourselves to others is no longer the overwhelming quest of life. We are no longer compelled to trample on others on our way up the ladder of personal identity and success. The loneliness of isolation is replaced by the companionship of authentic community.

The proper understanding of God's grace and my unique giftedness make me aware of my personal identity and worth and my total dependence and interdependence. These are not contradictory ideas; they are two sides of the same coin. By virtue of creation and redemption I am dependent on God's grace for all I am or have. "Renewing of the mind" enables me to understand the gracious quality of all of life. I now understand that I am a special creation of the King of kings who has designed and gifted me for unique kingdom service. Yet I am only one member of His body, which makes me *interdependent*. I depend on others' gifts to complete mine and to minister to me. Simply and magnificently, we need one another! We do not lose our personal identity by confessing our interdependence. On the contrary, we begin to discover it.

The members of the body are so closely interrelated that when one member suffers, the entire body suffers. When one rejoices, we should all rejoice together (cp. 1 Cor. 12:26). When any gifted member chooses to separate himself or herself from the body, they will soon become lifeless and useless. For example, we might comment that a brilliant pianist has gifted hands. Those hands separated from the body would serve no purpose. We have all watched gifted athletes who have arrogantly lost sight of the role of the entire team in their personal success. They soon become isolated, sullen, and ineffective.

We cannot function independently because God created us, uniquely gifted us, and placed us in the body just as He chose. You are part of a larger community, both by creation and by redemption. You cannot live out the Christian life in isolation. Your spiritual muscles will atrophy, and your gifts become useless unless they are exercised through ministry within the larger body of believers.

Principle of the Common Good

As noted earlier, everything in this section is based on an absolute truth—"since we have gifts that differ according to the grace given us," (Rom. 12:6). This sentence in the Greek requires that we add a verbal statement such as "let us use them" (NKJV) or "each of us is to exercise them accordingly" (NASB).

Two points can be made. Gifts are not given by God for our amusement, and thus they find meaning only when they are employed for His kingdom and glory. Second, they are not intended to amaze our friends with our spiritual prowess, and thus they are to be used for the common good of the body. The spirituals in Corinth arrogantly believed their gifts proved they were spiritually elite, and they wanted to display their gifts in a manner that would draw attention to themselves. In so doing, they were actually tearing down Christ's body, the church.

Paul develops this principle in greater detail in 1 Corinthians where he is required to devote three full chapters to the discussion of gifts. The entirety of chapter 14 focuses on desiring and using gifts with the ultimate concern of edifying the body. Gifts are God's gracious gifting of individual members of the body, enabling them to edify the body and serve God's eternal purpose.

We can be assured that God has sovereignly equipped His church to accomplish His purpose in every generation. Our creative King is gifting the church with new gifts in each generation based on the needs of the church to complete the task of reaching the nations. Further, no task is too great for the church that assists its members in discovering and employing their individual gifts. While I am certainly talking about the universal church, I am also talking about your church. When all the gifted members employ their gifts for the common good and the advance of the kingdom, not even the gates of hell can stand against the church.

Here are just a few of the wonderful truths we can learn:

- You are part of God's gifted body.
- You were created to be a colaborer with Him.
- No person is unimportant or insignificant in the work of the church.
- No task that God gifts and calls you to do is unimportant or insignificant.
- If it's important to God, it's important.

When you fully understand you are an integral gifted part of God's design for advancing His kingdom, it will change your life forever. God will not ask you to do anything He will not enable you to do. The church has often been called the largest volunteer organization in the world. This is not quite true. Our service is not an issue of volunteerism but one of living sacrifice.

A Brief Recap

The brevity of this passage allows us to see the key principles concerning giftedness in a summary fashion.

Paul first establishes the foundation for all gifted ministry in the presentation of the body and the renewing of the mind. Our bodies have been made alive through the new birth and are thus the only appropriate gifts we have to offer the King. The transformation of the mind enables us to break the bonds of conformity and know and do the will of God. This transformation enables us to see the graciousness of all life and thus our "gifted" potential.

Paul assures us that the service we offer to the King is living, holy, and acceptable. Our service is a daily and ongoing gift set apart unto the King and declared "acceptable" by Him.

The renewal of the mind enables us to discern our giftedness and to employ our giftedness for the good of the body.

Paul articulates five key principles of gifted ministry:

1. The principle of sound judgment
2. The principle of universal giftedness
3. The principle of unity through diversity
4. The principle of interdependence
5. The principle of the common good

QUESTIONS FOR REFLECTION

1. Since gifts function in the context of the human body, our first step to gift discovery and use is to present ourselves to God. Have you given the Lord all that you are without reservation? If not, what areas do you need to release to Him today?
2. Have you developed the practice of the daily renewing of your mind through prayer and regular Bible study? What steps are you willing to take to allow God to transform your mind, enabling you to understand your gifted potential?
3. Two dangers inherent in gifts is the tendency of overevaluation leading to arrogance and underevaluation leading to uselessness. Which side of the coin do you find yourself struggling with?
4. God has designed us to be interdependent not independent. Do you ever manifest a spirit of independence based on a false pride? What steps are you willing to take to find your place in the body?

7 | Gifted Leaders Equipping Gifted Members

A Study of Ephesians 4

Our children have always looked forward to family vacations. Most of us aren't really tourists so we mainly enjoy spending time just "hanging out." When my girls were younger, we had a tradition that became a part of each family vacation. We would work a jigsaw puzzle as a family project. Each year as the children grew older, our puzzles became increasingly complex. One year we purchased a puzzle that had numerous baskets of ripe strawberries. You can't imagine how many subtle shades of red there are in hundreds of strawberries.

When we dumped the pieces out on the table and turned them all upright, the task seemed impossible. There were so many pieces! Some of them were tiny, and all seemed to be smeared with bright red. The five of us started to work with little agreement on how to begin the daunting task. I recommended that we start with the border. Another family member wanted to begin with a large and prominent basket in the middle of the picture. Progress was painfully slow during the first few sessions of our puzzle time. However as we persevered, details began to emerge, and we became excited as the picture began to take shape before our eyes. Toward the end of the vacation, only a few areas of detail remained to be completed with the few pieces scattered on the table.

The study of spiritual gifts may for some of you resemble that family vacation puzzle project. The topic of spiritual gifts has been so confusing and volatile for some that they have simply avoided taking the puzzle pieces out of the box. However, once the decision was made to tackle this essential, perhaps puzzling, biblical topic, we had first to decide on a strategy for putting the various pieces of our study together.

Congratulations. We have already accomplished these first steps together, and we have even assembled much of the picture of gifts in the early church! We chose to follow a logical pattern of taking the various gift passages in their chronological sequence. In doing so, we have paid close attention to the historical setting in each case. Some authors have attempted to work this "gift puzzle" by arranging their material by topical categories. I prefer the chronological study because it requires us to deal with all the pertinent material in its entirety and in its original context. This process allows us to be faithful to the biblical text and avoid the temptation to read our own preconceived ideas into the text.

I hope that you have a clearer understanding of Paul's teaching and can see the picture take shape. Only a few points of detail need clarification. How do gifted members and gifted leaders work together? What is the result when the entire gifted body works in harmony? How can I determine my gift(s)? We will begin to assemble these last few puzzle pieces in this section.

The Ephesian letter is the last major passage we study. It contains a listing of gifts that appears to be somewhat different from earlier lists. One verse from this section is frequently quoted by pastors and laypersons alike. "He gave some . . . as pastors and teachers, for the equipping of the saints for the work of service, to the building up of the body of Christ" (Eph. 4:11–12). But what does that mean, and how does it work in today's church? How does this passage fit together with the picture of the gifted community we studied in earlier passages? Let's see if we can assemble the last few pieces of the puzzle.

The Setting of the Ephesian Letter

Ephesians is one of the most loved of all the Pauline letters. It contains beautiful passages about the believer's inheritance in Christ and our bold and confident access to the Father. In chapter 5 Paul paints an intimate picture of the church, comparing the love of a husband for his wife with that of Christ's love for the church. Believers of every generation have been strengthened and encouraged by the powerful description of the whole armor of God. I have always been moved by the two lengthy prayers that encourage the believer to appropriate all the resources available in Christ.

Nonetheless, the letter itself poses a few mysteries that must be solved before we can fully understand the key gift passage. As you read the letter, you may notice that the tone and style differ significantly from that of many of the other Pauline letters. The general tone of this letter and the lack of personal names and remembrances make it unlikely that Ephesians was written to a single congregation, particularly one intimately acquainted with Paul's ministry. Notice for example that in 3:1–2 Paul introduces himself by including a reference to his ministry to the Gentiles. "For this reason I, Paul, the prisoner of Christ Jesus for the sake of you Gentiles—if indeed you have heard of the stewardship of God's grace which was given to me for you."

This rather impersonal introduction of his ministry to the Gentiles stands in stark contrast to the intimate scene we find in Acts 20:36–38 where the elders from the church in Ephesus embraced Paul before he set sail from Miletus. "When he said these things, he knelt down and prayed with them all. And they began to weep aloud and embraced Paul, and repeatedly kissed him, grieving especially over the word which he had spoken, that they would not see his face again." Why would people so intimately connected to Paul be addressed as if they may have only heard of his ministry?

When you compare this letter to other Pauline letters like 1 Corinthians, you will discover that the vocabulary is also different from earlier letters. The language reflects the fact that Paul allows us inside his prayer closet as he prays for the church. Further, if you read this letter in conjunction with Colossians, you will discover that the content and even the phrasing of the two letters are similar. How do we account for these unique features of this letter addressed "to the saints who are at Ephesus" (Eph. 1:1)? Why were these two similar letters written and to whom?

A Possible Reconstruction of Events

Let's create a brief reconstruction of likely events. Colossians 4:12 tells us that while Paul was in prison he came into contact with Epaphras, a leader in the church at Colossae (Col. 1:7–8). Epaphras had informed Paul about the faith of the believers in Colossae and had enlightened him about heretical teachings that were causing confusion for the young believers in his church. Paul likely wrote Colossians at the request of Epaphras and the prompting of the Holy Spirit to deal directly with false teachings that were troubling the church in Colossae.

The news that heretical teachings were affecting this neighboring congregation must have caused Paul to fear for the believers in Ephesus and in other church communities throughout this region of proconsular Asia. Luke tells us that Paul's ministry impacted all who lived in Asia. "This took place for two years, so that all who lived in Asia heard the word of the Lord, both Jews and Greeks" (Acts 19:10). Many of the churches in this region probably owed their existence to Paul's missionary work in Ephesus. Thus, having written a letter to the church at Colossae, Paul seized the opportunity to write a more general and positive letter with the specific intent of stopping the spread of similar heretical teachings to other churches in the area.

Paul dispatched Tychicus, a beloved brother and faithful servant with the letters we refer to as Ephesians and Colossians (Col. 4:7–9). Paul still had one complicating factor with which he must deal. While Paul was imprisoned, Onesimus, a runaway slave, had been converted and had become a "beloved brother" (Col. 4:9). Paul felt compelled to return Onesimus to Philemon his owner, but he requested Philemon to free his former slave and treat him like a brother. You can read Paul's appeal in the letter to Philemon, which was also transported by Tychicus.

Here is a possible sequence of events. Tychicus and his traveling companion Onesimus traveled by boat bearing the three letters. They landed at the seaport in Ephesus and delivered the Ephesian letter with the instructions that it should be shared with other churches in proconsular Asia. It would have been natural that a letter from Paul intended to strengthen the churches in Asia Minor would originate from Ephesus, the central seaport location that had been Paul's base of ministry. This would also explain how the phrase "at Ephesus" (Eph. 1:1) became attached to this letter.

The original route for the distribution of the Ephesian letter would likely have been the seven churches linked together in the book of Revelation— Ephesus, Smyrna, Pergamum, Thyatira, Sardis, Philadelphia, and Laodicea. These churches had probably banded together for fellowship and friendship, forming a vital communication network for early believers. Their linking together would have formed a rather early edition of a "local association" of churches.

Once Tychicus had delivered the Ephesian letter, he proceeded directly to Philemon in Colossae by way of the Meander Valley. This route would have been more direct and less populous thus providing for greater safety as he delivered a "wanted" runaway slave. Once in Colossae, Tychicus returned Onesimus to his owner and delivered the Colossian letter to the church with the instructions that it be shared with other churches in their "local association."

Several references in Ephesians and Colossians make this reconstruction appealing. Colossians 4:16 indicates that Paul wanted the Colossians to share their letter with the Laodiceans and, in turn, read the letter arriving from Laodicea. "When this letter is read among you, have it also read in the church of the Laodiceans; and you, for your part read my letter that is coming from Laodicea." If we follow the route suggested by the seven churches mentioned in

Revelation, Laodicea would be the stop just prior to Colossae. Thus the letter coming from Laodicea is the Ephesian correspondence.

In the Colossian letter Paul expressed his concern for "all those who have not personally seen my face" (2:1), which suggests he anticipated persons reading the letter who had not been the direct recipients of his ministry. We have already noticed that Paul directed the Colossians to share their letter with those in Laodicea, but Paul may have anticipated an even more expansive audience. The churches receiving the Ephesian letter were promised a personal visit by Tychicus. "But that you also may know about my circumstances, how I am doing, Tychicus, the beloved brother and faithful minister in the Lord, will make everything known to you. I have sent him to you for this very purpose, so that you may know about us, and that he may comfort your hearts" (Eph. 6:21–22). Once Tychicus had completed his mission to Philemon, he could visit each of the seven churches, carrying a copy of the Colossian letter. In person he could explain the purpose of these unexpected Pauline letters and further encourage the churches as they stood for the faith.

This possible reconstruction helps explain one other significant text. In Ephesians 3:2 Paul refers to his stewardship related to Gentiles but assumes that they may have only heard about the events leading to his Gentile ministry. "That by revelation there was made known to me the mystery, as I wrote before in brief. By referring to this, when you read you can understand my insight into the mystery of Christ" (Eph. 3:3–4). What has Paul already written that, when they have the opportunity to read it, will explain the mystery of Christ? The answer is the Colossian letter that will be coming from Colossae via Laodicea. In other words Paul intends for Ephesians and Colossians to be distributed to all of the churches in proconsular Asia so that they might fully understand who Christ is and what role His church plays in revealing the fullness of God.

Heresy and Its Antidote

Since heresy prompted Paul to write Ephesians, we would benefit from understanding the nature of the heresy. The description of the Colossian heresy is complex, and a full investigation is not necessary for this present work. The problems addressed in the Colossian letter are so diverse that it seems unlikely that the concern was a single group of opponents with a set theological agenda. We discover here a young Christian community under pressure to conform to the beliefs and practices of both pagan and Jewish neighbors.

Apparently some teachers were claiming to possess a deep wisdom which gave them insight into the will of God (Col. 1:9–14; 2:2–4). They may have based their claims on visionary experiences (2:18). At the heart of the heretical teachings, however, was a devaluation of the person of Christ (Col. 1:15–20 and 2:8–10). The influences of pagan immorality were present along with some who argued that believers must practice self-denial (2:16–25). Their decrees were: "Do not handle, do not taste, do not touch!" (v. 21). All of these factors presented a challenge to the validity and vitality of the church. Was the church nothing more than another religious sect? Was Jesus the unique Son of God who fully reveals the Father? Ultimately, if Christ is not fully God, then the church itself is nothing more than another religious sect.

Many of these elements sound strikingly similar to some of the teachings we hear in our day. Little has changed when it comes to heresy! The church today is faced with many of the same concerns confronting the church in Paul's day. Paul insists that the proper functioning of the "gifted" church is essential to doctrinal integrity. "As a result, we are no longer to be children, tossed here and there by waves and carried about by every wind of doctrine, by the trickery of men, by craftiness in deceitful scheming" (Eph. 4:14). Gifts are not simply related to effective ministry; they are intricately related to the total life of the church.

The Context of Ephesians 4

The "therefore" in 4:1 indicates a clear and vital link between the discussion that follows and the instruction that precedes. Paul's first exhortation in this gift passage calls for believers to live in a manner worthy of their calling. The call to a worthy walk leads to a discussion of the vital necessity of unity based on their common belief and experience. This exhortation to a worthy walk resulting in unity is based on truths already explained in earlier portions of the letter.

Believers have been chosen, adopted, redeemed, forgiven, and blessed with every spiritual blessing in Christ (Eph. 1:1–15). Based on these profound truths, Paul prays that the eyes of their heart may be enlightened (1:18), enabling them to understand the hope of their calling, the riches of His inheritance, and the surpassing greatness of God's power made available to them. This power is of the same nature that God demonstrated when He raised Jesus from the dead and exalted Him to the right hand of the Father. Through the exaltation of the Son, the Father placed all things in subjection to Christ and placed Him as head over all things for the church. Why? The church is Christ's body and thus is designed to demonstrate the fullness of God in the same manner that Jesus did during His earthly ministry (vv. 15–23). Can you believe that? The church is destined to demonstrate the fullness of God to the world today!

Believers must never forget that we were once sons of disobedience (2:2), but God who is "rich in mercy" (2:4) made us alive together with Christ and seated us at His right hand in the heavenly places (2:6) with the intention of demonstrating the surpassing riches of His grace in kindness toward us (2:7). "For we are His workmanship, created in Christ Jesus for good works, which God prepared beforehand so that we would walk in them" (2:10). Did you know that you have been redeemed, empowered, and gifted so that God could demonstrate His grace through you as you accomplish the good works that He prepared for you before you were born? Can you see now why it is so critical for you to discover and employ your gifts in accomplishing God's purpose for your life?

> The church is Christ's body and thus is designed to demonstrate the fullness of God in the same manner that Jesus did during His earthly ministry (vv. 15–23).

People who were once separate from Christ, excluded from the commonwealth, strangers to the covenants of promise, without hope and without God are now members of God's household (2:11–18). "So then you are no longer strangers and aliens, but you are fellow citizens with the saints, and are of God's household, having been built on the foundation of the apostles and prophets, Christ Jesus Himself being the corner stone, in whom the whole building, being fitted together, is growing into a holy temple in the Lord" (2:19–21). Stop and meditate for a moment on this text. Do you fully appreciate what it means to be a member of God's household? Did you know that the church was of such historical import that it was built upon the foundation of the apostles and prophets with Christ as its cornerstone?

In chapter 3 Paul, with great wonder and humility, reminds his readers of his own calling to preach the gospel. The radical understanding of grace enabled a former persecutor, a man who considered himself to be least of all the saints (3:8) to preach boldly the unfathomable riches of Christ. But Paul is even more overwhelmed by the truth that he has been chosen to unveil a mystery that has been hidden in God. You might wonder concerning the content of this mystery. Listen and be amazed! "So that the manifold wisdom of God might now be made known through the church to the rulers and the authorities in the heavenly places. This was in accordance with the eternal purpose which he carried out in Christ Jesus our Lord" (3:10–11). Read that text again! Do you get it? From all eternity God planned to demonstrate His manifold wisdom through the church. This was carried out in Christ who came to earth to found the church (Matt. 16:18).

Are we ever guilty of treating the church as just another institution or organization? Do we fully understand what it means to be a member of the church, Christ's body? Do you ever "play church" by going through the motions of church activities without fully recognizing or using the resources made available to the church by the resurrected Christ? You are one of those resources! Are you using your gifts in and through the ministry of your local church? I sometimes hear people talk about loving the universal church, but they have no connection or ministry in a local expression of that universal church. That is like saying you believe in the universal concept of family but have no relationship to anyone in your own family.

The ministry of the church is of such kingdom import that Paul breaks into passionate prayer for believers of every age. He prays that we will be strengthened with power in our inner man so that Christ may fully dwell in our hearts (Eph. 3:14–17a). He prays that we might be able to comprehend the love of Christ which "surpasses knowledge" (v. 19). How can we know a truth that "surpasses knowledge"? The key is in this text—"with all the saints" (v. 18). Our relationship with "all the saints" enables us to know the unknowable love of Christ. Each of us has but a few small pieces of the massive picture of God's love. But as we come together in community, we assemble a more complete picture of God's love.

These specific prayer requests are again related to a single goal: "that you may be filled up to all the fullness of God" (v. 19). The church—yes, I am talking about your church—is intended to express God's fullness in your community and to the ends of the earth. In case you think the church is incapable of such a lofty goal, just listen to the end of the prayer. "Now to Him who is able to do far more abundantly beyond all that we ask or think, according to the power that works within us, to Him be the glory in the church and in Christ Jesus to all generations forever and ever. Amen" (vv. 20–21). More than we ask or dream! According to the power that works in us! Did you notice that when the church receives glory, Christ receives glory?

I hope you can see why it is critical that the church fully realize its God-given potential. I hope you can see why it is essential that you understand your gifted potential. The church is empowered to express God's fullness as individual members discover their gifts and fully employ them in building up the body in love.

My Worthy Walk in Community

Throughout our study of gifts, we have discovered the importance of community for personal spiritual development, and this passage is no different. The description of the worthy walk begins in 4:2 with the phrase, "showing tolerance for one another in love." This phrase describes the power of love to overcome the dangers inherent in human relationships. Living in community is difficult, and tolerance or tenacity is required. We are committed to Christ, and we are inextricably linked to one another. We refuse to give up on members of our Christian family. We must learn to live harmoniously as members of the same family if we are to take the message of the King to the ends of the earth.

> *The church is empowered to express God's fullness as individual members discover their gifts and fully employ them in building up the body in love.*

The attitudes necessary to "show tolerance"—humility, gentleness, patience, tolerance, and love—remind us of the fruit of the Spirit. This section is not about being virtuous; it is about living in harmony with the call of God on our lives. Living in community is so difficult that it requires the attributes that can only be produced by the Holy Spirit in the lives of those who have been saved by grace and have become the workmanship of God (2:8–10).

We can't fall into the trap of trying to produce these virtues by human effort. When we try to behave with humility, we either become frustrated with our inability to do so, or we become proud of our ability to be humble. When we try to be patient, we become anxious with our inability to be patient. When we try to produce any of the virtues of the Spirit through human striving, we become discouraged in our inability to change our old nature. These virtues are the divine work of the Spirit and come through surrender, not effort.

The various terms that Paul employs in verse 2 somewhat overlap in meaning. They were intended to combat arrogance, harshness, and intolerance in personal relationships. These virtues, because they manage personal relationships, are the necessary backdrop for the proper functioning of a gifted person in a gifted community. You may remember that in every community ministry passage we have studied, this emphasis on harmony in interpersonal relationships has been central. The proper functioning of the gifted body demands intimate, harmonious family relationships.

Humility and gentleness are linked together in the Greek construction. Humility is a distinctly biblical virtue. Humility was actually considered a vice in the Greek world of the first century. It was seen as a sign of weakness. Biblical humility is the opposite of complacency, conceit, and self-exaltation. It is not a pious, personal put-down. It does not express itself by the oft-heard remark, "Oh, I'm nobody! I am not gifted, and I have no value to the church." Such remarks are often little more than inverted pride. They beg for human encouragement and recognition and ignore the voice of God who affirms our true value and giftedness.

Humility is actually the *proper assessment* of oneself based on the understanding of our total dependence on the grace of God. Proper evaluation of one's giftedness rules out both arrogance and self-pity and enables us to be gentle in our relationships with others and effective in our ministry to the King. Understanding one's role in God's kingdom allows all the members of the body to work in complete harmony. Paul taught the Corinthians that they are members of one body to such an extent that when one member rejoices or suffers, all the members experience the same feeling (1 Cor. 12:25–26). Paul taught the Romans the same truth when he instructed them to think so as to have sound judgment based on God's allotment of faith (Rom. 12:3).

Humility, gentleness, and patience are the divine attributes, the practical expressions of love, which enable believers to forbear with one another and thus preserve the unity of the Spirit (Eph. 4:3). Love in all of its practical expressions must govern the Christian life and specifically personal relationships in the body. The theme of community relationships is so vital that Paul will return to it in Ephesians 4:17–32. In these verses he insists that believers must be renewed in the spirit of the mind, put on the new self, and behave in a Christlike manner precisely because we are members of one another.

Don't forget that the emphasis on community has been central to every passage related to spiritual gifts. In 1 Thessalonians 5 Paul admonished the brethren to esteem their leaders in love, to live in peace, to help the weak, to be patient with all, and to show forbearance when wronged. Faced with the exaggerated claims of the spirituals in Corinth, Paul placed the description of the authentic spiritual person at the center of the discussion of gifts in 1 Corinthians 13. He then proceeded in chapter 14 to demonstrate the practical effects of the outworking of love in the life of the gifted community. In Romans, Paul placed the discussion of gifts in the context of ethical behavior and underlined the necessity for proper evaluation. Don't miss the point! Gifts have meaning only in the context of community. Gifts must be used to express God's grace in and through the community to be authentic. Gifts, however dramatic, are never to be used to exalt or draw attention to the gifted person.

If we are going to work together as a gifted community, we must live in unity. In one breath Paul speaks of unity as a work of the Spirit, and in the next breath he exhorts the reader to preserve unity. Paul boldly affirms the basis of our unity by listing seven great unifying truths that all Christians hold in common.

> *Gifts must be used to express God's grace in and through the community to be authentic.*

Yet he challenges the gifted members to labor together "until we all attain to the unity of the faith" (4:13). Once again we confront the mystery of divine sovereignty and human freedom. Unity is a gift of the Spirit, but it must be maintained by all the gifted members working in harmony.

Paul's sevenfold expression of unity is one of the most eloquent compositions in all of Scripture. The first triad—"one body and one Spirit . . . one hope of your calling"—recalls several themes discussed in earlier chapters of this letter. "One body" refers to the church as the body of Christ. "One Spirit" is the Holy Spirit who indwells the individual members of the church and gives it unity. We sometimes forget that the church is not a building but a spiritual organism made up of people who have in common the shared experience of the Spirit. It derives its life, unity, and ministries from the Spirit, who is the gift of the ascended Lord. "One hope of your calling" (v. 4) means the hope that is received by virtue of one's response to the call to Christ. By virtue of our relationship to Christ, we have hope and purpose for now and for eternity (cp. 1:18).

The second triad—"one Lord, one faith, one baptism" (4:5)—reminds readers of the moment when they confessed Jesus as Lord and descended into the waters of baptism. This common relationship to Christ signified through baptism broke down every artificial barrier that could have been divisive. This same truth is clearly articulated in the Corinthian gift passage: "For by one Spirit we were all baptized into one body" (1 Cor. 12:13). There is no clearer statement of this truth than Galatians 3:26–28. "For you are all sons of God through faith in Christ Jesus. For all of you who were baptized into Christ have clothed yourself with Christ. There is neither Jew nor Greek, there is neither slave nor free man, there is neither male nor female; for you are all one in Christ Jesus."

Paul concludes the series of the great truths of unity with a reference to God whose essential oneness is the basis for the unity of His people. "One God and Father of all who is over all and through all and in all" (Eph. 4:6). Do you recall the focus of the final prayer of Jesus for His disciples? "I in them and You in Me, that they may be perfected in unity, so that the world may know that You sent Me and loved them, even as You have loved Me" (John 17:23). God Himself is the basis and source of our unity, and all that creates disunity disrupts and diminishes the work of the church, which was designed to express the fullness of God in its community and to reach to the ends of the earth. Does your church value unity? Does it live in such harmony that it expresses God's unity and fullness to the community?

We must now look to the historical situation of Ephesians to gain further insight into Paul's emphasis on unity. In 1 Corinthians Paul stresses unity in order to combat the individualistic attitude of the spirituals who desire to exalt themselves and choose one spiritual leader over another. In Ephesians Paul ties unity, fostered by the proper working of the gifted members, to the issue of doctrinal stability. Don't forget that Ephesians and Colossians were written to churches combating false teaching. When we study Ephesians 4:13–14 of this gift passage, we see that the goal of gifted ministry is unity of the faith which is, in turn, linked to doctrinal stability. "We are no longer to be children, tossed here and there by waves, and carried about by every wind of doctrine" (v. 14). Paul was aware that internal disunity created greater vulnerability to the "winds of doctrine."

While Paul stresses that unity is a gift of God mediated by the Spirit, he nevertheless impresses on his readers that unity is a goal toward which the church must strive. The phrase "being diligent to preserve the unity of the Spirit" (4:3) reminds the readers that while they cannot create unity, they can and must make every effort to preserve it. Unity must be pursued through the edifying use of the gifts. "In the bond of peace" (4:3) indicates that peace will be the result of living in love. Wouldn't you like to belong to a church where unity and peace abound? When you fail to discover and use your gifts, you actually create a fissure in the church's unity and weaken the ministry of the church?

The message of unity must be heard afresh in every generation. It is the only hope for churches and denominations alike. Diverse gifts and ministries should never be the cause of dissension. When properly appreciated and practiced, spiritual gifts should lead to growth and stability. Our inadequate or distorted understanding of gifts has often led to disunity rather than preserving the unity of the Spirit. When gifts are properly understood as manifestations of grace, sought with the edification of the body in view, and used for the good of the whole, the result will be humility, unity, edification, and peace.

The Language of Gifts

In this letter Paul clearly builds on his earlier gift teaching but adds several unique elements that aid in our total understanding of spiritual gifts. He connects gifts to the exalted Lord rather than the Spirit, ignores the traditional term *charismata*, and explains how gifted members and gifted leaders serve in ministry together.

Once again we are assured that all believers are gifted: "But to each one of us grace was given according to the measure of Christ's gift" (Eph. 4:7). Further, we are reminded that unity does not mean "uniformity." Paul uses the conjunction "but" to emphasize that unity, the topic of verses 3–6, does not negate the need for the diversity of gifts.

Some commentators ignore this passage in their discussion of gifts because the term *charisma* is lacking. Paul uses the root word *charis* along with another Greek word meaning gift (*dorea*) in verse 7 to speak of Christ's gift. Since terminology can be both confusing and divisive, let's look at the various terms Paul has used in the discussion of gifts. *Charismata* is the first word Paul used to refer to spiritual gifts in 1 Corinthians, where he used it in preference to *pneumatika*. *Pneumatika* comes from the root word *pneuma* meaning "spirit" and was used by the spirituals to emphasize their advanced spirituality. Paul, desiring to stress the graciousness (*charis*) and universality of gifts and thus combat spiritual arrogance, chose the word *charismata*. The use of *charismata* in 1 Corinthians has a corrective impact. Spiritual gifts prove nothing about the possessor but everything about the Giver.

> *Spiritual gifts prove nothing about the possessor but everything about the Giver.*

In Romans 12:6 Paul again uses the term *charismata* in a specialized sense to mean "abilities for service" or "spiritual gifts." The term *charisma* can be used, however, to mean simply "free gift" as in Romans 5:15, where it refers to the free gift of salvation. It is also possible for Paul to discuss the gifted ministry of members of the community without using the term *charisma* as he did in

1 Thessalonians 5. Thus the key is the content of the passage and not the presence or absence of a certain term.

When we look at the gift language here in Ephesians, we find an interesting modification which is related to the historical context of this letter. The phrase, "But to each one of us grace was given" (Eph 4:7) has precisely the same impact as "according to the grace given to us" in Romans 12:6. Each believer has been given an individualized expression of grace (*charis*) enabling him or her to accomplish ministry for the Head of the church. Earlier in Ephesians 3:2 and 7 Paul refers to his empowering for ministry to the Gentiles by the use of *charis* and *dorea* (gift).

In our present passage Paul indicates that the individualized grace for ministry is in accord with the "measure of Christ's gift." This statement is immediately explained by a quotation from Psalm 68:18. The phrase you should note is "and He gave gifts to men" (4:8). The word for "gifts" is *domata*, but in this context it has the same meaning as *charismata*. Paul found this word, already present in the psalm, to be an appropriate means of communicating the same truth—our abilities for ministry are free gifts and no basis for pride.

We should notice that Paul didn't appear to have the same hang-up with terminology that we do today. We hear someone use the terms *charismatic* or *Spirit filled,* and we draw lines that divide individuals and churches. This is contrary to the teaching of the New Testament and the Spirit who indwells the church. Every believer and every church, by virtue of their spiritual origin, are charismatic in the truest sense of the word. This does not mean that this individual or church must speak in tongues or practice the gift of miracle-working faith. It means that they have experienced the grace of the Lord Jesus Christ in salvation, and they possess individualized grace empowering them for ministry. Without this gracious empowering of God, no authentic ministry can be accomplished.

For those readers who would call themselves "charismatic," the fluidity of Paul's language should be a warning against labeling another church as "non-Spirit filled" because they do not manifest certain gifts. Perhaps you have heard one believer ask another fellow Christian, "Why don't you attend a church where the Spirit is alive?" Any such implication ignores the clear teaching of Scripture and harms the body. On the other hand, those who consider themselves "evangelical" and thus "noncharismatic" should be reminded that God's grace has endless diversity. We cannot force the Holy Spirit into the confines of our preconceived box. We are not called to stand in judgment over other believers. The key question in every church relates to the proper use of any and all gifts in terms of order and edification.

The Gifts of the Triumphant King

Paul focuses on the exalted Lord as the Giver of the gifts in our present setting because of the unique needs created by the heretical teachings in Asia Minor that devalued both Christ and the church. If we take a moment to review our earlier findings, we will notice that Paul's teaching concerning the Giver of the gifts differs slightly in each context. In 1 Corinthians, where there was an exaggerated emphasis on spirituality based on the possession of certain gifts, Paul pays particular attention to the ministry of the Spirit in the life of each and every believer. He indicates that the Spirit enables every believer to confess Jesus as Lord and baptizes each into the body. Thus the Spirit creates unity in the body that is fostered by the diversity of gifts, which He distributes to each as He wills. In Romans, where Paul writes with no specific problem in mind, he makes no explicit mention of the Spirit's role in dispersing the gifts. The emphasis in Romans is on God as the ultimate author of the gifts.

In our present passage the emphasis is on the exalted Christ. You will recall that, in our discussion of the heretical teachings that prompted the writing of Colossians and Ephesians, we looked at the emphasis in Colossians on Christ as the full expression of God (Col. 1:19). In verse 18 of that same passage, Paul declares that Christ is head of the church and the first-born from the dead enabling Him to come to have first place in everything. In the Ephesian letter Paul continues the theme of the ministry of the exalted Christ through the church by insisting that God placed everything under the feet of Christ so that the church would be empowered to express God's fullness (Eph. 1:22–23).

How does the exalted Christ express His fullness in the world and continue His ministry through the church? He gives gifts to men and women; and, in turn, He gives those gifted people to the church. Paul supports His emphasis on Christ as the Giver of the gifts by a reference to Psalm 68:18. If you look up Psalm 68:18, you will notice an important difference in the quotation. The phrase "you have received gifts among men" has been altered to read "He gave gifts to men." This change is important since it establishes the crucial point that Christ is the one who gives gifts to men. It is possible that Paul, under the inspiration of the Spirit, paraphrased the psalm, adapting it to suit his purpose. It is, however, interesting that the Targum on the psalm (an Aramaic translation or paraphrase of some parts of the Old Testament) contains the same alteration from "receiving" to "giving." Paul may have been familiar with this Targum to Psalm 68:18.

In any case the triumphant ascent, the rule of Christ, and the giving of gifts to people are the crucial elements that Paul wants to underline for his original audience. The emphasis on the exaltation of Christ, His dominion over all powers, and His consequent filling of all things through the church is emphasized in Colossians and Ephesians. Now by applying this psalm to Christ, Paul underlines the total sufficiency of the exalted Lord who has equipped the church for every ministry. This truth would strike a telling blow against any heresy that would devalue Christ or diminish His church. We face a world inundated by false teaching that would make the church of the exalted Lord only one among many options for spiritual truth. The world desperately needs to see the fullness of God displayed in and through the church today.

> *He gives gifts to men and women; and, in turn, He gives those gifted people to the church.*

In Ephesians 4:9–10 Paul adds commentary on the term "ascended" to make clear that Christ alone is the Giver of the gifts. The interpretation of these verses is a challenging matter and several solutions have been offered ranging from the descent of Christ in the incarnation, the descent of the Spirit at Pentecost, the descent of Christ into the grave, and the descent into hell between death and His resurrection. For our purposes it is not necessary to solve the question of what the descent means since Paul's primary emphasis is on the ascension.

Christ, who previously descended, has ascended triumphant over all powers including death and the grave and has been highly exalted by the Father in virtue of which he fills all things. "Far above all the heavens" has an impact similar to the phrase "far above all rule and authority and power and dominion" in Ephesians 1:21. The victorious, exalted Christ equips the church with persons gifted for ministry. This singular truth should shake us from the lethargy of playing church and create in us a desire to know and use the gifts that are provided by our Lord.

> *The victorious, exalted Christ equips the church with persons gifted for ministry.*

We can again draw attention to the thematic unity of Ephesians and Colossians by looking at a similar passage in Colossians 2:15. "On the cross he discarded the cosmic powers and authorities like a garment; he made a public spectacle of them and led them as captives in his triumphal procession" (NEB). In Colossians the triumph of Christ is linked to both the freedom of the believer (vv. 16–18) and to Christ's ability to supply all that is necessary for the growth of the church (v. 19). The emphasis on the relationship of the exalted Christ and the empowering of the church is also found in Colossians 1:1–20. This theme, mentioned in Colossians, becomes a prominent theme of Ephesians. What Paul mentions in Colossians 2:19 is fully explained in Ephesians 4:7–16.

Thus the discussion of the ascension in Ephesians 4:8–10 serves to clarify 4:7 by demonstrating the authority of the One who gives the gifts to the church. The members of the early church (or the church today) are not members of an insignificant sect. We are part of the universal church that is fully equipped by the Lord of the universe to reach all nations with the message that He is their rightful King. Paul wanted to make clear that anyone tempted to think that there are any other avenues to divine fullness should realize that the fullness of the Godhead dwells in Christ and He fills heaven and earth. The truly astounding and exciting news is that this fullness is only experienced on earth through His body, the church.

We cannot afford to play church! We cannot treat church as a spectator sport! We must discover and employ our gifts for the edification of the body and the reaching of the nations. They are gifts from the exalted Lord Himself. If we ever take seriously the truth that the exalted Lord fills the church, making it the place of full access to the resources of Almighty God, our churches and consequently our world will be transformed. I can never understand how someone can take church membership and attendance lightly with all that is at stake in the effective ministry of the church.

Gifted Leaders to Equip Gifted Members

Some Bible commentators suggest that the teaching in this section departs from Paul's vision for the church where all the members are gifted for ministry. They see here a stronger emphasis on structure and church hierarchy, and therefore they detect a separation between clergy and laity. (Such is clearly not the case.) We find here further clarification on how gifted leaders and gifted members work together for kingdom advance. This passage is clearly consistent with earlier Pauline teaching, but it adds an important clarification on how gifted leaders are to equip the gifted members to do the work of ministry thus leading to balanced and supernatural church growth.

As we study the text together, we will clearly see that all members are viewed as being equally gifted (4:7) and equally important to the growth of the body (4:16). The leaders have gifts that enable them to assist others in the discovery, development, and use of their gifts. Some Christians seem to behave as if pastors or trained staff members are the only persons in the church qualified to accomplish ministry. If someone is sick, their first thought is to send the pastor. If they have an unsaved friend, the pastor should lead him to the Lord.

Early in my ministry I was teaching a class on personal witnessing in a small church. I grew this class from an attendance of fifteen down to about five people. I was frustrated, and I fell into the trap of lecturing those present about the lack of commitment of those who were missing. Finally a deacon raised his hand and asked why I was teaching the members about witnessing. Noticing my absolute confusion, he declared that the church "hired" me to witness. This is only one example of how the conviction that the pastor (or trained staff) alone is qualified for ministry has paralyzed the church, burned out many pastors, and kept many gifted laity from the true joy of using their gifts in meaningful ministry.

The ministry of the New Testament church is a shared ministry in which the pastor has unique leadership functions by virtue of his gifts, one of which is equipping other gifted members for the work of service. Perhaps you are wondering why someone "gifted" to serve needs to be "equipped" to serve. The verb translated "equipping" contains ideas of both "preparing" and "making complete." Thus to say that a person is gifted in a particular area does not suggest that they do not need further preparation in order to enable them fully to use their gift. We recognize this truth when we insist that a person who feels called to full-time ministry should go to college or seminary to receive training for ministry. In the same manner, when we discover a gifted teacher, we don't simply arm them with a quarterly and thrust them headlong into a room of fifth graders. We provide training to enable them fully to use their gift. Spiritual gifts are given by the Spirit but can be developed by training and use.

The Gift List

The gift list in Ephesians 4 is unique, containing a twofold emphasis: gifts are given to people and, in turn, these gifted people are given to the church (v. 11). The listing of gifted leaders reminds us of 1 Corinthians 12:28; "And God has appointed in the church, first apostles, second prophets, third teachers."

What is unique about this list is that Paul only includes leadership, teaching, and proclamation gifts. Why? The answer is found in our understanding of the specific historical setting of this letter.

First let's review what we have learned from the earlier gift lists. In the first gift list in 1 Corinthians 12:8–10, Paul included only the extraordinary or ecstatic gifts which were desired by the spirituals to provide proof of their advanced spirituality. Paul's second list in that chapter (12:28), following the description of the church as a body of diverse members crafted by God Himself, expands the understanding of the breadth of abilities that might be included in a listing of gifts. He thus begins with apostles, prophets, and teachers and then adds two rather mundane service abilities—helps and administrations. In between he includes two of the dramatic gifts from the first list. His singular purpose is to broaden their understanding of the variety of abilities God might give for the building of His church.

In Romans 12:6, our control situation, Paul does not mention the ecstatic gifts but places an emphasis on service and leadership gifts. Notice that none of the lists are precisely the same, and none of the lists are complete. In each case Paul uses the gift list to illustrate, with contextual sensitivity, the diverse abilities that might be used for the edification of the body.

The emphasis on leadership, teaching, and service gifts is again apparent in Ephesians 4. The importance of the "service" gifts is clearly in view as Paul underlines the ability and responsibility of each member to contribute to the growth of the body. But the actual gift list is restricted to leadership and teaching functions because of the unique needs created by the threat of false teaching. Paul placed apostles, prophets, and others with teaching roles at the center of this passage to counteract the heretical teachings in proconsular Asia, which actually prompted the writing of this letter. Thus the common element shared by each person listed in Ephesians 4:11 is their role in teaching or preaching the gospel.

In Colossians Paul emphasizes the importance of apostolic teaching (1:5, 23; 2:6ff) and its expression through the ministry of men such as Epaphras, Tychicus, Onesimus, and Archippus. It is therefore appropriate that Paul's discussion of gifts in Ephesians would focus on unity of faith and stability in the face of false winds of doctrine and the scheming of men. It is equally understandable that Paul would place an emphasis on gifted leaders who were responsible for teaching and preaching.

Ephesians 4 is the only text in which Paul connects the use of the gifts to the maintenance of doctrinal stability (v. 14). May I once again reiterate an important truth: Paul never intended any gift list to be comprehensive, and he felt the liberty to tailor each to fit the specific need of the recipients of the letter.

The listing of evangelist and pastor/teacher are new to Paul's listing of gifts. He has included "new" gifts in each list. Had he written about this subject several more times, Paul would likely have listed other

> *Paul never intended any gift list to be comprehensive, and he felt the liberty to tailor each to fit the specific need of the recipients of the letter.*

gifts as the Spirit prompted and the situation dictated. Those who attempt to compare the various lists, number the gifts, and then group them around certain categories of ministry misunderstand the dynamic nature of Paul's teaching. God's desire and ability to empower His church for each new challenge are not static. God uniquely gifts His church for each new task and ministry as the need arises.

Certainly we can affirm that many of the gifts mentioned in Paul's lists remain operative as the mission of the church dictates their need. Gifts such as teaching, administration, and showing mercy, to name but a few, will be needed by the ministering church in every generation. Yet with new tasks to be accomplished and the advent of technological advances, many churches require people with skills and gifts in electronics or sound engineering to facilitate their ministry. Should we not think of these God-given abilities for service as spiritual gifts when they are rightly understood as gracious gifts from the Father and surrendered to His service for the edification of the body?

Before we move ahead to look at the results of gifted ministry, we should pause to note that there is an inextricable link between gifted leader and gifted member. As I visit various churches, I often sense a "we" versus "them" spirit concerning pastor and laity. Some pastors or staff members unconsciously talk about church members as "them." "Those folks just don't have any vision. I can't get them to do anything." On the other hand, I also hear church members talk about their pastor/staff as virtual outsiders. "We've got to be careful! The pastor is trying to change our church." We will never be what God called us to be until we understand that we are one body gifted by Christ to reach the nations.

The full weight of this letter is stunning. Through our relationship with Jesus Christ, we have been joined to His body. We give visible expression to our commitment to Christ by publicly professing Him and uniting with a local expression of His church. Our connection with this local body of believers unites us with the eternal and global work of God. We are given the opportunity to use our gifts to build upon the foundation established in the apostles and prophets, with Christ as the cornerstone (Eph. 2:19–22). The church has been filled, empowered, and gifted by the resurrected and ascended Lord who desires to express His fullness in the world through us!

The Results of Gifted Ministry

Both the short-term and the long-term goals of the full use of the gifts is "the building up of the body of Christ" (Eph. 4:12). The goal of edification of the body is so critical to the understanding of the ministry of gifts that Paul literally brackets the entire discussion as he repeats this goal in verse 16: "causes the growth of the body for the building up of itself in love." The gifted leaders have the task of equipping the gifted members for their unique work of service with the end result that the body of Christ is built up. It is a marvelous thought that the Head of the church both permits and enables us to play a role in the building up of the church.

The theme of edification is so central to the discussion of gifts that we would be wise to review the emphasis on edification from earlier gift passages. In 1 Thessalonians 5 the concept of edification is underlined by specific admonitions such as "admonish the unruly, encourage the fainthearted, help the weak, be patient with everyone. See that no one repays evil for evil, but always seek after that which is good for one another and for all people" (vv. 14–15). The goal of edification receives its fullest expression in the Corinthian correspondence, where Paul is combating the desire to use spiritual gifts in an unrestrained fashion to demonstrate one's spirituality. Thus the thrust of the entire fourteenth chapter is on seeking gifts with the greatest potential for edification and then using gifts already possessed in a manner that edifies the brethren. The goal of edification is stated succinctly in Romans 12:5 with the reminder: "So we, who are many, are one body in Christ, and individually members one of another."

The goal of edification runs throughout this passage and is developed in two positive directions, both of which are consistent with Paul's concern in writing the letter. Paul desires that the ministry of the believers will result in the building up of the body: (1) until they attain unity of the faith and (2) a full measure of spiritual maturity (Eph. 4:13). These two goals will enable them to stand against the unsettling waves of false doctrine and the trickery of deceitful scheming (v. 14). Once again we see that Paul applies his teaching to the needs of the communities being addressed.

The phrases "unity of the faith" and "knowledge of the Son of God" are bound together both by the Greek construction and by the context of the sentence. The themes of unity and knowledge receive special attention in both Colossians and Ephesians because of the need for these churches to stand together against the heretical influences present in proconsular Asia. The emphasis on knowledge and the mention of false teaching both indicate that "faith" should be understood as referring to the content of belief, that is to say "doctrine." Personal belief in Christ commits one to the objective truths that lead to that belief (Col. 2:6–7; Eph. 4:20–21). Sound doctrine is still the church's mainline defense against heretical influences that threaten its health and thus its growth.

This letter begins with a reference to Paul's desire that his readers grow in the "knowledge of the Son of God." In Ephesians 1:15–17 Paul indicates that he has not ceased to pray that they would receive "a spirit of wisdom and of revelation in the knowledge of Him" (v. 17). The knowledge of Him is further defined as (1) an understanding of the hope to which believers have been called, (2) the riches of His glorious inheritance in the saints, and (3) the immeasurable greatness of His power made available to the believer. Paul wants them to understand how utterly futile it would be to search for spiritual fullness apart from Christ, who is the fullness of Him who fills all in all.

It is easier to observe the mistakes of earlier generations than it is to learn from them. Why are so many people looking for spiritual truth in New Age teaching, cults, or psychic phenomena? Why is the New Age movement gaining such momentum? Who would have believed that one of the fastest growing "churches" of our day would originate with Oprah's television program and book club? Could it be that the church has failed to embrace and demonstrate the full knowledge of Christ? Have we failed to teach believers how to be filled with the Spirit and to appropriate the fullness of Christ?

Having said that we must be open to the empowering of the Holy Spirit and the fullness of Christ, I must add that we must avoid the subtle suggestion that some "experience" must be added to conversion in order to receive the fullness of power and blessing. We sometimes hear the teaching that one must receive a second work of grace or the baptism of the Spirit subsequent to salvation to know the fullness of God. Paul's emphasis in every letter is that the fullness of God is made available in Christ alone. The suggestion that salvation requires any other act to make it complete is a dangerous, nonbiblical one. Believers need to come to a more mature knowledge of the Son of God and thus more completely surrender themselves to the fullness already available in Christ; but you can be sure that God withholds nothing in His Son. We must continually and habitually seek the full flow of God's power through us by allowing His Spirit to convict and cleanse us of sin and then continually fill us with His presence.

The phrase "unity of the faith, and of the knowledge of the Son of God" is intended to stress both the need for unity in our Christian belief in the face of diverse winds of doctrine and the full sufficiency of Christ in the face of every claim to provide wisdom or spiritual power through another source. Paul points to the sufficiency of Christ to combat the immature behavior of those who were being blown off course by every wind of doctrine. They need only grow in knowledge of what is already available in Christ, not seek another spiritual experience. Yet the tendency remains! It is often easier and more emotionally stimulating to seek a mystical experience rather than practice the discipline necessary to grow in the knowledge of God.

The ultimate goal of the full use of gifts is growth to maturity, which is measured by the fullness of Christ (Eph. 4:13). To understand what Paul means by the fullness of Christ, it will be helpful to trace the use of this phrase throughout the Ephesian letter. In the first chapter Paul declares that God has seated Christ at His right hand and placed all things in subjection under His feet, making Him head over all things for the sake of the church (1:20–22). The exaltation of Christ results in the empowering of the church enabling it to be "the fullness of Him who fills all in all" (v. 23). In the third chapter Paul prays that believers would personally experience the fullness of God in terms of inner strengthening, the indwelling presence of Christ, and an overflowing abundance of love (3:14–19). When this abundance is manifest by the church, it will glorify Christ Jesus to all generations and forever (v. 21).

Now in Ephesians 4 Paul clarifies the way in which the fullness of God is actually experienced and expressed in the church. Christ descended to earth and ascended into heaven that He Himself might personally fill all things. He does this by the distribution of gifted persons to the church. The "fullness of Christ" therefore refers to the completeness already made available to the church, which must be attained by the full use of the gifts. Thus the fullness of Christ is at once a *gift* and a *goal*, a *blessing* and a *calling*. Through the discovery and use of your gifts, you are part of the process by which God manifests His fullness through the church.

"Fullness of Christ" serves as a focal point for this entire gift passage. Christ, who fills all things, fills the church and thus empowers it to express His fullness in the world. The phrase "fullness of Christ" gathers up all the elements of growth expressed in the phrases "unity of the faith," "knowledge of the Son of God," and "maturity to the measure of stature which belongs to the fullness of Christ." The actual process of growth "in all things" is accomplished through the proper and full use of the gifts, as each member works according to his own measure (v. 16). God provides His fullness through the gifting of individual believers whose gifted service, in turn, enables the church to express God's fullness in the world today.

Much is at stake in the proper understanding of spiritual gifts. Reading and studying this book cannot be simply an academic exercise fed by spiritual curiosity. While you may have begun this study to find out what the author might say about tongues or some other specific gift, I pray that your interest has gone much deeper. For the sake of the church and the nations, we must grow in the full knowledge of the Son of God and allow His power to flow through us as all members serve in their own gifted ministries.

> *God provides His fullness through the gifting of individual believers whose gifted service, in turn, enables the church to express God's fullness in the world today.*

In 4:14 Paul brings the goals and potentialities of the gifted community into sharp focus by contrasting them with the current issues facing the churches of proconsular Asia. To be blown about by every wind of doctrine is both childish and foolish when one understands that the church has at its disposal the full resources of the risen Christ. The use of "every wind of doctrine" points to the pluralistic religious climate of Paul's day and underlines the transitory value of these false teachings when compared with the eternal truth revealed in Christ. These winds will soon dissipate, only to be replaced by other false winds. The contrast between the mature man of verse 13 and the children of verse 14 could not be more striking. Children are unstable and thus prove to be easy prey for deceitful people.

Further Paul compares those seeking deeper wisdom through sources outside Christ to small rudderless boats that are at the mercy of the wind and the waves. I remember the first small rudderless boats I constructed as a child. I would throw them in the creek and run along the bank observing their progress. In truth, I spent more time wading in the creek attempting to free them from the debris that easily entangled them. Believers without a sound theological foundation are like rudderless boats. The gifted church is empowered to grow in every aspect into Christ and thus stand above the waves and winds of false doctrine.

The Proper Working of Each Individual Part

Paul concludes this section with a positive emphasis on the opportunity and responsibility of each member to participate in the growth of the church and the expansion of the kingdom. The ultimate goal is defined as growing in "all aspects into Him who is the head, even Christ." The phrase "all aspects" means wholly, entirely, and completely. Quite a goal, but we have been given the resources of the fullness of Christ, available to the church as the gifted members work in unity. With this goal in view, the gifts will be fully and necessarily operative until the return of the Lord, an emphasis Paul made earlier in 1 Corinthians 13.

Growth is fostered as members "speak the truth in love." What a contrast with the scheming false teachers who present *false doctrine* in a *deceptive* manner. The church grows through the proclamation of the *truth* in *love*. Spoken truth is necessary to curb the dangerous winds of false doctrine that threaten the church in every generation. But the speaking of the truth must always occur in the context of love. Notice the repetition of "in love" in Ephesians 4:15–16. "In love" describes the sphere of Christian life and ministry and the manner in which all ministry must be conducted.

The emphasis on love reminds us of 1 Corinthians 13 and Romans 12:9–21. Loving relationships are always central to the Pauline teaching on the discovery and use of gifts. The phrase "in love" actually links the teaching on gifts with the ethical teaching that begins in Ephesians 4:17 of this chapter. Growing into the fullness of Christ in every aspect not only means growth in unity and doctrinal stability, it involves ethical integrity as well. It is one thing to claim to believe that the Bible is without error; it is another to embrace fully and live out the truths it teaches.

The ultimate goal of all Christian growth is repeated in 4:16 but with new terminology designed to emphasize the present process of growth and every member's role in that growth. Paul gives a glimpse at the inner workings of the gifted community as it is in the process of growth. Therefore this verse serves as something of a summary. Paul brings together four prominent themes of gifted growth and relates each of them to the present work of the church in its journey to become all that it is empowered to become in Christ.

1. *The church is empowered to grow because Christ the triumphant King fills it.* The reference to Christ as the head of the church in 4:15 is intended to

direct the reader's attention to the practical implications of being the body of Christ the sovereign Lord. The energy (*energeia*) for growth comes from God through Christ. Christ empowers the body to edify itself in love. Paul articulates the same truth in 1 Corinthians 3:6; "I planted, Apollos watered, but God was causing the growth." This truth should ban forever the popular refrain, "I can't," or, "We can't." The source of our empowering should rule out all timidity when it comes to ministry.

2. *Although the growth comes from God, every body member is fully involved in the process of growth.* How is supernatural empowering communicated in the daily working of the church? The supernatural work of God is communicated on earth "by that which every joint supplies." The joint in the human body works like a fulcrum to magnify and direct the energy supplied by the muscle. The muscle power for Christian ministry is supplied by the Holy Spirit, but the gifted member is the joint by which the power of the Holy Spirit is focused and applied to specific earthly tasks.

I remember my discovery of the power of a lever and fulcrum. As a young boy, Dad assigned me the task of removing a large stump from the ground. It had been cut free, but it remained in its hole. I was too small to remove it by direct force. After watching me struggle for most of the morning, Dad showed

> *The muscle power for Christian ministry is supplied by the Holy Spirit, but the gifted member is the joint by which the power of the Holy Spirit is focused and applied to specific earthly tasks.*

me how to multiply my effort through the use of a lever and fulcrum. It seemed almost magical that such a simple tool could have such a profound impact on my puny efforts. You are the fulcrum, the channel through which God desires to focus His divine power and apply it directly in the world today. Your gifts provide the lever for God's activity.

We have looked once at Paul's declaration in 1 Corinthians 3 about God's sovereign activity in growing the church. If we look again at that same passage, we will notice that Paul's teaching there is consistent with his conclusion in this passage. He declares that Apollos and Paul are servants through whom the Corinthians believed (3:5). They were God's conduit for the application of divine power. The one who plants the seed and the one who waters are one, and each will receive a reward for his or her labor. He then broadens the scope of his discussion beyond Apollos and himself by warning that each believer must be careful concerning the materials with which he builds because each man's work will become evident since the quality of his work will be tested by fire. We are important to the activity of God in our church and in our world, and one day we will be held accountable for how we have used the time, energy, influence, gifts, and money He has given us for the building of His kingdom. Christians do not have an option as to whether they build; they only determine the quality of the material with which they build.

3. *The unity of the Spirit is necessary for diversely gifted members to work together for a common goal.* The emphasis on "every," "each," and "proper working" stresses the demand for unity and mutual support in the use of spiritual gifts. Spiritual gifts make us dependent on God and interdependent with one another. One member working alone can accomplish little and soon becomes spiritually impoverished due to a lack of edification from other members of the body. On the other hand, when one member fails to function, the entire body is hampered in its kingdom impact.

4. *The proper implementation of the gifts must always take place in the context of love.* The gifted community is not only distinguished by its full possession of gifts through which divine power flows, but it is also marked by its divine character. If we recall the thrust of 1 Corinthians 13, we will remember that the fullest expression of any gift has no spiritual value when love is absent. For example, we might discover an individual who is a gifted teacher, but who does not love students and thus does not teach in the spirit of love. Little or no edification occurs in this loveless application of the gift of teaching, and thus there is no growth of the body.

A Brief Recap

Paul wrote Ephesians and Colossians as a positive deterrent against heretical teachings present in proconsular Asia. For that reason Paul focuses on the authority of Christ, declaring Him to be the fullness of God. In the Ephesian letter Paul focuses on the church since any attack on Christ would also be an attack on the church. The church is fully empowered through the resurrection and exaltation of Christ to express His fullness in the world.

In a manner consistent with 1 Corinthians 13 and Romans 12, Paul places the functioning of the gifts in the larger context of Christian unity. Gifts must be used for the good of the body in the context of love.

Paul once again insists that all believers are gifted. The exalted King is the one who gifts the believers and then, in turn, gifts the church with those gifted people.

Consistent with the lists included in 1 Corinthians 12:28 and Romans 12:6–8, Paul emphasizes leadership and service abilities. The focus once again is on those gifts that are more easily employed for the edification of the church.

Paul gives a clearer understanding of the working together of gifted leader and gifted member. The leaders are gifted to equip the saints for the work of ministry. In the context this suggests gift discovery and development.

Once again Paul makes clear that every member can and must contribute to the building up of the body. Gifted members enable the church to grow up into every aspect into Christ. Because of the unique situation created by the winds of heretical teaching, specific attention is given to the growth in doctrinal maturity that will allow Christians to withstand the trickery and cunning craftiness of false teachers.

The Lord fills the church, enabling it to express God's fullness in the world today, by giving it gifted members.

QUESTIONS FOR REFLECTION

1. Does this passage describe you and your church? How?
2. Are a few leaders doing most of the work, or are all members serving according to their unique giftedness? Are ministry needs going unanswered? What?
3. Is there an appreciation for diversity of gifts? Give examples to explain your answer?
4. Does your church have a common goal and a sense of unity? Is everyone striving for the growth of the body in love? Give examples of how unity might be improved.
5. But the answers to such general questions about the church can leave us in a personal comfort zone. What are you doing that promotes unity in diversity in your church?
6. What areas of training would you be open to that might help you to discover and develop your gifts?
7. What are you willing to do to become a conduit of divine power?

8 | Gifts and My Life
Removing the Fear and Confusion over Gifts

When we grasp the depth of God's love in the giving of the gifts, it will move us to greater levels of commitment and service. God has placed everything in heaven and earth under the feet of the ascended Lord for the empowering of the church. He accomplishes this empowering by presenting the church with gifted members who are thus privileged to join the King as He advances His kingdom on earth through His church. If you have accepted Christ as your personal Savior, you are one of those people included in God's plan for the advance of His kingdom until all the nations are presented with the truth that He is their rightful King.

My goal is to see believers energized, and dormant churches brought back to life. I pray that in our lifetime we will once again be accused of "turning the world upside down." I can hardly contain my excitement when I think about the potential that could be tapped if we took seriously the power made available to us through the resurrection of Christ and the gifting of the church.

In this final section I would like for us to look back over our gifts journey and remind ourselves of what we have learned. I want us then to apply these truths to our own lives and churches. Hopefully we will learn how to discover and use our gifts in the greatest venture on earth, a venture that enables us to touch the world and impact eternity.

A Low Altitude Flyover

When I was pastor of First Baptist, Norfolk, I had a friend who would take me flying in his small Cessna. Since the cabin was not pressurized, we had to fly at relatively low altitudes. I actually enjoyed this low-level flying because it gave me a good overview of the land and at the same time allowed me to see some of the details I might have missed while driving through the land. In previous chapters we have been involved in a study of the details of Paul's teaching in each of the particular gift passages. To follow our travel analogy, those chapters allowed us to walk the streets of each city with Paul. In this section we will fly back over those communities from a slightly higher vantage point and thus get an overview of Paul's teaching on gifts.

Thessalonica

I treat 1 Thessalonians 5 as one of the earliest community ministry passages in the New Testament. In this situation Paul does not use the term *charisma* but the ministry of leaders and laity is clearly in view. Paul desires to undergird the work of the true leaders to ensure for the continued growth and stability of this group of new believers in his absence. He insists that the leaders must be loved and esteemed for the sake of their work. We cannot forget that kingdom work is more important than our individual prejudices and the small issues that might divide us. Further, he indicates that the leaders must labor among, have charge over, and give instruction to the church at large.

The brethren, in turn, are to admonish, encourage, and help. They must exercise these functions with patience and an attitude that seeks the good of one another and all people. The ministry of the church must always be established in the context of love and mutual respect. While Paul does not include a listing of gifts, he does warn his readers not to quench the Spirit or despise prophetic utterance. Instead they are to examine everything carefully and hold to that which is good.

We find here several seminal ideas that will become central to Paul's more developed teaching on the gifted community in later passages. The emphasis on leaders, every member ministry, and a loving mutual concern that requires everyone work together for the good of the community are central to all of Paul's later teaching.

Corinth

Our low altitude look at Corinth will take a bit more flying time since Paul devotes three entire chapters to the issue of the gifted community. It is, therefore, apparent that the situation in Corinth required and allowed Paul to more fully develop many of the ideas already presented to the church in Thessalonica.

The term *charisma* (spiritual gifts) appears here for the first time. Its selection and use must be understood in the light of the historical situation presented by the Corinthian community. There are people in Corinth who consider themselves to be "spirituals" (*pneumatikoi*), and they fortify their claim by pointing to their miraculous abilities (*pneumatika*). They believe that these gifts, such as tongues and miracle-working faith, are evidence that they already reign. We refer to this false teaching as "overrealized eschatology." We see it in evidence in those who proclaim the health and wealth gospel in our day.

The word *eschatology* refers to the study of the end time. Those who have an overrealized eschatology believe they already have everything heaven has to offer while on earth. Thus they argue that all Christians should always be healthy and wealthy. Paul's first corrective is to substitute the term *charismata* for *pneumatika,* thus indicating that all "spiritual manifestations" are actually expressions of God's grace. A proper understanding of grace should eliminate all boasting and spiritual elitism. Further, he indicates that all ministry gifts are intended for the present age of the church and thus will cease when Christ returns. Thus, the possession of gifts actually proves that one is still earthly and thus not spiritual in the sense that they already reign.

To counter the childish spiritual arrogance of these spirituals, Paul makes clear that the Spirit is at work in *every* believer. He enables them to confess Jesus as Lord and baptizes them into one body. He argues that every believer has been given a manifestation of the Spirit for the good of the body and thus the unity of the body depends on the proper functioning of all members. The use of the imagery of the human body as a picture for the working of the Christian community occurs for the first time here and provides an unforgettable picture of the value of every diverse member of the body. The bottom line is that the Lord composes the body as He desires, placing each member in the body according to sovereign design. Paul also uses the body imagery to demonstrate that those members who, from a human standpoint appear to be less important, are in fact to be afforded greater honor.

This final point is clearly applied as Paul includes a second and broader list of gifts which includes ministries such as leadership, teaching, and service. He actually numbers the leadership functions to draw special attention to them. The concept of a gifted community does not negate the need for leaders. This gift list broadens the concept of what one might view to be a spiritual gift. Paul begins with leadership gifts and concludes with service abilities such as administration and helps. He does include two of the gifts from the first list to demonstrate that he does not discount the miraculous functions. From this point on Paul focuses on the use of intelligible gifts in the gathered assembly because they are better suited for edification of the body. In chapter 14 he contrasts two speech gifts—tongues and prophecy—and indicates a preference for prophecy based on its intelligibility. The discussion of these two gifts has implications for the mature believers' desire for gifts. The person marked by love seeks to abound for the edification of the church.

Chapter 13 is the apex of Paul's argument, and it redefines the spiritual man. If the possession of a certain gift does not indicate one is a spiritual, what does? The answer is love, the character of Christ manifested in one's life. The description of love in verses 4–7 is contrasted with the description of the "spirituals," which has emerged in the first eleven chapters of 1 Corinthians. Chapter 13 establishes the basis for insisting that truly spiritual believers would desire those gifts which most readily edify the body. Further, it allows Paul to establish the pattern for the use and control of all gifts. Love is expressed in the life of the community in terms of edification.

In the final verses of chapter 13 Paul establishes that gifts are intended for the church in the "present age" and thus have meaning now as they are used to edify, but they have no meaning or purpose in the age to come. Thus they have no sign value that one already reigns in a spiritual sense. This passage does not prove the cessation of gifts, as some argue. In fact, it asserts just the opposite. Gifts will continue throughout the age of the church. They will cease when the perfect—the coming of Christ and the culmination of His kingdom—comes. Then we will see face-to-face and know as fully as we have been known. Love is the one reality of the present that continues unabated into eternity, and thus we should seek and employ gifts to express love in the present.

Chapter 14 demonstrates how the spiritual person as redefined in chapter 13 will seek and use gifts. Spiritual gifts should be earnestly sought since they enable one to express love (in terms of edification) in the life of the community. By using prophecy and tongues in a representative fashion, Paul demonstrates a clear preference for intelligible gifts when the church is assembled. The gift of tongues, uninterpreted, fails to communicate to both believer and nonbeliever alike. When interpreted, tongues can be of value to the church. However, once spoken audibly, tongues may be offensive to the unbeliever and thus a deterrent to evangelism. Therefore, Paul instructs the one gifted in tongues to avoid the risk by giving only the intelligible interpretation. This would avoid any audible use of tongues and thus avoid the risk of offending the unbeliever. The totality of chapter 14 suggests that Paul believes tongues are of value to the individual and thus more suited for private practice than for ministry to the assembly.

Specific regulations for controlling the use of gifts are only found here and are best understood in light of the Corinthian difficulties. Paul's desire is to establish order on a broad basis that would be acceptable to all. He first appeals to God's nature: our God is not a God of confusion. When gifts are used based on love, they will not create confusion. The individual can and must control the use of personal gifts out of consideration for the good of the body. Nevertheless, Paul establishes external regulations designed to silence anyone, male or female, who is not concerned for the edification of the body.

Rome

Since Paul had not personally visited Rome, we can look at this passage as something like a control situation in an experiment. Paul's insistence on sober evaluation; edifying use of gifts; and the listing of leadership, teaching, and service gifts can best be explained in light of Paul's recent confrontations with the Corinthian spirituals. Paul knows that the central concepts related to spiritual gifts and the ministry of all believers is of value to every community, but he also wants to guard against an arrogant and exaggerated understanding of gifts like that of Corinth developing in other churches.

Because of the nonpolemic nature of Romans 12, several points stand out. The foundation for discovering and using gifts is the presentation of the body and transformation of one's thinking by the renewing of the mind. The individual, who surrenders himself to God and is being transformed through the renewal of the mind, is able to see himself from God's vantage point and thus understand his gifted potential. Paul establishes five fundamental principles related to gifts—sound judgment, universal giftedness, unity through diversity, interdependence, and the use of gifts for the common good. The absence of gifts such as tongues and miracle-working faith and the general nature of some of the gifts listed, showing mercy and giving, make clear that Paul wants his readers to seek gifts most suited to the edification of the body.

Proconsular Asia

The unique emphases in the Ephesian gift passage are explained by Paul's desire to protect the churches in proconsular Asia from the spread of heretical teachings. Paul begins with an emphasis on the worthy walk and unity. His description of the sevenfold bond of unity is one of the most powerful and beautiful passages in all of Scripture. Paul declares that the triumphant Christ, the Lord of the universe, gives gifts to people and then personally gifts the church with these people.

Paul emphasizes leadership and teaching gifts because of his desire to establish the authority of the individual leaders of these churches and to ensure doctrinal stability. Nonetheless, Paul clearly indicates that all members are gifted, and therefore the body depends on the proper working of each individual part. Paul gives close attention to the goal of the gifts, which is the building up or growth of the body. Because of the heretical winds blowing in proconsular Asia, he ties the ministry of the gifts to doctrinal maturity. This mature growth will prohibit believers from being blown about by every wind of doctrine.

A unique but key aspect of the Ephesian letter is the emphasis on the exalted Christ who now fills the church, enabling it to express God's fullness in the world today. Paul felt privileged to unveil the mystery of the church, which for ages had been hidden in God. Now it is clear that it was and is God's eternal purpose to reveal His manifold wisdom through the church to the rulers and authorities in the heavenly places. The exalted Lord enables the church to accomplish this kingdom-sized task by giving gifts to men and then giving them to the church.

An Overview of Pauline Gift Theology

Let's set aside for the moment the emphases and applications that are unique to specific historical situations and try to summarize Paul's teaching on spiritual gifts.

- Every Christian is empowered by the Spirit to confess "Jesus as Lord" and is incorporated into the body of Christ expressed through fellowship in a local community of believers.
- Every member of the body of Christ is gifted for service and must discover his or her gift(s) and use them for the edification of the body.
- The gifts are the consequence of God's grace. As such, they indicate nothing about the believer's spirituality, but they point to God's gracious intention to equip His body for service.
- Every believer has a unique and necessary function in the body. Therefore all members are necessary, and all depend on the ministry of others in the body. This interdependence makes essential that members care for one another.
- All community life must take place in the context of love, including the desire for and use of gifts.
- Gifts have as their single aim the edification of the body and the glorification of Christ through His church.

- Gifted leaders must be recognized, esteemed, and obeyed so that all members may function in the context of peace. Leaders are to equip other gifted members to develop and use their gifts so that together they may build up the body in every aspect into Christ.
- The church is empowered by its Head, and there is no appointed task it cannot accomplish. The Great Commission is not a suggestion but a command that must and will be completed as the church discovers its empowering and giftedness.
- The gift lists are not static but are always and only illustrative of the sort of functions one might accomplish for the church through the gifts of the Spirit. The Lord will gift His church to accomplish its mission in every setting and in every generation.

Why Gift Discovery Is So Important

You may still have some questions concerning the relative importance of spiritual gifts: If gifts are so important, why wasn't I taught about them earlier? Can I be a productive member of the body and not know my spiritual gift? I've done OK for all these years; why should I bother with gifts now? These are important questions, and we need to address them honestly.

Gifts Are Important because They Are Gifts from Our Gracious Father

Our loving Father would not give His children anything that is not essential to their spiritual development and His purpose for our lives. When Jesus encouraged His disciples to pray, He gave them this word of assurance: "Or what man is there among you who, when his son asks for a loaf, will give him a stone? Or if he asks for a fish, he will not give him a snake, will he? If you then, being evil, know how to give good gifts to your children, how much more will your Father who is in heaven give what is good to those who ask Him!" (Matt. 7:9–11). In Luke's Gospel, we find the same encouragement to pray, but with this conclusion: "How much more will your heavenly Father give the Holy Spirit to those who ask Him?" (Luke 11:13).

The Christian has no cause to fear the work of the Holy Spirit. God's desire in giving gifts is to enrich your life and enable you to join Him as He advances His kingdom through the church. Spiritual gifts are your spiritual heritage. God desires to give abundant life as He gifts you for service. Look on your gift as a personalized expression of God's grace.

Gifts Are Important because They Enable You to Join the Father in His Kingdom Activity

The last challenge and commission the Lord gave His earthly disciples is the Great Commission. "Go therefore and make disciples of all the nations, baptizing them in the name of the Father and the Son and the Holy Spirit, teaching them to observe all that I commanded you; and lo, I am with you always, even to the end of the age" (Matt. 28:19–20). It is almost too wonderful to think that God has enabled us to join Him in His work. Spiritual gifts are the individualized expression of God's grace enabling you to participate in taking the good news of the King to the ends of the earth. Our ignorance, apathy, or fear concerning spiritual gifts may be a chief cause of the church's failure to accomplish the Acts 1:8 mandate.

We regularly hear that only 20 percent of church members are actively involved in the ministries of the church. If that number is anywhere close to accurate, we should not be surprised to discover that more than two-thirds of churches are plateaued or declining while there is an unprecedented spiritual hunger worldwide.

Here's a simple example that will illustrate the impotence of the average church. In most churches only 50 percent of the members are active, which means they attend on a somewhat regular basis. Of that active group, only 50 percent will be present on a given Sunday. Only 20 percent of those attending on a given Sunday will actually participate significantly in the mission of the church.

What if you were a football coach who had one hundred players on the roster? Sounds encouraging, doesn't it? When it comes time to receive a uniform, only half show up. Fifty players, that's not too bad! We can still have a two-platoon system and men on the bench if anyone goes down. But we have a problem! Only half of those who were willing to take a uniform actually come to a given game. Actually we have a bigger problem! Only 20 percent of those who come to the game are willing to take the field. You do the math! We won't win many games with five active players. You may argue that a larger percentage of those who showed up for the game would be willing to play. Let's be generous and double that figure. Still not enough willing players to field an entire squad! How many churches do you know where the present facilities would actually hold all those whose names are on the role if everyone attended on the same Sunday?

I do not believe that the average church member is lazy or apathetic about fulfilling the Great Commission. I think our failure to discover and use our gifts accounts for much of the lack of involvement. Many members assume they can do little, if any, ministry tasks.

Spiritual Gifts Are Important because They Lead to Meaningful Membership in the Body of Christ

In elementary school I had a friend with six fingers on each hand. I thought it was pretty neat. Who couldn't use an extra finger once in a while? When I called attention to his cool finger, he was embarrassed. I later discovered that this finger was useless and made him feel strange. Do you ever feel like an extra and unnecessary appendage in your church?

Tragically, many people do, and it keeps them from purposeful involvement. Those who feel like a useless appendage will become less active until they finally drop out and quit attending any church. Listen again to this passage we studied from Paul's first letter to the Corinthians. "But now God has placed the members, each one of them, in the body, just as He desired" (12:18). Does "each one" include you? You are not in the body by accident. God put you into the body with His own purpose in mind. Discovering your gift will help you understand your purpose.

Spiritual Gifts Are Important because They Enrich Your Personal Life

You matter to God's kingdom. When you come to grips with this truth, it will change your life forever. You were created by God, redeemed by His Son, gifted and empowered by His Spirit to serve alongside Him in the advance of His kingdom. How does that make you feel about yourself?

In the tract "How to Be Filled with the Spirit," Dr. Bill Bright related the story of the discovery of the vast oil field known as the Yates Pool.

> During the depression this field was a sheep ranch owned by a man named Yates. Mr. Yates wasn't able to make enough on his ranching operation to pay the principal and interest on the mortgage, so he was in danger of losing his ranch. With little money for clothes or food, his family (like many others) had to live on government subsidy.
>
> Day after day, as he grazed his sheep over those rolling west Texas hills, he was no doubt greatly troubled about how he would pay his bills. Then a seismographic crew from an oil company told him there might be oil on his land. They asked permission to drill a wildcat well and he signed a lease contract.

At 1,115 feet they struck a huge oil reserve. The first well came in at 80,000 barrels a day. Many subsequent wells were more than twice as large. In fact, 30 years after the discovery, a government test of one of the wells showed that it still had the potential flow of 125,000 barrels of oil a day. And Mr. Yates owned it all! The day he purchased the land he had received the oil and mineral rights. Yet, he'd been living on relief. A multimillionaire living in poverty! The problem? He didn't know the oil was there, even though he owned it.

The story is one of those good news-bad news accounts. The good news is that Mr. Yates owned incredible resources. The bad news is that he spent most of his life in virtual poverty because he was unaware of the vast wealth just under the surface. Many Christians waste countless years because they don't know about the wonderful resources available to them through the Holy Spirit. I am not just talking about people who have dropped out of church because they didn't have a sense that they belong or can make any impact through the church. I am also talking about those who are serving out of a sense of duty but without an adequate understanding of their giftedness. Serving outside your area of primary giftedness can often lead to frustration and burnout.

Spiritual Gifts Ensure Diversity and Provide for Unity

Unity and diversity are not opposites but necessary companions. God gives unique and different gifts through the variety of members for the edification of the body. The diverse gifts enable one member to edify and encourage another. This, in turn, enables the church to grow in unity and in maturity. Since no one has all the gifts necessary to enable the body to grow, the members are interdependent. This interdependence creates the need for unity and provides the impetus to pursue it as a goal. Fellowship and unity are the foundation for the effective operation of the gifts. At the same moment, the full functioning of the gifts creates unity in the church.

Spiritual Gifts Provide for Doctrinal Stability

In Ephesians we discovered that the full operation of the gifts leads to growth, which is measured by the "stature which belongs to the fullness of Christ" (4:13). This level of maturity ensures that we will not be tossed by the waves and carried about by every wind of doctrine. Those involved in service through the church will have an appetite for God's Word. In the physical world exercise ensures a healthy appetite. The same is true in the spiritual realm. Thus the stability provided through accountability to other members of the body plus regular study of God's Word leads to doctrinal integrity.

Spiritual Gifts Are the Means by which the Exalted Lord Fills the Church

We often talk about God's empowering or building the church, but we seldom ask how such empowering occurs in the real life of my church. The answer is that He gifts members and then places those members in the body as He chooses. The Pauline letters have a consistent theme. You may recall our discussion of 1 Corinthians 3 where Paul identifies himself and Apollos as servants with different roles through whom God is building the church. In that same passage he exhorts each believer to be careful how he builds.

In our study of Ephesians, we discovered the incredible truth that everything accomplished in the death, resurrection, and exaltation of Christ was for the church, enabling it to express the fullness of God in the world today (Eph. 1:20–23). This ability to express God's fullness is provided to the church as the exalted Lord gives gifts to individuals and then places them in the church (Eph. 4:7–11). Perhaps you are thinking, *But I choose the church and the place of service.* Here is the great mystery: Behind our choosing is the sovereign activity of God working in the lives of surrendered believers. Paul could affirm that He redeemed us to accomplish good works "which God prepared beforehand so that we could walk in them" (Eph. 2:10), and "God has placed the members, each one of them, in the body, just as He desired" (1 Cor. 12:18). God redeems you and gifts you and gives you to the church to fill it with His fullness. Incredible, isn't it?

Why Such Confusion?

If the gifts are vital to the church, why do so few believers understand the role of gifts? Why do so few know how to identify their gifts? I have been able to identify at least three basic reasons for the lack of understanding and resulting confusion.

Failure to Study and Pray

Paul instructed Timothy: "Be diligent to present yourself approved to God as a workman who does not need to be ashamed, accurately handling the word of truth" (2 Tim. 2:15). This basic insight could be applied specifically to the matter of spiritual gifts. Many Christians have not been challenged to study the texts concerning gifts of the Spirit. In fact: Paul begins the discussion of gifts in 1 Corinthians with a statement of fact: "Now concerning spiritual gifts, brethren, I do not want you to be unaware" (12:1). The Corinthians, in their spiritual arrogance, thought they knew all there was to know about gifts, but such was not the case. They had actually limited the work of the Spirit to only a few miraculous gifts and had failed to understand that teaching or administration was equally supernatural. We seem to forget that every spiritual activity is by definition supernaturally empowered. Much confusion still exists because we have not been serious students of the Scriptures related to the issue of spiritual gifts.

Some of our failure to study may actually be related to the lack of materials on the subject until recent years. My dad was a Baptist pastor, and I grew up in the church. I cannot, however, remember a special study related to the topic of spiritual gifts. Further, the church and its members have been guilty of preferring pablum over meat when it comes to Bible study. We have often ignored in-depth Bible study that requires us to read, think, and process what we are reading. I commend you for your diligence in working through this book.

The insights learned through any Bible study are the result of prayer. When we study God's Word, we must consistently ask Him to reveal its meaning to us. Further, the key to understanding your gifts is to ask the Father who gives the gifts. He is the final authority on the matter. James encourages us: "But if any of you lacks wisdom, let him ask of God, who gives to all generously and without reproach, and it will be given to him" (1:5). Do you lack wisdom concerning your giftedness and your role in the body? Have you asked the author of the gifts? Maybe it is a simple case that we have not because we ask not.

Fears and Concerns

Charisphobia is the fear that you might become a charismatic or someone might accuse you of being one. Some believers fear that surrender to the Spirit will cause them to lose control, and so they ignore the topics of the Holy Spirit and the gifts. A fear of gifts has often been the result of an exaggerated emphasis on tongues, healing, or other visible gifts that have created confusion and church splits. One can understand how such a fear can develop when you have a repeat of the confusion created by the spirituals in Corinth. The solution for that is not to ignore the gifts but to provide balanced teaching as Paul did in the Corinthian letters.

Some Christian leaders and teachers discourage gift discovery because of some dangers inherent in the gifts. They speak of the confusion produced by false teaching on gifts and point to the rationalization that sometimes occurs on the part of believers because of the misapplication of gift teaching. For example, someone might argue that they don't witness because they don't have the gift of evangelism. Finally they fear the self-deception that occurs among believers about their giftedness. I have a great respect for many of these teachers, and I agree with many of their concerns and warnings. I do not think the solution to this problem is to ignore the doctrine of gifts and thus impoverish the church; it is to provide balanced biblical instruction.

I want to add several other warnings. I continue to see people who allow their gift to create a sense of spiritual elitism. Another concern I have has to do with the confusion caused by some gift lists that too closely link gifts and personality temperaments. I have had people excuse their offensive behavior based on a presumed spiritual gift. They argue that they are curt or rude because they are prophets. Our gifts should never be used to excuse our intolerance or lack of concern for another. Gifts are always exercised in the context of love.

While such fears of abuse and confusion are real, they must not deter us from seeking and using our gifts for the good of the body. If anyone might have had an excuse to ignore the topic of gifts, it would have been Paul after his encounter with the spirituals in Corinth. Yet he counters the confusion by insisting that the Corinthians seek the higher gifts, and he includes fundamental gift teaching in other letters where appropriate.

I pray that this book helps to eliminate any fear that would prohibit you from seeking to discover and employ your gifts. You do not have to speak in tongues to be filled with the Spirit. You do not have to lose rational control to minister through your giftedness. Paul insists that the individual can exercise control over his own gifts. My prayer is that you will follow Paul's advice and seek those gifts that will best enable you to serve Christ in the local church. You are the means by which the exalted Lord gifts His church, enabling it to express His fullness in the world today. Don't fear, your Father delights in giving good gifts.

The Fuzzy-Thinking Factor

Have you ever looked at an image through a lens where you couldn't adjust the focus, and thus it remained slightly fuzzy? The recent proliferation of literature on spiritual gifts has created a fuzzy image for some. Are all the gifts mentioned in the New Testament still operative today? How many spiritual gifts are there? If you have read extensively on the topic of gifts, you will find that some authors argue for nine gifts, others include eleven, fifteen, sixteen, twenty, or twenty-seven.

Often the differences are accounted for because some authors include only the gifts listed in a particular list such as the one in 1 Corinthians 12:28–29. Other writers include gift-like abilities found in the surrounding text such as hospitality and voluntary poverty. A few writers include Old Testament passages and thus include abilities related to craftsmanship and musical abilities.

I agree with those who include craftsmanship and musical abilities although they are not included on any New Testament list. The mention of the Spirit and the language of Exodus 31:3–5 confirms the conclusion that these are abilities enabled by the Spirit. "I have filled him with the Spirit of God in wisdom, in understanding, in knowledge, and in all kinds of craftsmanship, to make artistic designs for work in gold, in silver, and in bronze, and in the cutting of stones for settings, and in the carving of wood, that he may work in all kinds of craftsmanship." Musical ability is often mentioned in the Old Testament, particularly the Psalms, but New Testament passages such as 1 Corinthians 14:26 ("each one has a psalm") and Colossians 3:16 ("admonishing one another with psalms and hymns and spiritual songs") support the conclusion that abilities such as composing and singing should be included as gifts available to the church.

When we notice that musical abilities do not occur on a gift list, it should remind us that the lists are illustrative and not exhaustive. Further it should warn us to avoid the tendency to try to force the work of the Holy Spirit to conform to our own preconceived ideas. The freedom of the Holy Spirit to empower a craftsman to meet the needs of building the tabernacle or to provide the apostles for the foundational work of the church should remind us that the gifts are provided to enable the people of God in every generation to accomplish the task of advancing the kingdom and fully expressing God's fullness.

This insight leads to two observations. The question of whether a gift found in the New Testament still remains active today is better answered by the question of whether it is still needed by the church today. For example, we could thus conclude that the foundational role of apostolic witness to Christ no longer exists in the same manner that it did in the first century. This would indicate that revelation in the sense of Scripture is no longer needed since God spoke fully in His Son. Modern-day prophets who attempt to communicate any revelation that adds to Scripture are speaking by some other spirit. Some work of the Spirit may have greater relevance to churches in various parts of the world than in the Western world. For example, Muslims who come to Christ often relate visionary experiences. Stories of healing are more frequently reported in underdeveloped nations. I think we can trust God to be God and to provide for His church in every setting and in every generation.

A second observation relates to the sovereign freedom God has to provide new gifts to the church in every generation. Perhaps the reason craftsmanship gifts were not mentioned on any Pauline gift list is that the church of the first century did not need gifts related to construction of buildings. In the same manner, the church today may need gifts not needed in the first century. It should not surprise us that God would distribute new gifts today as the opportunities of ministry require them or that different gifts might be found in various locations or churches. The Holy Spirit is free to give gifts as He desires, and His purpose is to enable the church to fulfill the Great Commission.

To avoid the confusion created by the various gift lists, I have chosen not to give any such list in this book. If you think such a list might be helpful to you, you can make one of your own by looking at the lists in the New Testament or you find other books that will provide such lists.[1] Use a gift list to assist you in discovering your gift if you find that it is helpful, but don't limit the Holy Spirit's creative work in your life. If you find that your passion and gift do not appear on any list, don't let that disturb you. Just thank God for your gift and ask Him how to employ it for the advance of His kingdom.

One other issue has created some fuzzy thinking as it relates to gifts is their relationship to "natural talents." Must our spiritual gift be a unique ability given after conversion with no connection to the talents that were part of us when we became Christians?

Spiritual Gifts and Natural Talents

Have you ever wondered how spiritual gifts are related to natural talents? Many authors argue that there is no relationship between gifts and natural talents. Peter Wagner, for example argues that we can't view gifts as "souped-up" talents.[2] I find the question of the relationship between the two an intriguing one in terms of both Scripture and actual experience.

It is possible that many people are not involved in meaningful service because they think their spiritual gift must be a totally new ability that is unrelated to any ability or experience prior to conversion. Yet I have met few people who give testimony to having received a totally new ability after conversion that is completely discontinuous with abilities possessed before conversion. If for the moment we set aside the more ecstatic gifts such as tongues and miracle-working faith, this would be true a great majority of the time.

We may have created confusion about spiritual gifts by distinguishing between natural and supernatural in the same way we do between secular and sacred. For the believer secular does not exist; everything for us is sacred. Thus we may ask about the author of natural talents—our birth gifts. Did Mother Nature create these abilities we call natural talents? Of course not. Mother Nature does not exist. God the Creator is the source of everything, including all our talents. The Bible indicates that God knit us together in our mother's womb (Ps. 139:13) and shaped us from birth (Isa. 44:2).

If we can agree that God is the source of all ability, why would it surprise us to discover that we were created with unique birth gifts that would someday enable us to serve God? Paul states, "For we are His workmanship, created in Christ Jesus for good works, which God prepared beforehand so that we would walk in them" (Eph. 2:10). If the good works we are intended to accomplish were prepared beforehand, is it not reasonable to think that we were created with these good works in view. Jeremiah, the Old Testament prophet, declared that before he was born the Lord knew him, consecrated him, and appointed him as a prophet (Jer. 1:2). Our birth gifts are transformed at conversion in the same manner as our physical bodies, enabling our bodies, including our birth gifts, to be used as instruments of righteousness (Rom. 6:12–13).

Before we proceed, you should know that I agree with those who insist that spiritual gifts are reserved for Christians. The unregenerate person has no part in the Spirit and thus has no comprehension of his or her spiritual potential. Such a statement does not exclude the fact that spiritual gifts and birth gifts may be related. I further agree that spiritual gifts are not energized or souped-up natural talents; they may, however, be birth gifts that have been transformed by the Spirit. I believe that most people will discover that their spiritual gift is consistent with their birth gift and thus they should explore their interests, talents, and passion to discover how they can best serve God.

For the sake of clarity let me break this into seven component parts.

1. We are created by God with unique purpose and design.
2. Our life experiences and opportunities become a part of God's benevolent gift to us that shapes our entire person.
3. At some point we experience spiritual birth which is accompanied by the transformation of our bodies, enabling all the members of our body to be of use in kingdom service (Rom. 6:12–13). Birth gifts may become spiritual gifts.
4. With conversion our spiritual blindness is removed, and we receive the Spirit so that we may know the things freely given to us by God (1 Cor. 2:12).

5. As believers we present our bodies to the Lord as a living sacrifice, acceptable to God, as our spiritual service of worship (Rom. 12:1).

6. The empowering of the Spirit transforms all of our abilities and life experiences, enabling us to serve God effectively.

7. We can now accomplish the good works God prepared for us before we were conceived.

Some of the ideas presented above are new and may need further explanation. Let's look briefly at Romans 6:12–13: "Therefore do not let sin reign in your mortal body so that you obey its lusts, and do not go on presenting the members of your body to sin as instruments of unrighteousness; but present yourselves to God as those alive from the dead, and your members as instruments of righteousness to God." At birth we receive our physical bodies as a gift from the Creator. Because of the spiritual blindness caused by sin, we may allow our bodies and its members to be used as instruments of unrighteousness. When we become Christians, the Spirit gives life to our mortal bodies, making them capable of service to God as instruments of righteousness. For example, the tongues and hands we now possess are the same ones we possessed before conversion but with a radical difference—they have been transformed by the Spirit. For that reason the members of our bodies can and must be given to God in service.

We have already discussed the importance of spiritual understanding in the discovery and use of gifts, but let's look at this step again in the context of gifts and talents. In 1 Corinthians 2:9 Paul declares that man has no concept of all that God has prepared for those who love Him. But conversion is accompanied by the reception of the Spirit who searches out the deep things of God (2:10). "Now we have received, not the spirit of the world, but the Spirit who is from God, so that we may know the things freely given to us by God" (2:12). The spiritual man is now able to discern the gracious quality of all of life. In 1 Corinthians 4:7 Paul, combating spiritual arrogance, pointedly asks, "What do you have that you did not receive?" Paul begins the section on gifts in the letter to the Romans with the same emphasis: "Be transformed by the renewing of your mind, so that you may prove what the will of God is" (Rom. 12:2).

Now that believers have come to understand the gracious nature of all of life, they present their entire being as an act of worship to God. Paul begins the gift passage in Romans 12:1–8 with the injunction, "Present your bodies a living and holy sacrifice, acceptable to God, which is your spiritual service of worship." Because of the transformation that occurs in conversion, the gift of our bodies is now acceptable to a Holy God.

The transformation of our bodies includes all our birth gifts and life experiences. This gift of oneself back to God is our "spiritual service of worship" (Rom. 12:1). Spiritual gifts are the abilities that enable us to serve God while in this physical body. Just as the Spirit transforms and energizes our physical bodies, He transforms and energizes all our abilities in such a manner that we can legitimately refer to them as spiritual gifts. This energizing of our bodies is accomplished by the infilling of the Spirit (Eph. 5:18). Thus we must continuously surrender our total selves to Him for service. When properly understood as the gracious gift of God and surrendered to Him in service, our gifts and abilities enable us to accomplish service already declared acceptable. What an incredible God! He creates us, redeems us, transforms us, and declares that our service to Him through our gifts is acceptable.

Let's think about a few possible examples. A teacher and a gifted musician begin to attend church. They hear God's Word and are converted. As they grow in understanding, they develop the desire to serve the Lord through His church. Further, the Spirit teaches them that their ability to teach and produce music is a gift of God and as such should be offered back to Him as an act of spiritual service. We should affirm these persons in their giftedness and encourage them to serve the body of Christ through their spiritual gifts.

You may ask if their teaching or singing is any different when understood and used as a spiritual gift. The answer is a resounding yes! First the purpose is different. They now sing or teach to edify the body and serve the King. This will mean that both the intent and the content are different. Second, the empowering in the use of their gift and its impact are different. They teach or sing with the empowering of the Spirit, and thus their gift has a supernatural impact. Finally, the end result is different. People will glorify the King and not applaud the instrument being used. When a talent is used, it glorifies the individual whereas when a spiritual gift is employed, it glorifies the Giver.

We might think of the apostle Paul who, as the chief of sinners, led others to join him in persecuting the church. Once saved, Paul's powerful personality, tenacious spirit, and gift to mobilize people for a cause were transformed and empowered by the Spirit.

> *When a talent is used, it glorifies the individual whereas when a spiritual gift is employed, it glorifies the Giver.*

This enabled him to lead others in a church planting movement of unparalleled proportions. Every aspect of Paul's experience, personality, and ability was transformed and thus became useful to God. *God wastes nothing!*

A couple of words of balance are necessary. I am not suggesting that God cannot give new gifts that have no relationship to our life or experience before redemption. He is God and is sovereignly free to gift us as He desires. Each of us should remain open to any new gift that God desires to give because He only gives good gifts. As I have indicated, most people will find that their spiritual gifts correspond to abilities given by God at birth. This is a both/and situation and not an either/or situation. Spiritual gifts may be both new abilities given after conversion and talents possessed prior but transformed through conversion.

You may be asking when a birth gift becomes a true spiritual gift. Good question and let's answer it by using TRUE as an acrostic. *Transformation* of the entire person occurs at redemption. This transformation includes birth gifts. *Recognition* of our spiritual giftedness is made possible by the Holy Spirit who now resides within us. *Use* of this gift is for the good of the body and the glory of the Lord. *Energization* for spiritual impact is accomplished by the infilling of the Holy Spirit. When these four criteria exist, we have a TRUE spiritual gift.

A Brief Look at Service through Gifts and Abilities

What if an individual is a member of the church but has never been truly converted and transformed? This person is attempting to employ natural talents to perform a spiritual or supernatural endeavor. This is like using a water pistol in a gun fight. It will ultimately lead to personal frustration and often to church dissension. For example, we might have a CPA who is an excellent accountant. He joins the church but is not actually born again. He wants to be of use to the church and becomes involved on the finance committee. His abilities make him a valuable member until one evening the committee is called upon to exercise faith as well as accounting sense. The man is perplexed because the discussion of faith seems unreasonable. He is still thinking with a natural mind uninformed by the Spirit and using a natural talent that has not been transformed. It is unwise and dangerous to give a ministry role to a person who has not been converted.

Another scenario could depict an individual, let's say a musician, who has been converted and has come to understand that his ability is a gift from God.

One Sunday he is called upon to sing a solo. In a moment of spiritual immaturity and pride, he seizes the moment to display his ability rather than to edify the body. He is using his gift without the infilling of the Spirit. The results of such activity will be carnality and spiritual arrogance. In this case the use of a spiritual gift will not result in edification but rather will lead to fruitless activity and may actually create dissension in the body. Corinth provides a clear example of a community where some members were using spiritual gifts in human strength and for personal gain. Their motivation was to be seen or heard.

The Lord desires that each believer offer himself fully to God and use his gifts with the infilling of the Spirit for the good of the body. This will result in the unity of the body, the edification of the church, and the glory of God as His kingdom is advanced. In our next section we will look at biblical and practical steps to assist you in discovering and developing your gifts.

A Brief Recap

We began with a brief review of all the gift passages we have studied together and then looked at an overview of Pauline gift theology. You may want to review the nine summary statements on gift theology.

We established that gifts are important for numerous reasons related both to the individual and to the ministry of the church. Thus gifts cannot be ignored since they are an expression of the Father's love and crucial to His plan for the advance of His kingdom.

We looked at issues that have caused both confusion and fear as they relate to spiritual gifts and attempted to answer those concerns from a biblical standpoint.

A major area of confusion is related to the relationship between natural talents and spiritual gifts. We concluded that talents are birth gifts from the Father and are often the area in which we will discover our giftedness. You might want to review the seven component parts of how a birth gift is transformed into a spiritual gift (see page 185). It remains possible for the Father to give us new gifts as the church has need of them.

We discovered that God may distribute the gifts differently in different churches and in different parts of the world. We can trust God to provide everything that is necessary to enable His church to complete His Great Commission.

Questions for Reflection

1. Look back at the overview of Pauline gift theology and write them in your own words.
2. In your opinion which is the most critical reason gift discovery is important for you and your church?
3. Do you still have any fears or reservations about asking the Father to reveal your gift(s) to you? What are they?
4. Is there an ability that you have always listed under "natural ability" that might be your area of spiritual giftedness?

9 | Discovering and Developing Your Gifts

The Process of Gift Discovery and Deployment

We have carefully examined the biblical texts concerning spiritual gifts, and now let's put together the last few pieces of our puzzle and complete the picture. You may already be involved in serving God through your gifts, but you have a hunger to know if you can serve Him more effectively by developing your gifts. Some readers, however, may still be looking for help in discovering their gifts. We will now look together at some guidelines for gift discovery and development.

Most people will find that there are four distinct steps in the process: (1) discern, (2) surrender/empower, (3) develop, and (4) employ. The following discussion will clarify each step. Let me encourage you not to rush through this section or the process of discovery. Be patient and allow the Holy Spirit to reveal Himself to you, and in so doing, He will make you aware of your unique giftedness. Our greatest desire is to know the Giver and not just to discover our gifts.

I have taken for granted a few fundamentals that we need to review before we embark on the discovery process. You must be a Christian to possess and use spiritual gifts. Being a Christian doesn't mean belonging to a church or denomination; it means belonging to God. To become a Christian we must be born again by the Spirit of God. To do that you must agree with God about your sin problem, willingly turn from your sin, and acknowledge Jesus as your personal Savior. If you are not certain that you have made such a commitment, turn to the Appendix and allow the Holy Spirit to guide you.

You must trust the Holy Spirit to give you good gifts. You have no need to approach this process with fear. Rather, you should have joyous anticipation, knowing that the Father created you uniquely for Himself. You must desire to know and to use your gift in service. God is not interested in satisfying our curiosity; He wants to enable us to become all He intended us to be. He wants us to join Him in advancing His kingdom. This is a good time for a motive check. Why do you want to discover your gift?

The Process of Discovery

We have looked at 1 Corinthians 2:9–16 on several different occasions. You might want to read it once more from your own Bible. Paul begins with the assurance that God has prepared for us things too wonderful for natural man to conceive. The natural man will never understand them, but the spiritual man can know them because he has received the Holy Spirit. God wants you to understand your gifted place in the body, and He alone can reveal that to you. I will give you several practical ideas for hearing God speak, but I want to be both clear and candid—only the Holy Spirit can reveal your gift.

You may be wondering if this study will include a gift survey to assist you. The answer is yes and no. I will include what I refer to as an "open-ended" gift survey. It does not include a list of specific gifts with several questions about each, but rather it includes questions related to the needs of your church, the passion of your heart, and the activities that bring you fulfillment.

I have not found traditional gift surveys to be helpful for several reasons. First, some Christians have used them as a shortcut to gift discovery. This has caused them to ignore the role of concerted prayer. Seek the Giver, not the gift, and you will not be disappointed. Second, a survey which has a set number of gifts may cause you to overlook gifts not included on a particular survey. Surveys are designed based on a selected number of gifts. That list will necessarily reflect the conclusions of the person designing the list. Every list has a static quality and thus does not have any place for new gifts God may be giving His church to enable it to accomplish its mission in its unique context. Third, the use of a survey may cause the user to practice a subtle form of "gift projection." It is usually not difficult to tell which gift, from a set list, is being treated by a particular question. Therefore, if you desire a certain gift, you can answer the questionnaire in such a manner to score high in that particular gift.

I have found myself doing the same thing on personality or leadership inventories. I answer questions thinking about how I would like to respond or lead in a given situation. I am projecting my desired style onto the inventory. In the same manner it is possible to take a gift inventory and discover that we score high in the area of our *desired giftedness* rather than our *actual giftedness*.

Some Christians have found that surveys have been helpful to them. A survey can work like an aptitude test administered by a guidance counselor. That is, it can provide helpful suggestions. If you choose to supplement the material I give you with such a tool, approach it as a prayer guide, answer honestly, and be willing to allow the Holy Spirit to direct you to gifts outside the inventory.

1. *Place a priority on Prayer.* James 4:2 tells us: "You do not have because you do not ask." Is it possible that you have never asked God to reveal your giftedness? So why not ask Him right now? However, you shouldn't rush the process. Keep on asking, keep on seeking, keep on knocking, and claim the promise that He will answer. I am saddened to discover that many Christians would rather spend thirty minutes filling out a gift inventory than thirty minutes talking with their Father about their giftedness. In our world of instant gratification, we want answers right now. Enjoy your time with God; seek the Giver and not the gift.

If you have been asking and you are still unsure, you might want to do a motive check. James 4:3 says, "You ask and do not receive, because you ask with wrong motives, so that you may spend it on your pleasures." Are you seeking to know your gifts so that you can become more effectively involved in kingdom activity, or are you looking for a spiritual prize? Be transparent as you talk with your Father; He knows your thoughts and intents. Ask Him to give you a pure heart and the desire to edify the body through your giftedness.

2. *Consider the needs of your kingdom community.* We know that the purpose of the gifts is to enable us to advance God's kingdom activity through the church, and further we know that He has placed us in the body as He chose. Thus, it seems obvious that a primary clue concerning our giftedness is the ministry needs of our own church. In fact, I believe that this may be the clearest indicator of one's giftedness. God's desire in giving the gifts is not to exalt our ego but to edify His body. Have you ever noticed that if you ask several people about the greatest need of the church, you will receive several different answers? Do you know why? We tend to see our church's needs through the lens of our own giftedness.

As you pray, you can ask yourself several questions: What area of need in my church causes me the greatest concern? What one need continues to surface in my prayer time? What do I see God doing in and through my church? God generally distributes gifts consistent with His present activity. When we discover God's activity, we put ourselves in proper position to discover our gifts.

Ask the Father to allow you to join Him in His activity and to use you to meet a particular need, and you will likely discover your gift.

3. *Look carefully at your passion.* What would you like to do to advance the kingdom through your church if there were no boundaries? You don't have to fit any preexisting slots for service such as those opportunities listed in the church bulletin or on the Web site. In one church, after I preached a message on discovering your gifts through the understanding of your passion, a lady caught me in the hallway after the service. Excitedly she asked, "Were you serious about your message?" "Yes," I replied, a little cautiously. "Good," she responded, "I resign." Seeing my absolute confusion and panic, she explained. "I have been the head of the preschool for years, but I have always wanted to teach the handicapped. I'll finish the year in preschool, but with your blessing I want to start a class for people who are handicapped." She did just that, and our church was recognized for having one of the first classes for people who have handicaps in Virginia.

In another church setting I was visiting a young couple who had been considering First Baptist. After hearing their personal testimonies, I asked them; "If the Lord were to place you in First Baptist, what would you most like to do to serve Him?" I assured them that they didn't have to fit any of our slots in the Sunday school organization or the choir. She hesitated before she spoke. "If I tell you my real passion, you will laugh," she said. I assured her I would never do that. She finally indicated that she was a drama major in college and that she had always wanted to use that gift for the Lord. I could hardly believe my ears. We had several people who had indicated their desire to be trained in drama, but we had no one gifted to lead them. We had been praying for God to provide someone with her gifts. Isn't God good? He is always on time, and He gives us a passion commensurate with our gift(s).

4. *Look for fulfillment.* Many Christians labor under the misconception that if they are doing the will of God they must be miserable. When I was a youth, I was convinced that if I ever fully surrendered my will to God's will, He would send me to deepest Africa where I would live in a mud hut, fend off snakes, and eat rotten monkey meat. My overactive childhood imagination had been fueled by too many missionary stories from Africa. Nevertheless, my childhood fear was real and expressed the concern that serving God must be laborious and painful or it isn't true service. Let's be honest; some of our service in any area is demanding, and some things we do in ministry we do out of obedience. Yet our service to the Lord through our gifts should be fulfilling and invigorating.

Many Christians who experience burnout do so because they are serving in areas where they are not gifted.

In my own ministry I find fulfillment through my preaching ministry. I enjoy everything about the preaching task from the preparation to the delivery. Throughout my ministry I have been called on to preach multiple times each Sunday and each week. When I completed three messages on a Sunday morning, I was physically spent, but I was also fulfilled by the use of my gift. Counseling is another matter altogether. After a couple of hours of heart-wrenching counseling, I am ready for the sauna. That's not my gift. By the way those missionaries I mentioned who told the stories about fending off the snakes were joyous because they were fulfilled in their gifted ministry.

5. *Listen for honest affirmation.* Many times the Holy Spirit will use the affirmation of other believers to assist you in discovering your gifts. As you pray for discernment, think about the times when someone has indicated that an action of yours has ministered to them. It may have been when you sang a solo, took them a meal, or sent them a note. It might also be helpful to seek the counsel of your pastor or a mature Christian friend. Explain that you have been earnestly seeking to find your place in the body and then ask them if they have seen any areas of giftedness in you. The counsel of friends should then be confirmed by the Holy Spirit as you pray.

6. *Try several areas of ministry.* If you are still struggling to find your place of service in the body, experiment with several areas of ministry. I am sure there are people who will allow you to serve alongside them for a short time to see if God gives you a passion and a gift for the particular area of ministry. If you think about it, experimentation is the way we discover other areas of interest and ability. For example, you might not have known that you had an aptitude for cooking, art, or gardening if you had never attempted those activities. Try several areas of ministry in your church and seek confirmation from the Holy Spirit.

Here are a few clues that may help you determine your gift through service. Am I effective in this area of ministry? Have others affirmed me in what I am doing? Do I find fulfillment? Am I thinking about the needs of those I am serving throughout the week? Don't be discouraged if you don't discover your gift the first time. It may take several attempts before you find your place. In the meantime, you will be making new friends in the church and growing in your relationship with your heavenly Father.

7. *Fill out the inventory.* I promised to provide an open-ended survey that might help in gift discovery. As indicated earlier, our God is infinitely creative

and is thus capable of granting new gifts for kingdom activity. At times our gifts are latent and lay just below the surface of our consciousness simply waiting for us to unearth and develop them. Some people discover that what they have considered to be a natural talent is in truth a birth gift from God. Through the process of conversion and the filling of the Holy Spirit, these birth gifts can be used for service to the King. You must only present them to the King for His service and allow Him to produce results through you.

You could fill out the survey in a matter of minutes, but I warn against rushing through the process. Get a piece of paper and view this as a prayer guide.

The Open-ended Survey

1. What do you perceive to be the greatest need of the church?
2. If there were no barriers and no ministry slots to fill in your church, what would you most like to do to advance the kingdom of God?
3. What do you do that encourages others?
4. In what areas of service do you find satisfaction, fulfillment, and energy?
5. What ministry area generates the greatest sense of enthusiasm and excitement?
6. List things you have done that have caused people to say, "You do that well," or, "You ministered to me."
7. What area(s) of service do you think about when you are talking to your heavenly Father about the needs of the Christian community?
8. Which training classes have created the most interest for you?
9. List areas of service you have attempted, and ask yourself which seemed most comfortable to you.
10. What needs do you see in your own church or community that aren't being met? Which one causes you greatest concern?
11. Do you find yourself praying regularly for a particular need? What need?
12. What birth gifts do you have that could allow you to meet these needs?
13. Are you willing to surrender any and all abilities the Spirit reveals to you to the Lord? Are you open to training opportunities to develop your gifts?
14. If you are still struggling to list gifts and abilities that you might use for the kingdom, ask the Holy Spirit to give you the ability necessary

to meet the unique need that most burdens you. Find a prayer and accountability partner to pray with you.

A Final Word on Discovery

Now that you have finished reading the section on gift discovery and working through the discovery process, you may be somewhat unsure of how to proceed. You may be thinking that nothing has happened or that you don't feel any different. If you were expecting an overwhelming ecstatic experience, you may be disappointed. We can't live our Christian lives based on experiences and feelings; we live them based on God's Word. Moments of ecstasy do occur in the spiritual life, but they are given according to God's design and usually have little to do with our giftedness for service.

If you are still unsure of your gift, enjoy the journey and begin immediately with the experimentation process. Ask leaders in your church to suggest areas where you might get involved in the ministry of your church. As you serve in different capacities, ask God to confirm for you the area of your giftedness.

For example, people may say, "You have the ability to make everyone feel at home." That may be a hint that your area of giftedness would enable you to serve as a hostess or greeter in your small group. Maybe your gentle way and warm smile are just what a nervous guest needs while trying to find a seat for the first time.

We have already established that God can transform and empower birth gifts into spiritual gifts for service. Perhaps you have a real gift for sewing. Most churches are looking for people who can make banners or help with costumes for a Christmas play. Perhaps you could even make clothes for your benevolent ministry. For the artistic person, how about set design for a play or improvement of the church Web site? What ministries are available for those with technical skills? Have you considered running a soundboard? Do you enjoy working with children? I know your church can provide training that will help you develop the gift to work with young people. If you have a gift of organization, you could put it to use organizing babysitters for single moms.

If you are an idea person who is not good with the details, I have good news. For every idea person there will always be detail-loving people with strong administrative gifts who will be thrilled to put flesh on your ideas. That is the value of the diversely gifted body. I am one of those idea people, and I have been privileged to work with many detail people in the local church, the seminary, and now the Executive Committee of the Southern Baptist Convention.

Do you see a need in your church that is not being addressed? Perhaps the Lord has gifted you to be a pioneer in a new ministry area. Tell the pastor and key lay leaders about your concern and your willingness to serve in this new ministry.

If you are not comfortable standing before a group and talking but you love to express yourself on paper, consider starting a newsletter or helping with an existing one. Offer to write for the church Web site. I once had a lady in the church who could find grammatical errors on nearly every page of our newsletter. She had a habit of circling them in red and delivering her edited copy to the secretary. I suggested that it might be more productive if she agreed to proof the newsletter before it went to press. Thus she could use her gift for edification.

Are you the kind of person who has a list for everything? Your administrative prowess could be used in numerous areas of service. Consider volunteering to assist in the office during the week. Small groups within the church are always in need of people who can keep an accurate record of class members while juggling guest slips. You may be thinking that this is not an important task. I beg to differ! Many people are spiritually wounded because they had needs that went undetected precisely because no one noticed when they began to be chronic absentees.

If you love to make a joyful noise unto the Lord but you confine your singing to the shower, why not consider the music ministry? It doesn't matter that you are not a soloist; not everyone in a praise group or choir needs to be a soloist.

The river of possibilities for gifted service is endless. Do not fear! God has given you a life raft of His assurance. Every believer is gifted, and if you use your lifeline of prayer, He will never let you drown in the pond of confusion in your search to discover your gift. He desires the best for His children. He loves you so much that even before you were born He prepared the good works you were to accomplish. He created, redeemed, and empowered you for service to Him that He has already declared acceptable.

The Process of Surrender and Empowerment

How does the filling of the Holy Spirit relate to the discovery and deployment of gifts? That is a great question which is not often treated by many who write on gifts. I hope these few paragraphs will help you to understand why you must continually ask the Spirit to fill you with His presence.

First, let me assure you that God withheld nothing of the Spirit from you when you were converted. You do not need a "second work of grace" or a "baptism of the Spirit." You were baptized by the Spirit the moment you were saved. The Holy Spirit both convicts and converts (John 16:8, 13). He baptizes or assimilates us into the body (1 Cor. 12:13). The terminology *baptism of the Spirit* should always be related to the discussion of conversion. The baptism of the Spirit describes the process of conversion and immersion of the believer into the life of Christ and His body, the church. It is possible that you may not have appropriated all of the resources provided by the Spirit simply because you have not been taught how to do so. In other cases, persons have been reluctant to surrender to the infilling of the Spirit because of some preconceived notion of what might occur at that moment of surrender.

Second, the infilling of the Spirit is not a once-for-all-time experience; it is a daily process of surrender and infilling. In Ephesians 5:18–19 Paul writes, "And do not get drunk with wine, for that is dissipation, but be filled with the Spirit, speaking to one another in psalms and hymns and spiritual songs, singing and making melody with your heart to the Lord." When one is drunk with wine, his behavior is altered. It may cause a person to be overbearing, rude, or even belligerent. In contrast to the filling with wine, the infilling of the Spirit should alter a believer's behavior in a positive way. The infilling of the Spirit enables the believer to live joyously and edify others.

> *The baptism of the Spirit describes the process of conversion and immersion of the believer into the life of Christ and His body, the church.*

The Greek word translated "be filled" literally means "to fill to the full." In other words the Holy Spirit fills our life to the very top so that nothing is wanting in the measure of our spiritual fullness. Do you remember the emphasis on "fullness" in the Colossian and Ephesian letters? You may recall that Paul indicates that Jesus is the "fullness" of God (Col. 1:19). In Ephesians Paul teaches us that everything accomplished through Christ was done so that the church might be "the fullness of Him who fills all in all" (1:23). The church becomes what it was intended to be when its gifted members are continually filled by the Spirit.

You may have noticed that I have used the expression "continually filled." The verb is a present passive imperative. The present tense emphasizes the continuous nature of the activity. It is not a one time event but a moment-by-moment surrender of ourselves to the control and empowering of the Holy Spirit. The passive voice indicates that we are the recipients of the activity of the Holy Spirit and as such we are to surrender ourselves to His control. The imperative indicates that this is not a suggestion or an option to Christian living; it is a command and a necessity. We can accomplish *nothing* for God apart from His Spirit. This is not an option because the fullness of the body is dependent on the infilling of the members!

When you read the biographies of great Christian leaders, you will find that all will refer to a time when they fully surrendered themselves to God's purpose and power. They may use different language to refer to this event, but all alike have a point of reference when they surrendered themselves fully to the work of the King and were filled up with the Spirit. They began to walk in the Spirit and to serve in the power of the Spirit. The infilling of the Spirit is a must for every believer who desires to use his or her gift in service to the King.

Have you ever heard someone talking about another person preaching or teaching with "unction"? That word may be a little dated for some. Have you heard someone refer to a musician being "anointed" or "empowered"? Perhaps you have commented on a sermon or song that "blessed" you. All of these expressions point to the use of gifts in full surrender to the Holy Spirit. The lack of the constant infilling of the Holy Spirit explains why we can serve in the area of our giftedness with little or no impact.

Perhaps the idea of "being filled with the Spirit" is new to you. It should not be feared but sought. Our Father knows how to give only good gifts (Matt. 7:11). "Being filled" is simply a daily, or moment-by-moment, process of surrender and appropriation of the Spirit's presence and provision. Remember the Holy Spirit came to indwell you the moment you received Christ. "Your body is the temple of the Holy Spirit" (1 Cor. 6:19). He indwells us as our new manager and desires to control and empower us. He desires to keep our old sin nature at bay. Because the old nature wants to reestablish the rule of our own flesh and natural desires, we must volitionally allow the Spirit to animate our physical bodies.

Let me suggest a simple three-step process. (1) Because you cannot personally defeat the old nature, you must daily agree with God about your sin (confess) and then turn from that sin (repent). You might want to compare this act with the process of exhalation. We breathe out by agreeing with the

Father about our sin. This process allows God "to cleanse us from all unrighteousness" (1 John 1:9). We cannot be full of sin and the Spirit at the same moment. (2) Once we have thoroughly completed this act of confession, we must ask the Father to fill us once again. Some people like to make this act more specific by asking God to fill their minds, their tongues, their eyes, and their hands as they move through the members of the physical body that can be used by the adversary or by the Spirit. This is sometimes likened to the process of inhalation. You are now breathing in the life-giving power of the Spirit. (3) Finally, you must present yourself (your very body) to your new manager (Rom. 6:13). The Spirit doesn't infill you to amuse you but to use you. This process should be repeated each morning and at any moment during the day when you discover that sin has separated you from the presence of the Father and the empowering of the Spirit.

Unless we are filled with the Spirit and walk daily under the control of the Spirit, we will not function according to our gifted potential. When we attempt to control our fleshly desires or minister in our own strength, we will always be frustrated and impotent. In a carnal or sinful state we are often tempted to use our bodies and our gifts for our own purposes rather than for the edification of the body.

The constant infilling of the Spirit provides the supernatural empowering for the effective use of our gifts and keeps us focused on their proper use for the edification of the body. The Holy Spirit produces both the fruit of the Spirit (Gal. 5:22–24), enabling us to exhibit Christ's character, and the gifts of the Spirit, enabling us to serve in His body. For that reason the Spirit-filled person will always desire and use gifts to edify the body and glorify Christ.

> *For that reason the Spirit-filled person will always desire and use gifts to edify the body and glorify Christ.*

If you have never actually asked God to fill you with His Holy Spirit, why not stop and follow these simple steps. Ask the Holy Spirit to reveal all sin and then agree with God about your sin and joyfully turn from it. Ask God to fill you with His Spirit. Present your body to Him in service. Listen to His voice as He guides you throughout the day and shows you opportunities to join the King in His activity. You are not seeking a mystical experience, but you are obeying God's Word.

The Process of Development

I pray that you have a new level of understanding of the goodness of our God who created us in His image and for His kingdom, redeemed us by His grace, gifted us and empowered by His Spirit, and selected us for service to Him that He has already declared acceptable. Further, I pray that you are beginning to understand how important you are to God and to His community, the church. The resurrected Lord has enabled His church to express God's fullness on earth by giving to it gifted persons who, when they serve according to their gifted ability, enable the church to grow up into Christ. You are one of those gifted members!

Think about it this way. You may never have thought of yourself as having great value to the church. Now you have had the opportunity to look into the Word of God and discover that God created you with good works in mind and has gifted you to accomplish those works by His power. Let's assume, for example, that you have worked through the gift discovery process and have discovered that you have a gift for teaching and a concern for the youth in the community. You have sought and received confirmation about your giftedness from your pastor, staff, and other mature Christian friends. What do you do with this new information?

You may think the answer is obvious, and you volunteer to teach a youth class. Not a bad place to start! What would be the response of your pastor or minister of education? No doubt they will be thrilled, but hopefully they will not arm you with material and thrust you headlong into a class of adrenaline-filled young people. You will likely be required to undergo some training before you are unleashed with your newly found gift. Why? The church wants to ensure that your ministry experience is a positive one for you and the young people you are going to be serving. The use of your teaching gift will be enhanced by training that improves teaching skills, provides you with theological depth, and personal maturity. This leads us to the last two steps in using our gifts, development and employment.

Some people seem to think that spiritual gifts preclude training and development. They interpret using gifts as a spiritual activity and training as a human convention. We occasionally hear echoes from a past generation who believed that theological education was a worldly contrivance, unnecessary for the man filled with the Spirit. You may have heard someone argue that they didn't need to prepare their sermon or lesson beforehand; they would just rely on the Spirit when they stood to speak. I understand what they are suggesting but would argue that the Holy Spirit works in the study or in the seminary classroom.

Our God deserves our best and thus we must participate with Him in the full development of our gifts.

I hasten to add that all the training a church or seminary can provide will not compensate for the absence of a particular gift. Once again we find that we are not dealing with an either/or issue but a both/and one. Each church needs to help people discover their gifts and rely on the Spirit *and* then help them develop those abilities to their fullest extent.

Paul mentions spiritual gifts on two occasions in the Pastoral Epistles. On both occasions, he exhorts Timothy to develop the spiritual gift which was in him. "Do not neglect the spiritual gift within you, which was bestowed on you through prophetic utterance with the laying on of hands by the presbytery. Take pains with these things; be absorbed in them, so that your progress will be evident to all" (1 Tim. 4:14–15). The warning not to neglect the gift, accompanied by the admonition to "take pains with these things," indicates that gifts may atrophy through lack of use and development.

In his second letter to young Timothy, Paul writes, "For this reason I remind you to kindle afresh the gift of God which is in you through the laying on of my hands" (2 Tim. 1:6). The phrase "for this reason" links this verse with the previous discussion of the faith heritage passed down to Timothy from his grandmother and his mother. Timothy had been nurtured in the faith by these women and gifted by God for service. The idea of "kindling" reminds us of a fire that has not recently been stirred and thus no longer burns brightly. It is possible for our devotion to God to lose its passion and our gifts to become less than effective. How then do we rekindle the fire of our gifted service? Paul mentions that power, love, and discipline have been given to Timothy. It is the power of the Holy Spirit, the love for God and the brethren, and our spiritual discipline that will keep our gifts at their maximum strength. God has given us all the resources we need to keep our gifts at full power through discipline and development.

You may have noticed the mention here of the laying on of hands. Scholars differ as to whether a unique pastoral gift was given by the Spirit at the moment of the "laying on of hands" or whether the "laying on of hands" was simply a way the early church chose to recognize those who had demonstrated gifts for pastoral ministry. Some persons see here the roots of the service of "laying on of hands" practiced today in the ordination for pastoral leadership. Whatever the case, it needs to be stated that the gifting is an activity of God. Man may be the instrument through which God works, but He is the source of all spiritual empowering and doesn't rely on the hands of any particular man.

We find a similar linking of gifts and development in Ephesians 4:11–16 where Paul discusses the work of the pastor/teacher in terms of "equipping of the saints for the work of ministry." Earlier in the passage (v. 7), Paul affirms that all believers have received a grace gift. In verse 16 he demonstrates that the growth of the body depends on the proper working of "each individual part." If we want to serve at peak efficiency, we must rely on the Spirit and take advantage of every opportunity to develop our gifts through training, service, and discipline.

Gifts Are Developed by Training

Let's think back on our illustration of the teacher who recognized that her ability to teach was from the Lord and wanted to use it in the ministry of the church. She should seek whatever training opportunities the church makes available to those called to teach.

Every church can learn from the process we use for our teachers and apply it to other areas of gifted service. For example, the church could offer hands-on training for those gifted in the use of audio or video equipment. Most churches already offer training for those who desire to use their musical gifts through the church. Numerous programs already exist for training those gifted in evangelism. The church that is serious about helping people fully use their gifts will need to think creatively about providing training in other areas of gifted ministry.

Gifts Are Developed through Use

Experience has taught us that muscle, memory, and strength are developed by consistent use. Children throw a ball thousands of times to develop their ability to throw with accuracy and speed. Use of your spiritual gift is enhanced through practiced use. We have already looked at Paul's admonition to young Timothy to be absorbed in the development of the gift within him. All of us have sat under the instruction of a new teacher or pastor who valiantly struggled during their first months only to become very accomplished at the use of their gift in time. Use is the key to development.

Each local church must therefore provide opportunities for people to develop their gifts through use. You can perhaps see the dilemma this poses for the local church. How do we ensure that proper care is provided for persons who are impacted by those who are in the process of developing their gifts? We could illustrate from the world of medicine. We are all excited to see young doctors who are in training, but we may be a little less enthusiastic when we discover that they are going to be "practicing" on us. We can take this illustration a step further and suggest a model for the church. Usually young interns are accompanied by more mature doctors who oversee their work, ensuring quality care while providing on-the-job training. Churches need to develop in-service training for persons who are developing their gifted ministry.

I grew up in a relatively small church where youth week was an annual event. During that week our church allowed youth to teach classes, lead the choir, sit in on deacons' meetings, preach, and perform other such tasks. It worked well for us because the adults with whom we were serving helped us prepare to perform the task and stood by in case we needed assistance. Guess which ministry I was elected to perform? Right you are—I was the youth week pastor. It helped that my dad was the pastor and assisted me with sermon preparation. I am certain that many of my delivery mannerisms are based on imitating him in the pulpit.

When I attended college, I had the privilege to serve as part-time youth pastor at Calvary Baptist church in Winston-Salem. The pastor, Mark Corts, allowed me to join him as he performed numerous pastoral functions. We visited the hospitals, made evangelism visits, and even talked about sermons and Bible studies we were preparing. I look back on these early ministry opportunities and realize that all these events allowed me to discover and develop my spiritual gifts.

This mentorship model of on-the-job training is found in programs such as Evangelism Explosion, Continuous Witness Training, and Faith Evangelism. Those being trained to witness are accompanied and coached by others who have more experience in sharing their faith. We need to apply the principle of on-the-job mentoring to all areas of gifted ministry. Each teacher should be challenged to enlist and develop another gifted teacher. Persons involved in the caring ministry of the church should equip others who have the gift to care for people's needs. Gifted musicians could coach developing musicians. We must provide both means and opportunity for the development of gifts through guided use.

Gifts Are Developed by Spiritual Growth

Since gifts are spiritual by definition, it stands to reason that their use will be enhanced as the believer grows in spiritual maturity. The gifts for ministry are the expression of His infilling presence and power. Thus as we grow in our personal relationship with God, we will know better how to appropriate His power and employ our gifts for the common good. Our desires become more mature, and thus we are less likely to seek a platform to prove our spirituality and more likely to seek a place of service to the brethren.

Paul defined his spiritual quest: To "know Him and the power of His resurrection and the fellowship of His sufferings" (Phil. 3:10). Our goal is not simply to discover and develop our gifts; it is to *know Christ.* As we grow up in every aspect into our Head, who is Christ, we will grow in our ability to employ our gifts for the good of the body of Christ. Our desire to use our gifts unselfishly will be purified, and our gifts will be fully energized as we learn to walk in the Spirit.

Many gifted believers may enjoy limited effectiveness because they neglect the basic spiritual disciplines such as prayer, Bible study, personal worship, and meditation. I can give personal testimony that the use of my gift of preaching/teaching is impacted by my personal spiritual maturity. Additional study, dramatic fervor, and innovative approaches to preaching cannot compensate for the lack of spiritual empowering. Think for one moment about your most effective ministry moments. Did they come when you were conscious of the employment of a certain gift, or did they come when you were ministering out of the overflow of your personal relationship with Christ?

All gifted believers must learn that our need for empowering is total and constant. We must have a regular and consistent personal Bible study time. We should follow Paul's direction to pray without ceasing. Without prayer we will soon become dry and lifeless, and the effectiveness of our ministry will be impacted. We need the corporate experience of worship and fellowship with other believers. Through interaction with other body members, we expose ourselves to the gifts and ministry of others who will assist us as we grow and bring reproof and correction when necessary. There are no Lone Ranger Christians. Any gifted member who isolates himself from the rest of the body will soon become lifeless and useless like a branch severed from the life-giving nurture of the tree.

The Process of Employment

Our ultimate concern is for the effective employment of our gifts for the glory of God and the good of the body. Spiritual gifts are practical, functional, and congregational; and therefore we cannot complete our study of the gifts without considering their proper use. At this point we could quote the popular slogan: Just do it! It is time for you to engage your life in the greatest adventure possible on this planet. You can employ your gifts through the church for the advance of the kingdom until every single person on this earth has had the privilege of hearing about their rightful King. You can live with eternal impact. Your earthly gifts can be employed by the King and empowered by the Spirit with eternal consequences.

Gifts Are Employed to Serve Others

Gifts are not given for our spiritual amusement or for the amazement of others; gifts are given to enable individual members to edify the body of Christ. They are an expression of God's grace given by the exalted Christ to equip His children to build up His body, the church. The gifts provide the supernatural ability enabling each one of us to minister in such a manner that our lives will have an eternal impact. The gifts enable us to care for one another and to fulfill the Acts 1:8 mandate as we take the message of the kingdom from our Jerusalem to the ends of the earth.

> *Your earthly gifts can be employed by the King and empowered by the Spirit with eternal consequences.*

In 1 Corinthians 12:25 Paul declares that gifts have been given so "that the members should have the same care for one another." Our mutual care in turn provides for and maintains the unity of the body. Unity is the essential foundation for the functioning of the gifts and, in turn, the proper use of the gifts ensures unity.

When gifts are properly employed, your church will resemble the "no need" church described for us in the book of Acts. "And all those who had believed were together and had all things in common; and they began selling their property and possessions and were sharing them with all, as anyone might have need" (2:44–45). All the needs of the body can be met as every member employs his or her gift to serve others.

Gifts Are Employed for the Fulfillment of the Great Commission

Spiritual gifts enable the local church to minister to its community and to the world. Every church is called and empowered to fulfill the Great Commission in all four quadrants described by the Acts 1:8 mandate. This task begins in Jerusalem, but it must extend to the ends of the earth. Don't you find it exhilarating to know that your church is part of a global strategy that will have eternal impact?

While every church must be committed to fulfilling the Great Commission, not all will employ the same strategy. The strategy of each church must be based on its context and its unique gift makeup. "But now God has placed the members, each one of them, in the body, just as He desired" (1 Cor. 12:18) suggests that God may gift different churches in different ways. For example, one church may feel led to reach singles; another may feel a burden for women who are pregnant out of wedlock. In each case God will provide the gift mix that will enable them to accomplish the task He has called them to do.

The church of the future will seek to determine its gift mix before it defines its particular approach to fulfilling the Great Commission. It will base its structure on the design the Lord has given through burden and unique gifting rather than a traditional or denominational program. Often churches have been more committed to running programs than asking whether those programs actually enable the church to fulfill its God-given passion and mission.

When we acknowledge that God Himself designs each local church as He desires, it will help us to be more tolerant of churches that provide ministry in a manner that is different from our own. If the unity of an individual church depends on the diversity of its members, why do we insist on sameness within the broader body of Christ? A clearer understanding of the sovereign activity of God in giving the gifts should enable local churches to feel the freedom to fulfill their call without necessarily offering all the ministries offered by a sister church. It will also require that we *cooperate* rather then *compete*. It is sad that church growth has sometimes led people to boast about "who's largest" rather than to join hands in advancing the kingdom. Remember, gifts properly utilized by the individual or the church will exalt the Giver and not the possessor.

The implications are obvious: (1) We must spend more time in prayer to determine the leading of the Spirit for the ministry of our church. (2) We must help members to discover, develop, and deploy their gifts for the glory of the King. (3) We must look to our gift mix for the key to our Great Commission strategy. (4) We must seek opportunities to cooperate with other like-minded churches for the sake of the kingdom.

Gifts Are to Be Employed under the Authority of the Local Church

Since gifts are given to edify the body, they must be used under the authority of the local church. You may recall that the arrogant abuse of gifts for self-promotion in Corinth had actually been destructive to the unity and ministry of the church. Paul placed guidelines on the use of gifts in order to ensure that they were used for the building up of the body. He may have anticipated that some of those who considered themselves to be spirituals would have been reluctant to accept any external authority which might limit the use of their gifts. "But if anyone does not recognize this [teaching], he is not recognized" (1 Cor. 14:38). Simply stated, he has no right or platform for the use of his gifts to glorify himself.

First Timothy 4:14 provides another example of the authority of the church regulating the use of gifts. "Do not neglect the spiritual gift within you, which was bestowed on you through prophetic utterance with the laying on of hands by the presbytery." Three points are worthy of note: (1) Timothy was qualified to lead the church at Ephesus based on his gift. (2) His gift, qualifying him for leadership, had been affirmed by another gifted leader, possessing the gift of prophecy. (3) Timothy functioned under the recognition and authorization of the elders.

As indicated earlier, the laying on of hands was the recognition and legitimization of a gift rather than the bestowal of the gift. This passage has implications for the modern-day practice of ordination. When the local church ordains someone to ministry, that church affirms the candidate in terms of calling and giftedness for ministry. Those ordained, in turn, express a willingness to submit their ministry to the authority of the local church. At present most churches practice ordination primarily for pastors, deacons, or elders. Perhaps we should rethink our practice in light of the biblical emphasis on the giftedness of every member and have a service of recognition for each area of gifted ministry. Once people have discovered, developed, and expressed a desire to serve based on gifts, the church should in some manner authorize them to serve. A ceremony similar to ordination might give greater emphasis to the gifted ministry of the church.

The purpose of placing gifts under the authority of the local church is to ensure that they are used to edify the body rather than glorify the individual. The local church provides the checkpoints, balances, and accountability necessary for proper use of all gifts. Even those who exercise gifts whose impact may be broader in scope than a single local church need to minister under the covering of a local church. For example, the evangelist, musician, church planter, or missionary needs a vital connection to the local church. First, the results of this person's work must ultimately be sustained by the local church. Second, those gifted to serve beyond the context of a single local church need for the church to minister to them. Third, accountability is essential at every level for gifted ministry. Accountability to a local body will greatly reduce the chance of personal or ministerial disaster. The long-term results of ministry without connection to the local church will be minimal at best.

Keeping the context of the church clearly in view creates the desire to seek those gifts that will enable us to edify the church. It should put an end to the "free agent" status of those who seek to exercise gifts with no concern for impact on others. Churches have been split by someone starting a small-group Bible study without the knowledge or support of recognized church leaders. These "unauthorized" studies all too frequently degenerate into gossip sessions about current leaders and fail to focus on edification of the body. Some even develop blog sites to criticize current leaders and practices of the church. Such a use of the gift of teaching outside the body often leads to church splits rather than advancing the kingdom. I have heard of churches where someone attempted to exercise gifts of healing or deliverance without the knowledge of church leaders. Such a practice is unbiblical and harmful to the body. A litmus test for the use of every gift is the edification of the church.

Gifts Are Employed for the Glory of God

Perhaps you are thinking that the statement above is so obvious it doesn't need to be said. It is never trite to indicate that our purpose on this planet is to advance God's kingdom by His power and for His glory until His return. We were created for God's glory. We were gifted and empowered at His pleasure and for His glory. The stewardship of all of His good gifts should advance His kingdom and give Him glory.

I have long loved the prayer of Paul for the church at Ephesus recorded in Ephesians 3:14–21. He prays that believers will be strengthened with might through His Spirit, that we will experience the indwelling of Christ, know the love of Christ with all the saints, and be filled up to the fullness of God. Why does Paul pray with such passion for the church? He gives us the answer in his benediction. It is all focused at God who is able to do exceedingly abundantly beyond all that we ask or think. How does God accomplish this? "According to the power that works within us" (3:20). God accomplishes His kingdom activity on earth through us with the end result that God receives glory in the church and in Christ Jesus. When the church is edified through the use of our gifts, God is glorified.

Never underestimate the impact of the edifying use of your gifts for the glory of God. Go ahead—discover, develop, and employ for the glory of God and the edification of the body. You can live a life that impacts eternity!

A Brief Recap

In this section we have looked at the process of discovery and development of our gifts so that we might employ them with the greatest kingdom impact.

Under the discovery of gifts we looked at seven specific actions: (1) Place a priority on prayer. (2) Consider the needs of your community. (3) Look carefully at your passion. (4) Look at what brings you fulfillment. (5) Listen for honest affirmation. (6) Try several areas of ministry. (7) Fill out the gifts inventory.

The key to development of our gifts is our personal surrender to the control of the Holy Spirit. Surrender involves a three-step process. We confess and repent of our sin. We ask the Father to fill us with His Spirit. We present ourselves, our very bodies, to our new manager.

To be at their maximum effectiveness, gifts must be developed. They are developed through training, use, and spiritual growth.

The bottom line in relationship to spiritual gifts is their employment for the good of the body and the glory of God. Gifts are to be employed to serve others, to enable the church to fulfill the Great Commission, and always for the glory of God. They must always be used under the authority of the local church.

Keep these keys in mind:

- Seek spiritual discernment. Spiritual gifts may be birth gifts given by God before conversion and now recognized as spiritual gifts and surrendered to the King for His service. Gifts may be new abilities given to meet specific needs in your church. Remember that you have the Spirit of God—"that we may know the things freely given to us by God" (1 Cor. 2:12). Ask God to reveal your gifts and your place in His body.
- Practice the daily infilling of the Spirit. This process will allow the Spirit to produce His fruit in your life and will ensure that the use of your gift will be fully empowered. Further, He will enable you to see and participate in God's activity through the use of your gift.
- Submit your gift(s) to the lordship of Christ. When you commit your gift to His lordship, it is His to use as and when He desires. You will serve at His direction and not your own initiative.
- Seek to abound for the good of the body. This focus ensures that your motives are pure and your heart is set upon the building up of the body of Christ.

- Use your gift in the context of the body of Christ. All gifts are given for the common good. Ask your pastor/staff and other lay leaders to help you find a place of service in the church. If your gift enables you to minister beyond the walls of the local church, it should still be used for the edification of the body and accountable to the church.
- Remain open to training for the full development of your gifts. God has gifted the pastor/teacher to assist the saints in developing their gifts for service.

QUESTIONS FOR REFLECTION

1. It is possible that you may not agree with all the findings or conclusions of this book. We rarely find any book we agree with fully. I think we can agree that God has given the church both a great calling and full empowering for service. What ways are you willing to seek a more meaningful involvement in the life of your church?
2. Did you fill out the gift inventory? If not, why not do so right now.
3. What steps are you willing to take to be trained for effective ministry? What training opportunities offered by your church are most interesting to you?
4. Are you willing to get involved? Make an appointment in the next several weeks to talk with someone in leadership that can help you find a place of service.

Spiritual Gifts
and Spiritual Warfare

Spiritual warfare is a topic seldom covered in books on the discovery of spiritual gifts. The topic of spiritual warfare has been both neglected and abused. Some ignore the issue while others see demonic influence and power at work in every event and end up blaming the devil for every failure in their spiritual life.

Be assured that spiritual warfare is real and that every believer enters the arena of spiritual conflict the moment they become born-again believers. Paul reminds the Ephesians: "For our struggle is not against flesh and blood, but against the rulers, against the powers, against the world forces of this darkness, against the spiritual forces of wickedness in the heavenly places" (Eph. 6:12).

It is my conviction that the conflict becomes more intense the moment we begin to serve the King and advance His kingdom through the effective use of our spiritual gifts. In a sense we become a greater threat to Satan once we understand our gifted potential and make a commitment to advance God's kingdom by His power and for His glory.

For example, Paul insists that the pastor, the spiritual head of the flock, should not be a new convert. Why, you might ask? "And not a new convert, so that he will not become conceited and fall into the condemnation incurred by the devil" (1 Tim. 3:6). The pastor, because of his ministry, becomes a prime target for the adversary. Satan can use a pastor's authority or success to tempt him to pride, so as to defeat him and render him ineffective in kingdom activity.

I have long feared that one of the greatest dangers of those who claim to be part of the charismatic movement is the tendency to encourage new believers to seek the gift or sign of tongues. This particular gift is such that it renders the mind unfruitful (see 1 Cor. 14:14). In this ecstatic state the naïve young believer may be more open to demonic influence. The new convert is often unprepared for spiritual attack and may become an early and unnecessary wounded warrior of spiritual conflict. Noncharismatic churches face a similar danger when they enlist young believers for ministry roles without any instruction on spiritual warfare. This may account, in part, for the rapid burnout of many new believers who are thrust into ministry without opportunity to grow in maturity.

In recent years, much has been written about spiritual warfare. The church seems to be struggling for balance on this topic. For years we paid too little attention to this topic, and now we may well be in danger of overemphasizing it in some quarters. For that reason, I will not attempt an exhaustive treatment of this topic, but will give you five principles every kingdom citizen needs to know.

Be Focused on the Victor Rather than the Vanquished

As Christians we are to focus on the victorious King rather than the "usurper king" who has already been defeated. Many books on spiritual warfare spend far too much time focusing on the work of the adversary, rather than showing believers how to appropriate their victory in Christ. If we are not careful we can unwittingly give too much attention to the enemy.

Several years ago a godly missionary shared with our church concerning her mission work. She had been born in Communist Russia. God had delivered her from Russia and from her spiritual bondage. At great personal risk, she had worked to provide Bibles and other physical materials to the pastors who worked with the underground church. Her work placed her in dangerous and ungodly situations. After the spellbinding presentation, someone asked her if she had seen a lot of demon activity. Her answer was simple but profound. She stated that she did not focus on Satan's activity; she focused on the sufficiency of Christ. That's good advice for all of us.

The government trains people to discover counterfeit bills by requiring them to spend hour upon hour studying the real thing. By constantly handling the genuine article, the counterfeit becomes obvious both to the eye and the touch. Do not focus on the adversary; keep your focus on the Lord. Heed James's advice: "Submit therefore to God. Resist the devil and he will flee from you" (James 4:7). The essential first step in spiritual warfare is to submit to God.

Be Assured Spiritual Warfare Is Real

We cannot pick what part of Scripture we choose to believe. We must take the Bible seriously when it speaks about the work of the adversary. Satan is real and he desires to destroy the work of the church as it advances God's kingdom on earth. Paul's description of the adversary and the armor of the believer in Ephesians 6 were not intended for dramatic effect. Paul wrote the instructions so that the believer would be thoroughly equipped for every good work. In a similar manner, Peter warned the brethren; "Be of sober spirit, be on the alert. Your adversary, the devil, prowls about like a roaring lion, seeking someone to devour" (1 Pet. 5:8).

Be Aware of the Schemes of the Devil

The devil works through the twin tools of deception and temptation. He attacks us through the lust of the flesh and the desires of the eyes. We can understand why Paul instructed the Corinthians to take every thought into captivity (see 2 Cor. 10:3–5). Further Paul indicates that the devil sets a snare for the unsuspecting believer (see 2 Tim. 2:26). Satan works his schemes by attacking us through our mind, will, emotions, and fleshly desires. Thus he can work through our anger (see Eph. 4:27), pride (see 1 Tim. 3:6–7), and other such emotions to tear down the work of the church. He loves to create dissension within the body. He glories when he can create a negative attitude among believers. He can tempt us to sins of the flesh that can render our ministry ineffective. Remember, Satan's battle is with the Lord and he attacks Him by attempting to render His body, the church, ineffective. If Christ expresses His fullness through the church by presenting to her gifted members, it stands to reason that Satan's battle plan includes discrediting those same gifted members.

Be Prepared

Don't be surprised by the attacks of the adversary. Expect them and be prepared. To be thoroughly equipped we must continually be filled with the Holy Spirit. We have already discussed how you can be filled with the Spirit. Follow the steps suggested earlier for being filled with the Spirit. Link these together with these simple suggestions.

First, confess your sins and trust God to forgive them and cleanse you from all unrighteousness. Confess with specificity and regularity. You don't have to

215

wait till an appropriate prayer time to confess. The moment the Holy Spirit convicts you of sin, agree with Him about your sin, and turn from it and to Christ. This is like breathing out. Now "breathe in" by asking the Spirit to fill you.

Second, put on the full armor of God. The armor is well-described in Ephesians 6:10–19. I suggest you actually visualize the armor as you prepare yourself for the day. For example, pick up the breastplate of righteousness and strap it to your chest through prayer. Take each piece, in turn, and appropriate it through specific prayer. Thus armed, you are prepared to stand in God's victory.

Remember, we are not instructed to do battle with Satan. We are told to resist Satan and to stand victoriously in Christ's victory. I am somewhat uncomfortable with the teaching that encourages Christians to "bind" Satan. Christ has already defeated Satan. Our role is to submit to Christ so that we can stand in His victory. I find no biblical examples where believers are commanded to speak to or rebuke the adversary. Not even the archangel Michael dared pronounce judgment against the devil (see Jude 9). Concentrate your focus on the Lord and allow Him to deal with His defeated foe.

Third, we must stand with the whole army of God. Not even the best-equipped soldier would be foolish enough to go into battle alone. The single-handed army is the fiction of movies. We are not to stand alone against the adversary. We are to stand with God's army of believers. We are a dependent and interdependent people. We are totally dependent upon the Spirit for life and empowering and we are interdependent upon other members of the body since we are intricately linked to one another by our common head.

Be Sure You Are Filled with the Spirit

We are constantly tempted to fall into the trap of thinking we can do something for God by our own strength. This is especially true when we are called upon to serve in the area of our greatest giftedness. Usually, this will be a task we have done hundreds of times before, like teaching, singing, witnessing, or giving. Thus, it is easy to think we can handle this little task on our own. This is one of Satan's best tactics. Believe it. We can accomplish no spiritual task based on human ability or strength.

If you are not thoroughly convinced, listen to the Master. "Truly, truly, I say to you, the Son can do nothing of Himself, unless it is something He sees the Father doing; for whatever the Father does, these things the Son does in like manner" (John 5:19). The moment we attempt to use our gifts in fleshly power we will see an immediate loss of power and effectiveness. We will grow weary in our service and become easily discouraged. Apathy followed by desertion is the logical next step. Too much is at stake for us not to be fully empowered.

Do you understand now why Jesus instructed His first-century disciples to wait until they received power from on high?

If you feel you need additional instruction on the topic of spiritual warfare, see Dr. Jerry Rankin's excellent book *Spiritual Warfare: The Battle for God's Glory* (Nashville, TN: B&H Publishing Group, 2009).

Appendix

The promises of this book are based on one's relationship to Christ. If you have not yet entered a personal relationship with Jesus Christ, I encourage you to make this wonderful discovery today. I like to use the very simple acrostic—LIFE—to explain this, knowing that God wants you not only to inherit *eternal* life but also to experience *earthly* life to its fullest.

L = LOVE

It all begins with God's love. God created you in His image. This means you were created to live in relationship with him. *"For God loved the world in this way: He gave His One and Only Son, so that everyone who believes in Him will not perish but have eternal life"* (John 3:16 HCSB).

But if God loves you and desires a relationship with you, why do you feel so isolated from Him?

I = ISOLATION

This isolation is created by our sin—our rebellion against God—which separates us from Him and from others. *"For all have sinned and fall short of the glory of God"* (Rom. 3:23 HCSB). *"For the wages of sin is death, but the gift of God is eternal life in Christ Jesus our Lord"* (Rom. 6:23 HCSB).

You might wonder how you can overcome this isolation and have an intimate relationship with God.

F = FORGIVENESS

The only solution to man's isolation and separation from a holy God is forgiveness. *"For Christ also suffered for sins once for all, the righteous for the unrighteous, that He might bring you to God, after being put to death in the fleshly realm but made alive in the spiritual realm"* (1 Pet. 3:18 HCSB).

The only way our relationship can be restored with God is through the forgiveness of our sins. Jesus Christ died on the cross for this very purpose.

E = ETERNAL LIFE

You can have full and abundant life in this present life . . . and eternal life when you die. *"But to all who did receive Him, He gave them the right to be children of God, to those who believe in His name"* (John 1:12 HCSB). *"A thief comes only to steal and to kill and to destroy. I have come that they may have life and have it in abundance"* (John 10:10 HCSB).

Is there any reason you wouldn't like to have a personal relationship with God?

The Plan of Salvation

It's as simple as ABC. All you have to do is:

A = Admit you are a sinner. Turn from your sin and turn to God. *"Repent and turn back, that your sins may be wiped out so that seasons of refreshing may come from the presence of the Lord"* (Acts 3:19 HCSB).

B = Believe that Jesus died for your sins and rose from the dead enabling you to have life.

"I have written these things to you who believe in the name of the Son of God, so that you may know that you have eternal life" (1 John 5:13 HCSB).

C = Confess verbally and publicly your belief in Jesus Christ. *"If you confess with your mouth, 'Jesus is Lord,' and believe in your heart that God raised Him from the dead, you will be saved. With the heart one believes, resulting in righteousness, and with the mouth one confesses, resulting in salvation"* (Rom. 10:9–10 HCSB).

You can invite Jesus Christ to come into your life right now. Pray something like this:

"God, I admit that I am a sinner. I believe that You sent Jesus, who died on the cross and rose from the dead, paying the penalty for my sins. I am asking that You forgive me of my sin, and I receive Your gift of eternal life. It is in Jesus' name that I ask for this gift. Amen."

Signed:_____

Date:_____

If you have a friend or family member who is a Christian, tell them about your decision. Then find a church that teaches the Bible, and let them help you go deeper with Christ.

Notes

Chapter 1, An Insider's View of the Emerging Church

1. Stuart Hample and Eric Marshall, *Children's Letters to God* (New York, NY: Workman Publishing, 1991).

Chapter 2, A Visit to Corinth

1. Much of the information on the city is from the excellent commentary by Gordon Fee. *The New International Commentary on the New Testament; The First Epistle to the Corinthians* (Grand Rapids, MI: Eerdmans, 1987), 1–4.

2. Not all translations will follow the interpretation of verse 13 that I have suggested. Some read "combining spiritual thoughts with spiritual words" (NASB). Most translations will indicate that some words such as "men," "thoughts," or "words" must be added from the context. The contrast with the natural man in verse 14 and the entire flow of the argument makes the translation used the most likely.

Chapter 3, Redefining Spiritual Gifts

1. Some commentators attempt to connect this warning to the practice of tongues or praying in an unknown language. They suggest that there was concern that someone speaking in an unknown language might actually curse Jesus. All attempts to make such a connection are pure speculation. Further, it is important to note that the matter of praying in an unknown tongue has not yet been introduced in the preceding discussion, which means such an allusion, without greater specificity, would have been missed by the first-century reader.

2. If you want to discover how you and your church can have eternal impact, you might want to look at the trade book and 40-day study of my book *Eternal Impact: The Passion of Kingdom-Centered Communities*.

Chapter 4, The Spiritual Person Redefined

1. Rick Love, *Muslims, Magic and the Kingdom of God* (Pasadena, CA: William Carey Library, 2000), 156–58.

2. Cynthia A. Strong and Meg Page, editors, *Ministry Among Muslim Women* (Pasadena, CA: William Carey Library, 2006), 210–13.

3. I want to thank Curtis Horn for this invaluable insight concerning Paul's personal illustration.

Chapter 5, Guidelines for Gifts in the Gathered Assembly

1. James D. G. Dunn in his excellent book *Jesus and the Spirit* argues that "distinguishing of the spirits" refers to the ability to evaluate the source and content of prophetic utterance. (London: SCM Press, Ltd, 1975), 233ff.

2. In his insistence that the first prophet be silent when interrupted, Paul differs from the regulation of Quran, 1 OL VI, 10; "One shall not speak in the midst of the words of his neighbor before his brother had finished speaking," Quoted from H. Braun, *Quran und das Neue Testament* (2 vols.) (Tubingen: J. C. B. Mohr, 1966), I 196.

3. B. Hall, "Paul and Women," *Theology Today*, vol. 31 (1974), 55.

4. J. B. Hurley, "Did Paul Require Veils or the Silence of Woman? A Consideration of 1 Cor. 11:2–16 and 1 Cor. 14:33b–36," *Westminster Theological Journal*, vol. 35 (1973), 190–220.

Chapter 8, Gifts and My Life

1. Kenneth O. Gangel, *Unwrap Your Spiritual Gifts* (Wheaton, IL: Victor Books, 1983); Rick Yohn, *Discover Your Spiritual Gift and Use It* (Wheaton, IL: Tyndale House, 1974); and Jack W. MacGorman, *The Gifts of the Spirit* (Nashville, TN: Broadman Press, 1974).

2. C. Peter Wagner, *Your Spiritual Gifts Can Help Your Church Grow* (Ventura, CA: Regal Books, 1974), 86–87.